ordinary graces

WORD GIFTS FOR ANY SEASON

Grace   *Strength*   *Gratitude*   *Life*

Lucinda Secrest McDowell

ABINGDON PRESS
NASHVILLE

Jan 18

ORDINARY GRACES
WORD GIFTS FOR ANY SEASON

Copyright © 2017 by Lucinda Secrest McDowell

Library of Congress Cataloging-in-Publication Data

Names: McDowell, Lucinda Secrest, 1953- author.
Title: Ordinary graces : word gifts for any season / Lucinda Secrest McDowell.
Description: Nashville : Abingdon Press, [2017] | Includes bibliographical references.
Identifiers: LCCN 2017031648 (print) | LCCN 2017035434 (ebook) | ISBN
   9781501841835 (e-book) | ISBN 9781501841828 (pbk.)
Subjects: LCSH: Meditations. | Grace (Theology)
Classification: LCC BV4832.3 (ebook) | LCC BV4832.3 .M34825 2017 (print) |
   DDC 242—dc23
LC record available at https://urldefense.proofpoint.com/v2/url?u=https-3A__lccn.loc.gov
   _2017031648&d=DwIFAg&c=_GnokDXYZpxapTjbCjzmOH7Lm2x2J46Ijwz6YxXCKeo&r
=ox0wiE5wyqlD4NWBvXI_LEW57Ah1_xv-dTElReAYRyw&m=FtsMc_XbUS3ELz869mCh
f3aNF0GXS8toVz4gVYYhcVQ&s=kkRYAOmf8auJrT3I7oWpYhI2TvFG7Nh45CNYQf22H
co&e=

17 18 19 20 21 22 23 24—10 9 8 7 6 5 4 3 2 1
MANUFACTURED IN THE UNITED STATES OF AMERICA

Copyright page continued on page 265.

*I dedicate these word gifts to **you**.*
For the striving, here is Grace.
For the weary, here is Strength.
For the anxious, here is Gratitude.
For the broken, here is Life.

❦

"From his fullness we have all received grace upon grace."

~ John 1:16

❦

For the clear shining of Thy face
That lightens this our dwelling place;
*And for the flowing of Thy **grace**,*
Alleluia.

~ Amy Carmichael (1867–1951)
"Praise to Our Sovereign Lord"

Contents

Grace

---

*So grant, I pray Thee, Lord, that by Thy **grace***
The fragrance of Thy Life may dwell in me,
That as I move about from place to place,
Men's thoughts may turn to Thee.

~ Amy Carmichael
"Christ's Fragrance"

1. Grace

From his fullness we have all received **grace** *upon* **grace**.
~ John 1:16

> *Sometimes I blurt out words that hurt other people. In trying to hide my insecurity, I become bossy, controlling, and impatient. With ears tickled by the praise of others, my mood can fluctuate from joyful to despondent on the whim of someone's opinion. But I don't want to be this way! I often wonder if anyone will ever really love me.*

I was "that girl."

Striving. Enslaved. Rigid. Yes, a Christ-follower. Carrying around God's gift of grace, but never bothering to open it and embrace its richness as a way of life.

The *last* person you'd expect to be writing a book offering the many gifts of God's ordinary graces.

But here I am.

Transformed by an encounter with Jesus, who stooped and lifted me out of my pit, relocating me to holy ground. The humbled recipient of a gift I don't deserve and could never earn by my own efforts—God's amazing grace. It cost me nothing (except surrender), but it cost Jesus everything.

Saul was the *last* person you'd expect to be picked by God to change the world.

Oh, he had plenty of academic and professional credentials. Lots of knowledge and ambition. Self-confidence in spades. Problem was, Saul was batting for the wrong team. He hated followers of the Way and was complicit in the stoning murder of Stephen, "spewing out murderous threats against the Lord's disciples" (Acts 9:1).

Hopeless, right? Not in God's sight.

God saw something in Saul that could be used for the Kingdom. Instead of punishing him, He waylaid Saul on the road to Damascus and assured the early Christians, "This man is the agent I have chosen to carry my name before Gentiles, kings, and Israelites" (Acts 9:15).

That one act of grace turned Saul the persecutor into Paul the missionary of Christ.

Do you feel like the least likely person to be gifted with a life of love, grace, and purpose? You are in fine company with me and with Saul. Receive that second chance, and out of your own undeserved freedom, begin to look at others with fresh eyes of compassion and mercy.

The New Testament Greek word *charis* is translated "grace" and "favor," and is the root of *charisma*, for "gift." Grace gifts abound. They are everywhere, just waiting to be opened. I discover them in ordinary places, like in the people who touch my soul because of their courage, kindness, or self-sacrifice. I even find them in the challenges that simultaneously turn my world upside down and change me from the inside out.

Mostly I discover these ordinary graces through His Word. *Each word is a gift.* Waiting to be received and incorporated into our hearts and actions.

To me, "ordinary graces" are surprising gifts that come to me while I'm simply living my story. If I am in a hurry, I will miss them. If I am distracted, I will ignore them. But for anyone weary from effort yet thirsty for more, God offers **grace**, **strength**, **gratitude**, and **life**.

Let's open these gifts, one day at a time.

My child, welcome to this place of grace. Just come as you are. These gifts may change your life—My love, acceptance, and grace. For you. Not because of anything you've done. But simply because you are.

2. Table

*So Mephibosheth ate at David's **table**, like one of the king's own sons.*

~ 2 Samuel 9:11b

A few years ago, a nationwide poll asked, "What word or phrase would you most like to hear uttered to you, sincerely?" The answers were:

1. I love you.
2. You are forgiven.
3. Supper is ready.[1]

Sometimes grace looks a whole lot like supper. At someone else's table. But before we can sit down, we must first be acknowledged, known, and invited. Not overlooked.

My eldest son, who has intellectual disabilities, has spent a lifetime overlooked by certain people who refuse to see beyond the exterior to the fun, wise, giving, and kind person he is.

I wish you could see his ear-to-ear smile when anyone invites him to have a meal with them, whether in their home or at a restaurant.

Invited.

And so my mama's heart feels deeply when I read about Jonathan's son Mephibosheth. Lame in both feet, Mephibosheth spent much of his life in the shadows. Although the grandson of King Saul, this young man was not turning down invitations to parties.

But as God continued to work in the heart of the current king—David—this king suddenly remembered a long-ago promise. "David asked, 'Is there anyone from Saul's family still alive that I could show faithful love for Jonathan's sake?'" (2 Samuel 9:1).

Needless to say, an unexpected summons to the king frightened young Mephibosheth. But David's news surprised him: "Don't be afraid . . . because I will certainly show you faithful love for the sake of your father Jonathan. I will restore to you all the fields of your grandfather Saul, and you will eat at my table always" (v. 7).

Mephibosheth was shocked and could hardly believe that he was being treated like one of the king's sons. Even as he grew older, he was part of the royal household. "Mephibosheth lived in Jerusalem, because he always ate at the king's table. He was crippled in both feet" (v. 13).

Is this a reminder that you perhaps need to follow through on a long-ago promise to someone?

How about beginning with an invitation to share table time—a simple homemade soup or even dessert at a local coffee shop?

Grace is said at tables because grace happens when we gather around a table.

> The meal is such a common biblical image that it beckons us to think of our table literally as a table of redemption, where healing occurs for the downcast, where joy is shared in Christ, and where the gospel is modeled to the unbeliever. Meals put people at ease and lower anxieties. The path to being heard by those who do not know Christ sometimes begins over an authentic dinner conversation.[2]

"Lord, thank you that your love for us is never wasted. Keep us rooted in your word, eating at your table, and praying by your Spirit, so that we may remember when we fail that we are part of your family not because we deserve to be but because you want us. Amen."[3]

Who is waiting to hear you say, "Supper is ready!"?

My child, I know how it feels to be left out. Deliberately snubbed. Passed over. But I am always with you. And perhaps today there is someone somewhere who needs your invitation to the table. In sharing My love with the uninvited, you may just draw them to the One who never turns anyone away.

3. Comparing

Isn't everything you have and everything you are sheer gifts from God? So what's the point of all this **comparing** *and competing? You already have all you need.*

~ 1 Corinthians 4:7 MSG

- "I can't believe the Joneses are vacationing in Europe, and we can't even get to the beach."
- "Why did she get a book contract when I've been writing longer than she has?"
- "I sent the steering committee my résumé, but they chose a younger person with less experience."

Don't do it, friend.

Compare. Compete.

Because it is simply a dead end. Personally. Professionally. Spiritually.

God has called you to follow Him, glorify Him, and further His kingdom through your own unique story. Not hers.

Can you trust Him for that? A chance to live out the grace you received as a free gift?

Paul reminds us today, "Isn't everything you have and everything you are sheer gifts from God?" We were created, redeemed, and sustained so that we may live our unique stories—yes, with all the mess, mistakes, meanderings, and even miracles.

Those who need to know us will be put in our path by a sovereign God.

Her success does not mean my failure.

A few years ago, Tracie was thrilled to be invited to speak at a large women's conference. But as she sat in the hotel lobby and observed the other speakers, her confidence began to slip away. "I began wondering whether the other speakers were more experienced than I was, if their messages would be more encouraging than mine, . . . if they were more successful in their ministries, if the attendees would like them better, on and on it went. As I compared myself to these women, my mind was filled with thoughts of insecurity and inferiority."[4]

Every time we compare ourselves with someone else, we are in danger of believing the lie of rejection—that our own lives are not important.

Did you think you were the only insecure person around?

Everyone suffers from comparison. "So much of our own unhappiness is rooted in assuming that someone else is living the happy life we want. The person you're measuring your life up against? She is measuring her life against someone else's. And someone is comparing herself to you! It's a whole cycle of comparison that doesn't end until someone says enough is enough."[5]

Okay, I'll say it: "Enough is enough!"

Here's how I fight the comparison battle:

1. I truly believe that I am loved and chosen by God.
2. I obey what He is calling me to do and be.
3. I encourage, promote, and lift up others. I go first.
   I pray to be a generous and grace-filled person.

You were not created to be her.

Isn't that a relief? Now, go forth and become the very best version of yourself, by God's grace.

My child, I planned you long ago. You are the unique creation I love and desire to help bring the kingdom of heaven here on earth. Yes, with all of you that is still "in process." With that hidden strength and blossoming wisdom. So, child, don't ache to be like her. She has her own story, and it is not yours. Be you.

4. Among

*The Word became flesh and made his home **among** us. We have seen his glory, glory like that of a father's only son, full of grace and truth.*

~ John 1:14

Two thousand years ago, people were confused, hurting, angry, and impatient. They wanted relief. They wanted results. Perhaps what they really wanted was a savior. Someone to solve all the problems in the world and thus make their lives easier.

They had already tried just about everything, including following their own instincts, going after whatever would satisfy, even as a temporary fix. But it wasn't enough. Our way usually isn't.

I look around and wonder if our behavior and rebellion are any different from those of people back then, when our Creator intervened so radically in human history. Sure, some of our complicated problems have different names and higher technological sources, but the hearts of men and women are continually seeking.

After what seemed like silence for more than four hundred years, a loving God did a radical thing to reach down into the world He had made, which had subsequently tossed Him aside.

He came.

God became incarnate as Jesus Christ, the Son, and entered into our mess, helpless as a baby, unknown and ordinary. "[He] moved into the neighborhood" (John 1:14 MSG).

To be among us.

Not *over* us, spouting truth from on high. But down here, where life is gritty and grace is gulped by desperate people wanting to belong. *Among.* Walking down the dusty streets with beggars and women of the night. Confronting corrupt temple holy men even as the ordinary worshiper became discouraged by church politics. Making His home in our homes. Dwelling in our midst and eventually in our very hearts.

"His answer was a man. One man who came and loved us. He loved us—face to face, hand to wound, eye to eye, belly to the table, sitting-and-sweating-with-us close. He loved with words. With actions. With truth. He loved large. He loved small. Out of love for the Father and for us, he died to himself every minute of every day."[6]

This is huge.

That One who is all-powerful and all-knowing would draw close to someone just like you and me. And yet Jesus-among-us is exactly what we celebrate every Christmas. The glory in the manger.

Where is God in your life? Is He still "up there" out of sight, out of reach, impossible to communicate with?

Or do you know Him "here"? Christ among you? A breath prayer away from solace and sanctuary?

If you don't yet walk on the "with God" journey, you can begin now.

Invite Him in and stay close. Speak to Him of your concerns and your joys. Ask Him for power when yours gives out. Ask Him for love to share with the unlovely. Rest with your head on His lap, and in obedience do hard things that will display His glory to the world.

This is why God sent Jesus. To be among us.

My child, when I first came to earth, things were in turmoil. People had been waiting a long time. For something. They were not expecting that something to be Me. My desire is to always "dwell among you" so that you will know you are not alone. I come every day. Often in the unexpected. I am here.

5. Servant

*I became a **servant** of the gospel because of the grace that God showed me through the exercise of his power.*

~ Ephesians 3:7

"Everyone wants a revolution. No one wants to do the dishes."

This sign hung in a radical Christian community house. And I both grin and shudder at its words. Because they are so true.

We want to do Important Things. We love the idea of *being* a servant—that is, until we actually have to *serve*.

Do you have a servant's attitude toward both tasks and relationships? Jesus clearly taught that "Whoever wants to become great among you must be your servant. . . . For even the Son of Man did not come to be served, but to serve, and to give his life as a ransom for many" (Mark 10:43-45 NIV).

Throughout these verses the original New Testament Greek word used is *diakonos*, which is translated "servant" or "minister"—the root word for "deacon." But if you break down the word—*dia* = "thoroughly" and *konis* = "dust"—the completed definition is to "thoroughly raise up dust by moving in a hurry, and so to minister."

What a word-picture of a servant!

Some of the dearest servants I've known became that way through ordinary graces in the midst of their brokenness.

They discovered that when we receive grace at our lowest point, we are then empowered to serve others. "If we, like others who have known pain, are intact today with a heart's desire to serve, it is not because of anything in us. We have simply received grace. We take no credit for it. How can you boast about a gift?"[7]

Oswald Chambers says that "to serve God is the deliberate love-gift of a nature that has heard the call of God. The call of God is essentially expressive of His nature; service is the outcome of what is fitted to my nature.

The Son of God reveals Himself in me, and I serve in the ordinary ways of life out of devotion to Him."[8]

Paul speaks today of becoming a servant "because of the grace that God showed me." What grace gifts compel you to want to serve others?

Are you willing to live as a servant in the midst of ordinary graces?

One willing, young mother still struggles with how this is embodied in her own life today . . .

> And so this is what I need now: the courage to face an ordinary day—an afternoon with a colicky baby where I'm probably going to snap at my two-year-old and get annoyed with my noisy neighbor—without despair, the bravery it takes to believe that a small life is still a meaningful life, and the grace to know that even when I've done nothing that is powerful or bold or even interesting that the Lord notices me and is fond of me and that is enough.[9]

Perhaps it's time to be willing to kick up a bit of dust for the Kingdom.

My child, serving others may be your most important job today. The task no one sees or applauds. Behind the scenes. Not post-worthy. What is that hard thing you must do today? I will help you serve. Gladly.

6. Empty

*"Don't call me Naomi, but call me Mara, for the Almighty has made me very bitter. I went away full, but the Lord has returned me **empty**."*

~ Ruth 1:20-21

One day her life included a husband and two grown sons. But how quickly she found herself all alone, describing her current identity with two words.

Bitter. Empty.

Naomi had followed her husband, Elimelech, to Moab, expecting good things—a fresh start for their family, away from the famine of Bethlehem. But tragedy struck, first with the death of her husband, then with the deaths of *both* sons, leaving her with only two foreign daughters-in-law.

And an empty heart.

How easy to praise God and trust God when we are full—full of health, full of purpose, full of friends and family. Full of good food! Oh yes, full is a desirable place to be.

Empty means nothing. No home or people to fill it. No job and no money. No vision or purpose to keep going. Just a hole.

Bitter blaming ensues. The same God who was the giver of the good now becomes the culprit who has ruined our lives. Naomi certainly felt this way—enough to change her name to *Mara*—"Bitter."

But bitterness is a dead end. One that can eat us alive, from the inside out.

> Naomi had every right to feel angry, abandoned, rejected, unprotected, uncared for, and unfairly burdened in life. After all, life wasn't what she had expected and her heartaches were many. . . . She loved God and her faith had been strong, but now she felt unseen by Him. Unloved. Her new name person-

ified the status of her new opinion about herself, her life, and her God.[10]

When we are empty, we are desperate to be filled. We want something to make up for the loss. A rebound relationship. An excessive habit to numb the pain. A get-rich-quick scheme that sounds too good to be true. Because it is.

But God usually has a different plan if we will turn to Him. "And to know the love of Christ that surpasses knowledge, that you may be *filled* with all the fullness of God" (Ephesians 3:19 ESV). He wants to fill us with Himself, the only one who can truly satisfy.

Naomi's path included a return to Bethlehem with nothing to show for her life except her Moabite daughter-in-law and a hunger of body and soul. But these women persevered and pursued a new life—including a legacy of hope Naomi could pass down.

Do you walk around empty, depending on others to fill you up with meaning, blessing, or purpose?

When we're living on empty, we tend to suck all the life out of everyone we meet. Our neediness grabs the nearest thing to fill our craving for love, acceptance, and worth. "The more we fill ourselves from His life-giving love, the less we will be dictated by the grabby-ness of the flesh. Being full of God's love settles, empowers and brings out the best of who we are."[11]

Losses and emptiness are inevitable in life. But the God who created us longs to satisfy us completely. Thus, we are empowered to move forward from wholeness rather than from empty desperation.

And though He may surprise us with His methods, He can be trusted. Just ask Naomi and Ruth.

My child, I know that loss makes you feel empty. And sometimes bitter. But I am the one who will fill those holes. With something new. Someone new perhaps. I have a long-term plan based on your ultimate good and My own glory. Be willing to journey to a new land. I will send companions.

7. Gift

*Every good thing given and every perfect **gift** is from above,*
coming down from the Father of lights, with whom there is no
variation or shifting shadow.

~ James 1:17 NASB

When I was a little girl, my Christmas list was designed entirely around the Sears catalog, complete with page numbers for clarity. Of course, as a kid, I only expected one or two of the numerous things listed to actually end up under the tree. But at least I could strongly hint.

Even now, one of my sons requires a specific wish list from me.

To him, a gift is something you purchase, wrap, and enjoy watching the recipient open while capturing it all in a photo. He gets frustrated if I say "Surprise me." So, I work with him by writing down the exact title of a book I've been longing to read, when in reality I'd be just as pleased if he took me out on a breakfast date.

This year, all I long for is world peace. Seriously.

Beginning with our own fractured country and extending all around the world, down to the smallest family unit who has forgotten what drew them together with love in the first place. My wish list is full of intangibles, and it looks very similar to my prayer list.

For me, the best gifts are time together making memories, enjoying a concert, or gathering for a picnic. An ordinary excursion that holds moments of discovery and delight. Such treasures usually arrive in the somewhat tattered packages of people who look a lot like those on my prayer list.

Grace gifts are not *rewards*.

Instead of climbing the ladder, perhaps we should kneel, as F. B. Meyer vividly observed a century ago: "I used to think that God's gifts were on shelves one above the other, and that the taller we grew in Christian character the easier we should reach them. I find now that God's gifts are on shelves one beneath the other, and that it is not a question of growing taller but of stooping lower, and that we have to go down, always down, to get His best gifts."[12]

God is the One who stooped to "graciously give us all things" (Romans 8:32 NIV). He began with Jesus Himself.

Do you view Jesus as your greatest gift ever received from a loving heavenly Father?

"It is not just at the Cross, or even in the Resurrection, that Jesus represents the grace, the gift-giving-ness of God to us. In every miracle, every parable—simply by being in the world at all—Jesus is proclaiming 'God is good, he loves giving, and I'm here, among other things, to prove it.'"[13]

In today's Scripture, the New Testament Greek word for "gift" is *dorema*. Often this is something given to honor someone, but it is also used to refer to the gift of salvation by grace from God. Elsewhere the word *charisma* is used when referring to a free gift of grace or a calling.

Perhaps the most important thing about gifts (whether tangible or intangible, and most certainly the best gift of Jesus) is that we receive them, recognizing the Giver of all—the "Father of lights."

Today you and I have been given the most precious gift of life. "Another day to give gifts and to receive them. To love and be loved."[14]

Just receive.

My child, my love language is gifts. And though they rarely come wrapped in paper and bows, they are nonetheless bestowed with great compassion. And celebration. Because I love to give. Open your hands and tear into all the goodness and grace I'm sending your way today, beginning with life itself.

8. Beloved

"I'll call nobodies and make them somebodies; I'll call the
*unloved and make them **beloved**."*

~ Romans 9:25 MSG

I remember the moment I finally got up enough nerve to say aloud, "I am God's beloved." Now this is my primary identity.

After half a lifetime of wrestling with unworthiness, I finally received the gift our Scripture speaks of today—God's unconditional love, which transforms those who feel unloved and forgotten into His beloved.

From then on, we are called to live loved.

"It's not deciding in my mind *I deserve to be loved*. Or manipulating my heart to feel loved. It's settling in my soul, *I was created by God, who formed me because He so much loved the very thought of me. When I was nothing, He saw something and declared it good. Very good. And very loved.* God's love isn't based on me. It's simply placed on me. And it's the place from which I should live . . . loved."[15]

Have you forever been changed by the love of Christ?

Fil Anderson was just walking along the beach one day when suddenly a young boy with Down syndrome ran toward him, then hugged and kissed him. Though startled, he remembers feeling that God was saying, "That little boy was a picture of my wild love for you. The way he looked into your eyes is the way I have always looked at you. That beaming smile on his face is how you make me smile. The way he wildly screamed with glee is how I feel about you. The way he kissed you only begins to express the love that is in my heart for you. I am totally crazy about you."[16]

God is totally crazy about you and me too.

Which should make every other title or status or label pale in comparison to *beloved*. Those are ever changing, but God's love will always be the set point of who I truly am.

> Jesus came to share his identity with you and to tell you that you are the beloved sons and daughters of God. . . . You were the beloved before your father, mother, brother, sister, or church loved you or hurt you. . . . God loved you before you were born and God will love you after you die. This is who you are whether you feel it or not.[17]

To know this and truly believe it will enable us to live loved.

It was a decisive moment in Jesus' life—the divine affirmation at his baptism: "This is my beloved Son, in whom I am well pleased" (Matthew 3:17 KJV). That identity defined and empowered Him all His days on earth.

Believing today's verse can also be a decisive moment in our lives as well—the day we received the gift of a new name—*Beloved*. And began thus to live out our calling. "Turn around and believe that the good news that we are loved is better than we ever dared hope, and to believe in that good news, to live out of it and toward it, is of all glad things in this world the gladdest thing of all."[18]

Just call me *Beloved*.

My child, what have you been called? Loser? old? unattractive? clueless? wannabe? Maybe people didn't actually say those things, but in your heart you heard them. May I change the script? From now on will you listen only to My voice—the one that calls you Beloved? Because that is the essence of who you are. Loved. By Me.

9. Truth

*As the Law was given through Moses, so grace and **truth** came
into being through Jesus Christ.*

~ John 1:17

Vicki told me the truth, but it was hard to hear it.

Because, frankly, sometimes the truth hurts.

In this instance, it was I who had unintentionally hurt someone's feelings. And so, like Nathan to King David, who couldn't recognize his sin with Bathsheba, my friend was basically saying to me the equivalent of, "You are that man!" (2 Samuel 12:7).

Sometimes we have to say hard things—truth—but with great grace. Jesus is our model for this delicate balancing act—"grace and truth came into being through Jesus Christ."

Have you mastered the balance between grace and truth?

Some of us have become grace-givers. Since coming face-to-face with our own sin, we know how much grace we require just to put our feet on the floor each morning. We make every effort to extend that to others, that they might be transformed by Christ's compassionate love.

Others of us are primarily truth-tellers. Our deep sense of justice simply requires it. Surely this is a biblical response to a holy God. Only, sometimes the truth we project is not received in a productive manner.

Rob Renfroe tells the story of two pastors, one replacing the other, who had served the church a long time. When asked if she hated to see the old pastor leave, one member said, "I think the change will be good for the church. Frankly, I was tired of all the hellfire and brimstone."

The questioner then asked, "So the new pastor doesn't talk about hell?" And she replied, "Oh, he talks about hell. But when he does, there are tears in his eyes."[19]

Vicki's eyes were moist when she admonished me. I'm sure she had prayed before approaching me, asking God to help her "[speak] the truth with love" (Ephesians 4:15).

What steps could you take today to learn the delicate dance of truth and grace? First of all, pray about the situation—political, cultural, relational, spiritual. Ask God to make His truth clear to you, and pray that you might be a gentle steward of it. Then, go to God's Word not only about the issue itself, but for continued guidance in your own behavior. Finally, approach the person with a humble attitude—he or she will be able to know if your intention is for his or her good or for your own satisfaction.

> Sometimes truth is hard to hear, but God speaks truth into our lives not to tear us down but to build us up; not primarily to make us feel guilty but to move us to confession and repentance so we can experience forgiveness; not to take life from us but to bring us into the abundant life that is ours in Jesus Christ. . . . When God gives us truth to speak into another person's life, it's not so we can stand above her and wag a finger in her face. It's so we can stand beside her and put an arm around her shoulder.[20]

My child, yes, the truth can be hard to hear. And even harder to live. But it is truth based on My Word. Will you dig deep to discover it, hidden among the many voices of your day, and then graciously share it with all you encounter? I promise to be in your voice and your actions.

10. Merciful

*Nonetheless, the LORD is waiting to be **merciful** to you, and
will rise up to show you compassion. The LORD is a God of
justice; happy are all who wait for him.*

~ Isaiah 30:18

Celebrity sightings in Nashville mean different things to different
people.

When we recently walked into a nearby restaurant, we observed a family
sitting in the corner booth. My daughter, who is an actress, immediately
saw her friend, Grammy winner Marcus Hummon, who had directed her
in a play. But my eyes immediately went to his wife, Becca Stevens, the
founder of Thistle Farms (a community of women who have survived oppression, violence, and prostitution), and one of 2016's CNN Heroes.

Becca understands ordinary graces—especially when it comes to helping
abused and marginalized women find new identity and purpose through
Christian support. In fact, she is all about our word for today—*merciful*.

"Thistle Farms is centered on the belief that women survivors of trafficking and violence proclaim mercy so profoundly, that through their healing a whole community can find healing. Being a conduit of healing is tied
to the church's mission to proclaim mercy, and to help the world become a
place where love and justice grow."[21]

Our verse today comes from the story of the Israelites, who knew what
to do, but chose another path. Can you relate? It seems that two thousand
years later, many of us still believe that we have a better plan—than God.
And so, we get sucked into a culture that promises to satisfy, but only leads
us farther away from the place we most want to be.

Here are just a few of the words God calls his children in Isaiah 30:
"they are . . . shame and disgrace" (v. 5), "unwilling to hear the Lord's
teaching" (v. 9), and they "trust in oppression and cunning" (v. 12).

Are you also in desperate need of mercy?

There is hope. Because our verse today begins with that wonderful conjunctive *nonetheless*, which means "in spite of that."

God is waiting to be merciful. To show compassion.

As I write today, our country is celebrating a man who gave his life for justice, mercy, and love: Dr. Martin Luther King Jr. However you may choose to observe this holiday, I hope we will all remember that Christ was the motivation for Dr. King's work.

> Unless we battle injustice, stand for the outsider, the oppressed, . . . risk our lives so others can have life, we can't happily bear any of the grace in our own lives—*because the grace we've been given, is always meant to be given.*
>
> You won't be able to bear the grace of your own life, unless you come bearing grace and hope and justice and kindness and life and joy *to everyone in your life.* Your life breaks in the deepest ways—unless you lighten your soul by giving forward some of the grace you've been given.[22]

Mercy is the compassionate, steadfast love of God for sinners, delivering us from the curse of death to union with God through Christ our Savior.

To whom will you be merciful today?

My child, I know you weep when you witness stories of brokenness, betrayal, and evil in the world. I weep too. And then I seek to offer both justice and mercy. As you pray about your own voice and actions, may you know My power and presence each time you risk offering compassion to those in great need. You did it to Me.

11. Enslaved

But now that you know God—or rather are known by God—
how is it that you are turning back to those weak and miserable
*forces? Do you wish to be **enslaved** by them all over again?*

~ Galatians 4:9 NIV

Once freed, why would someone turn back to that which enslaved him or her?

Though seemingly counterintuitive, this is a frequent phenomenon. It happened in Paul's day and it happens today.

More than forty years ago, at the end of a six-day bank siege in Sweden, four hostages were released, and it became evident that the victims had formed some kind of positive relationship with the very people who had captured them. Thus, Stockholm syndrome was born.

With Stockholm syndrome, during captivity, instead of despising their imprisoned existence, kidnapped victims actually develop a psychological alliance with their captors as a survival strategy. Lines blur and terror morphs into dependence. They trade true freedom for a false sense of security. "The hostages are in denial that this captor is the person who put them in that situation. In their mind, they think this is the person who is going to let them live."[23]

Do you ever find yourself secretly longing for people or practices from your past? Even after you've decided to follow the ways of God? Why do we do that? Because no matter how degrading, what has become familiar seems preferable over change. Even if fear or shame takes hold, we grasp any small gesture and hope it means love and acceptance.

Now that we are new creatures in Christ, surely it's okay to risk just a taste of that poison—we can leave it anytime, right? It never occurs to us that we've become enslaved.

We had discovered how to live by grace, not striving. But now we are back to craving approval, compromising values and virtue, and foolishly trying to live in two worlds. As one man confessed, "At different times on the journey I have tried to fill the emptiness that frequently comes through a variety of substitutes—writing, preaching, traveling, television, movies, ice cream, shallow relationships, sports, music, day-dreaming, alcohol, etc. Along the way I opted for slavery and lost the desire for freedom."[24]

The good news? The gift of grace is still ours—our failures in faithfulness don't have to be terminal.

It's time to end your Stockholm syndrome with the world.

It was never treating you with honor or love. You just thought that stuff was the best life had to offer, so you allowed it to lead you, noose around the neck. A slave.

No more. Jesus has already set you free.

Now live in that freedom. Because you can. And because you must.

My child, do you remember how those chains felt? That impossible addiction? That enabling relationship? Remember how I helped set you free? Now, breathe deeply. You do not want to return to that place, no matter what lies are twirling around in your brain. My grace has set you free, and I will help you continue to walk as a child, not a slave.

12. Morning

*Lord, in the **morning** you hear my voice. In the **morning** I lay it all out before you. Then I wait expectantly.*

~ Psalm 5:3

Bono, the musician, once asked Bishop Desmond Tutu how he managed to find time for prayer and meditation. His reply? "What are you talking about? Do you think we'd be able to do this stuff if we didn't?"

What he was doing? As the chairman of the Truth and Reconciliation hearings in South Africa, he heard daily reports of gruesome atrocities. Having received daily strength during his morning prayers, this courageous man was thus able to accomplish seemingly impossible tasks.

What are you facing today?

Whatever it is, will you spend time with the Lord first thing in the morning—lay out your concerns and "wait expectantly"?

"If your day starts off wrong, it stays skewed. What I've found is that getting up a little earlier and trying to have an hour of quiet in the presence of God, mulling over some Scripture, supports me," Bishop Tutu explained.[25]

Even if we cannot have hours of quiet each day, most of us can usually arrange our schedules to awaken a bit earlier to spend some time listening, praying, and focusing on Scripture, such as the one-word-a-day devotional you are reading now. Of course, we can pray and study any time of day, but there is something particularly empowering about dedicating the day ahead to the Lord.

> In the absence of words—and before any words have been spoken—my soul is calm and clear like the stillness of a quiet pond. . . . As wonderful as it is to be in the light, morning solitude has taught me that it is even better to be there when the light comes. Being there helps me "make contact" with

this God who comes and is always coming . . . like the sun . . . when it is time.[26]

Tailor your own time to whatever works for you—the acronym **TRIP** helps me focus:

> **T—Thanksgiving.** Begin your morning by thanking God, the Giver of all good gifts. Read Scripture, psalms, a devotion, or a Bible reading guide. Keep a gratitude list.
>
> **R—Repentance.** Start each new day with a clean slate. Tell God where you have failed Him; ask and receive His forgiveness. Then move forward in a new direction.
>
> **I—Intercession.** Pray over the names of family, friends, neighbors, and leaders. Intercede for the suffering around the world, wars, recent devastation, political concerns, church or work challenges. Pray "Thy will be done."
>
> **P—Plans.** Conclude as our verse says: "I lay it all out before you." Go over your schedule, aware of divine interruptions. Ask God to be with you especially in those times.

"The clock is to go all day, but there is a time for winding it up," said Charles Spurgeon in addressing the priority of morning prayers. "These times of regular communion with God wind us up for the rest of the day."[27]

Good morning!

My child, every day I offer a gift—clean white pages of a life on which to write your unique story. So greet the morning as what it is—a fresh start. Come to Me for words of encouragement and challenge. Bring to Me both your praise and your entreaties. And then go forth filled with joy.

13. Worthy

*Live a life **worthy** of the calling you have received.*

~ Ephesians 4:1 NIV

Leah struggled every day of her life to feel worthy.

The man she loved—her husband, Jacob—loved her sister, Rachel, more. So, Leah prayed she would have children, to prove to both her husband and her father that she was worth being loved and pursued. Who would ever see beyond her weak eyes into her soul, one created in God's image?

Leah felt unworthy because she had been rejected.

> Rejection steals the best of who I am by reinforcing the worst of what's been said to me. Rejection isn't just an emotion we feel. It's a message that's sent to the core of who we are, causing us to believe lies about ourselves, others, and God. We connect an event from today to something harsh someone once said. That person's line becomes a label. The label becomes a lie. And the lie becomes a liability in how we think about ourselves and interact in every future relationship.[28]

The labels of *unattractive* and *unwanted* prevented Leah from believing she was worthy of love. But God saw her real beauty and responded with a grace gift. "When the LORD saw that Leah was unloved, he opened her womb" (Genesis 29:31).

As He extended kindness to her in her despair, she finally found her own worth.

> Leah had been letting people name her, label her, define her. She was letting other people determine her value. She needed to see her value as God saw it and to receive God's grace as he wanted her to receive it. Leah needed to love herself through his love. . . .

> Leah began to say, "There's only one whose affirmations I ulti-
> mately need. And his affirmations aren't earned. They're given
> to me by grace."[29]

Today's verse calls us to live worthy of the life God has fashioned for us. The New Testament Greek word used here is *axios*, which means "having the weight of another thing of like value." The one who is worthy is not a lightweight. But substantive.

"Some of us pretend to be perfect, instead of admitting that behind the image we feel as small and unworthy as we ever have. The soul's worth, though, doesn't come from earning or proving."[30]

It's only when I understand God's unconditional love that I can embrace the worth of my own soul, because each soul is worthy of love, created by and in the image of the God of love.

At no time do I experience this truth more vividly than when my friend Christopher Dukes sings "O Holy Night" at the Christmas Eve candlelight service in our New England church, established in 1635. How can I help but feel rescued at these poignant and promising words?

> Till He appeared and the soul felt its worth.
> A thrill of hope—the weary world rejoices,
> For yonder breaks a new and glorious morn!
> Fall on your knees!
> O hear the angel voices!
> O night divine. O night when Christ was born![31]

Christ has appeared. Live worthy of His call on your life. Because He knows you. He sees you. And He loves you.

My child, did you know you are a pearl of great price? You are of supreme value. To Me. So that means that when others toss you aside as less-than, it's their problem, not yours. Listen only to My voice. And live loved.

14. Say No

For the grace of God has appeared that offers salvation to all
*people. It teaches us to **say "No"** to ungodliness and worldly*
passions, and to live self-controlled, upright and godly lives in
this present age.

~ Titus 2:11-12 NIV

I admit it. I went to see the same Broadway musical four times this spring.

Primarily because my talented daughter was performing in it. But I also kept going back to see another actress in her Tony-nominated scene of a gambling-addicted nun singing "Never Can Say Goodbye" to a slot machine. This was a seventies spoof, and she did a spot-on imitation of someone with the inability to resist temptation.

She simply could not spit out the word *good-bye* and leave the source of her addiction.

While played for laughs, it uncomfortably reminded me of my own inability to say no. Except that my addiction is too often to those activities and commitments that keep me overbusy, preoccupied with affirmation from others, and seeking titles designed to prop up my sense of worth.

Before I take time to consider whether an activity fits with my priorities, before I even pray, all too often the word yes comes out of my mouth.

Today's verse says that God's grace teaches us how to "say 'No'" to certain things so that we might live the godly life to which we are called.

What do you need to give up in order to receive such a gift?

Once we know our purpose and priorities, we can line up every opportunity next to those criteria. Some people struggle with this because they don't want to disappoint people. With each new request perhaps they need to remind themselves, *This thing I am being asked to do will not get me more love. And this will not help me meet my purpose.* "I'm committed to a particular, *limited amount of things in this season, and if what's being asked of me isn't one of those, then it stands in the way."*[32]

During the busy month of December, I was on a book deadline and thus limited my festivities to just the final holiday week when family visited. That meant saying no to everything else except teaching and writing my book. Saying no to lovely parties and concerts. Things I sincerely wanted to do. People I genuinely wanted to see. But it was a good choice to help keep holiday stress at bay.

To remain settled in my soul.

If our criterion is pleasing people, then we are lost. We must realize that every yes means a no to something else simply because we have limitations.

But that's a good thing. And it can be life-giving.

It does get easier. "The first times I had to say no were excruciating. But as you regularly tell the truth about what you can and can't do, who you are and who you're not, you'll be surprised at how some people will cheer you on. And, frankly, how much less you'll care when other people don't."[33]

Should you say yes or no to this thing that is facing you today?

I cannot advise you. But I urge you to take every detail to the Lord in prayer. He will give you His wisdom.

Follow His leading and embrace the gift of peace.

My child, I'm glad you love to say yes when needs come your way. However, an important part of maturity is recognizing that you have limits. Instead of struggling against constraints, see them as signs pointing you to the best, not just the good. Breathe deeply. Say no. Now you can say yes to the best.

15. Compassion

*"So he returned home to his father. And while he was still a long way off, his father saw him coming. Filled with love and **compassion**, he ran to his son, embraced him, and kissed him."*

~ Luke 15:20 NLT

Let's say you've done everything wrong.

Demanded money from people who love you. Turned your back on familiar for the lure of exotic. Flirted with vice and grabbed forbidden pleasure. Bought lots of stuff and tried to buy friendship. Eating, drinking, partying.

All along thinking that maybe *this* will finally fill the hole. The one in your heart that longs for more.

But it never does.

Until that day you turn around—alone, filthy, starving, and totally lost. And all you can think about is that your father's home is looking pretty good about now. But returning is out of the question. You are defeated, shamed, dirty, broke, outcast.

Not the sort of homecoming you once imagined.

But you have nothing. And nothing to lose. So you start the journey with faltering steps. Drawing closer to familiar terrain, you slow down.

Your father is running toward you.

A *compassionate* father. This is a word derived from two Latin roots: *cum* (with) and *pati* (to suffer). To show compassion means actually entering into someone's struggle and coming alongside his or her pain—to "suffer with."

The word used here in New Testament Greek is *splagchnizomai,* literally defined as "to be moved in the inward parts." Today we believe the physical seat of our emotions is the heart or brain, but the Greeks believed that all emotions were centered in the splagchnas—heart, lungs, liver, and kidneys.

Rembrandt's painting *The Return of the Prodigal Son* hangs in the Hermitage in St. Petersburg, Russia. Upon seeing it for the first time, Henri Nouwen said:

> My intense response to the father's embrace of his son told me that I was desperately searching for that inner place where I too could be held as safely as the young man in the painting.
>
> With his son safe within his outstretched arms, the father's expression seems to say . . . , "I am not going to ask you any questions. Wherever you have gone, whatever you have done, and whatever people say about you, you're my beloved child. I hold you safe in my embrace. I hug you. I gather you under my wings. You can come home to me."[34]

Are you ready to come home to the community of faith?

If so, look no further than your heavenly Father, who is ready even at this moment to welcome you. This is the very reason Jesus told the parable of the prodigal son—to make it clear that a compassionate God joyously welcomes repentant sinners into His house. "What a word of encouragement, consolation and comfort! We don't have to sift our hearts and analyze our intentions before returning home. Abba just wants us to show up. We don't have to be perfect or even very good before God will accept us."[35]

Home.

My child, have you been running from Me, even in your heart? I know there is much that beckons, many who entice. But your Father's house is the best refuge of all—the dwelling place for your soul. Will you turn around. And return? I have never left and will run to welcome you with open arms. There is much compassion here for any wounded wanderer. Come home.

16. Peer Pleasing

Is it not clear to you that to go back to that old rule-keeping,
peer-pleasing *religion would be an abandonment of everything*
personal and free in my relationship with God? I refuse to do
that, to repudiate God's grace.

~ Galatians 2:21 MSG

"Remember, you are living for an audience of One."

That is my friend Steve Hayner's great reminder of our goal—to glorify our most important "audience"—God.

Not that our listeners be spellbound. Not that our tribe be satisfied. Not that our social media reach be expanded. Not that our personality be embraced.

We were not called to follow Christ, build the kingdom, and please people. Paul learned this the hard way. By accumulating the accolades (from people) he almost lost the Audience (of God).

But grace changed all that. And Paul could never go back. "I refuse to do that, to repudiate God's grace."

Pastor Pete Briscoe says the Galatians were being taught Jesus plus law:

> Yes, get started with Jesus, but then you must keep performing in order to go from there. Paul kept trying to pull them back to that primary relationship. But the church often subtly reinforces the opposite. "Ok, you're saved, that's great. Now do this, this, this, and this." I've always had a taste of grace, but over the last few years I've decided to bathe in it. And that has been, as far as my emotional and spiritual life, revolutionary.[36]

In a recent survey of twelve hundred pastors, 91 percent admitted to people-pleasing tendencies.

One people-pleasing pastor, who says he is now in recovery, elaborates. "Pleasing people, of course, is not necessarily a bad thing. And some professions, by their very nature, draw people into them because they offer opportunities to help others. That desire, however, often makes us susceptible to the type of people-pleasing that becomes problematic."[37]

Problematic people-pleasing is when outside affirmation guides us more than inner conviction.

Due to a false sense of responsibility, we then take ownership for everyone else's feelings. We commit to too much because we don't want to let anyone down, yet in the process of not being able to fulfill unrealistic expectations, we let everyone down.

My mantra for too long: "I just want everybody to be happy."

Which is, of course, absolutely impossible.

> You may have a reputation for being the nicest person in the world because the operating principle in your heart is to have a reputation for being the nicest person in the world. Not only is that a manifestation of pride and therefore a sin; it also makes our lives miserable (living and dying by the approval of others), and it usually hurts those who are closest to us (who get what's left over of our time and energy after we try to please everyone else).[38]

Grace is Jesus plus nothing.

So let's not add to that, okay? "Grace is the gift of God's own presence and action in His creation. Through grace God forgives sins and transforms the believer into His image and likeness."[39] Our job is to be faithful to the call. God's job is what happens next.

Can you live out grace, not contingent on how people respond?

Only if your identity is as a beloved servant.

"If pleasing people were my goal, I would not be Christ's servant" (Galatians 1:10 NLT).

My child, you will never please everyone. No matter how fast you dance. And juggle. And try to keep the rules. That's why you are encouraged to live by grace. Which means I already chose you. Already love you. Already find you pleasing. Love people, but don't look to them for purpose and definition. I'm your audience.

17. Sinful

*God's law was given so that all people could see how **sinful** they were. But as people sinned more and more, God's wonderful grace became more abundant.*

~ Romans 5:20 NLT

I loved archery at summer camp.

My goal was to hit the target. If not on the actual bull's-eye, then at least on the target somewhere. I would position the arrow, keep my eyes on the exact spot I was aiming for, firmly pull back on the bow, and let it go.

More often than not, I missed.

Do you ever miss the mark in your spiritual life?

The Bible actually calls that sin. Really. The New Testament Greek word used in today's verse comes from the world of archery—*hamartia*. Both this noun and its verb form, *hamartano,* describe our nature for sin.

Jesus didn't actually use the word sin very often, but Paul made up for it. "All of us have sinned and fallen short of God's glory" (Romans 3:23 CEV).

"Sin is missing the mark, falling short like an arrow that does not reach its target, failing to follow God as we ought to, making the wrong choice. There are times when we do this willfully, but often our sin flows out of our brokenness—our sin nature."[40]

My own definition for sin is "choosing my way and not God's way." We all do that. Yet the more we sin, the more He shows up with grace gifts.

> The great surprise in the Bible is not that it depicts human beings as sinful. Human history continually reinforces the fact that sin never changes. We may dress it up and call it by different names—disorder, dysfunction, addiction—but the traps and temptations have not changed much. The truth is there is nothing "original" about sin—it's all been done

before. The only real surprise in life is God. The Bible reveals God as loving, holy, and merciful, a God who is constantly seeking sinners. He promises that he can take whatever we give him—all that is flawed and broken and wrong—and create something new and beautiful.[41]

Those of us who have come to grips with real sin in our lives cannot help but be sensitive toward others we observe headed down the wrong path. We long to tell them our stories, with the hopes that they won't have to make the same mistakes we did. That they might see grace for what it truly is—a lifeline of hope and healing. Having been rescued, we are tempted to throw out that lifeline, even when others aren't looking to be helped.

Why do we hesitate? Because sin is not a popular word in our cultural language today.

"Sin is sin because it is disobedience to God, because it exerts our independence from the God who gave us life and to whom we belong. Even if our attitude does not harm another person, if it misses the mark of God's will for our lives—if it is contrary to what brings glory to God—then it is sinful."[42]

Bull's-eye.

My child, I know sin is not a politically correct word these days. Yet sin is real—every time you choose to go another way, rather than Mine. The fallout of sin is pain and death, for many in an ever-widening ripple. But there is an antidote—My grace. Come to Me on your knees, and I will forgive and prod you forward. Toward the mark.

18. Encourage

*May our Lord Jesus Christ himself and God our Father, who
loved us and by his grace gave us eternal **encouragement** and
good hope, **encourage** your hearts and strengthen you in every
good deed and word.*

~ 2 Thessalonians 2:16-17 NIV

Sometimes it's the small things that encourage us the most.

The esteemed artist Benjamin West, founder of the Royal Academy in London, was encouraged by the simplest of gestures. It happened when he was six years old and was looking after his infant niece, Sally, while his mother and older sister went into the garden.

Captivated by the sleeping child's smile, he endeavored to draw her with pen and ink. As he heard the women returning, and not sure if he would be in trouble, he tried to hide his activities. But Benjamin West's mother asked to see what he had been doing. He timidly handed the drawing to her and asked her not to be angry. On the contrary, Mrs. West was delighted with the drawing and exclaimed that he had "made a likeness of little Sally." And with those words she stooped down and kissed her delighted little boy on the cheek, unknowingly launching his career.[43]

One act of encouragement. Someone knows us and believes in us.

In today's Scripture Jesus is the source of encouragement—"who loved us and by his grace gave us eternal encouragement." He knew we needed that fuel to keep moving forward with hope.

And the apostle Paul reiterated, "So continue encouraging each other and building each other up, just like you are doing already" (1 Thessalonians 5:11).

Paul gave gratitude for the encouragers in his own life: "May the Lord show special kindness to Onesiphorus and all his family because *he often visited and encouraged me*. He was *never ashamed of me* because I was in chains.

When he came to Rome, *he searched everywhere until he found me*" (2 Timothy 1:16-17 NLT, emphasis added).

> Quite a man, this encourager-friend of Paul's. He had the ability to be loyal, to provide cheer, and do deeds of kindness. He knew the right things to say, the appropriate things to do. That's why Paul wrote of being warmed and strengthened in spirit when Onesiphorus came to see him. Fear, doubt, and gloom drift away when you have a friend like this who can make you feel loved, appreciated and worthy.[44]

Did you know that you encourage others with the way you greet them, express appreciation, give a motivating word, stoop to listen to a sorrow, offer a prayer for strength, or give of your time and resources?

Onesiphorus is not a household word. When asked to name an encourager from the Bible, most would say Barnabas, whose name actually means "Encouragement." But when Paul was in prison, Onesiphorus showed up and still claimed him as a friend. And when Paul was hiding out in the vast city of Rome, fearful for his very life, Onesiphorus was the one who turned over every stone to find him.

I doubt he ever knew the extent of his grace-filled actions.

May the encouragement we receive from others be the fuel to prod us into spreading it generously throughout our needy world.

My child, remember how you felt when she remembered your name? When he gave you that important assignment? We thrive by encouragement and die without it. Look around. Who needs an injection of support and confidence? Why not pass along My grace gift of courage to someone else today?

19. Shame

*"The one who trusts in him will never be put to **shame**."*

~ 1 Peter 2:6 NIV

She was full of shame and had been for years.

You would never know it to look at her. Many who carry heavy burdens of shame easily mask the inner pain that haunts them.

But she had aborted her baby. Decades ago. She had cried out to God, along with the psalmist, "You know my shame and my disgrace" (Psalm 69:19). "Each day I habitually reminded myself of my secret, mentally beating myself up and constantly listening to the lies. . . . Here's the thing: God wasn't telling me I should be ashamed; I told myself that. God didn't say He couldn't love or forgive me; I told myself that. God didn't say I deserved to be unhappy and endure difficult circumstances; I told myself that."[45]

Shame is a prison full of lies, and the inmates are vast in number. But God wants something different for His people. Today's verse says that those who trust "will never be put to shame."

How can we break out of such a prison? By first understanding what shame is. And what it is not.

"False shame can come from being a victim of abuse. We have shame about our bodies, whether from body-image struggles or from the sting of discrimination, poverty, or family instability. False shame malforms us and keeps us isolated, hiding, fearful, and unable to believe that God or others love us."[46]

True shame is a "vague, heavy cloud that determines your identity and never goes away. The behavior or external appearance of the person may or may not look good. However, inside that person is a big, empty hole."[47]

The cure for both? To accept the love, mercy, and grace from a Christ who has rescued us from death and set us free from captivity to any sin, real or imagined.

His is a story of redeeming love, bringing beauty for ashes. The prophet Isaiah wooed the fickle Israelites with this promise, if they would only return to their first love: "Do not be afraid; you will not be put to shame. Do not fear disgrace; you will not be humiliated. You will forget the shame of your youth" (Isaiah 54:4 NIV).

If these words resonate with your soul, let the tears flow, kneel, and offer yourself afresh to the One who knows you best and loves you most.

Then, come to our imperfect community of Jesus followers. You are welcome here. An old hymn goes, "If you tarry till you're better, you will never come at all."[48] So, run to the arms of Jesus and to any who are willing to be Jesus-with-skin-on for you.

"The remedy for shame is not becoming famous. It is not even being affirmed. It is being incorporated into a community with new, different, and better standards for honor. It's a community where weakness is not excluded but valued."[49]

Welcome to the community of the unashamed.

My child, you need hide no more. I feel your pain; I know your tears. And the burden of shame you have been carrying is preventing you from the life I desire for you. Will you lay it down—the regret, the sin, the shame? And let Me carry it. You do not have to do life alone—join others who limp and love.

20. *Feet*

*So he got up from the table, took off his robe, wrapped a towel
around his waist, and poured water into a basin. Then he began
to wash the disciples' **feet**, drying them with the towel he had
around him.*

~ John 13:4-5 NLT

Filthy feet.

The primitive sandals the disciples wore did little to protect them from
the mud and dust that composed the dirt roads and alleys they traveled on
their way to the upper room.

The custom in biblical days was to have a servant wash the feet of each
guest before he or she entered the house. Sandals would be left at the door.
But on this night, as the disciples entered, there was no servant or willing
guest to do the dirty work.

Until their rabbi—Jesus—shocked them all by doing the unthinkable:
washing their feet.

"The disciples were speechless while he quickly and efficiently performed the servant's task, first pouring water from the pitcher over each
pair of feet, allowing the basin on the floor beneath to catch the water and
dirt that flowed down, then wiping the man's feet dry with the towel he
had wrapped around his waist as an apron."[50]

How would you feel if Jesus began washing your feet today? Recoil in
horror? Protest in pride? Cry from vulnerability?

Peter, seeking to cover his own pride with a varnish of false humility,
protested "You shall never wash my feet!" (v. 8 NIV).

I can just imagine Jesus' kind eyes as He explained why this process was
important to establishing their forever bond. "Unless I wash you, you have
no part with me" (v. 8 NIV).

Peter knew at that moment that he wanted it all—complete cleansing!

"Then, Lord . . . not just my feet but my hands and my head as well!" (v. 9 NIV).

We cannot truly serve others unless we first allow the humbled and exalted Savior to serve us. It might be helpful to think of ways Christ has cleansed us in order to prepare us for service. In that process, were we willing or did we hold back in pride?

This story illustrates Paul's words in Philippians 2:5-8: "Adopt the attitude that was in Christ Jesus: Though he was in the form of God, he did not consider being equal with God something to exploit. But he emptied himself by taking the form of a slave, by becoming like human beings. When he found himself in the form of a human, he humbled himself by becoming obedient to the point of death, even death on a cross."

That Scripture was read in our wedding ceremony, setting forth the goal to love each other with a humble, serving heart.

"Whatever we do in Jesus' name, we begin on our knees before our friends and neighbors, serving them, and conclude looking up to heaven, praying to the Father. Washing dirty feet and praying to the Holy Father bookend our lives. We can't live Jesus' resurrection life and can't do Jesus resurrection work without doing it within the boundaries that Jesus set."[51]

Perhaps it's time to take off your shoes.

My child, sometimes I just love to surprise folks. Catch you off guard. Remind you that the way up is down. My best friends didn't understand when I began to wash their feet, but perhaps you do. May you be reminded that vulnerability and allowing others to minister to you can be the open door for launching out as a servant yourself. Barefoot.

21. Works

*But if it is by grace, it is no longer on the basis of **works**;*
otherwise grace would no longer be grace.

~ Romans 11:6 ESV

Works can't save us.

They are merely the fruit of living in the grace we so undeservedly received from Christ.

The only work required for salvation is to believe. But if you've wrestled with doubt, then you realize it can be hard work to make a decision to trust God with your very life. However, once Christ lives in our hearts, He calls us to join Him in His work.

"For it is by grace you have been saved, through faith—and this is not from yourselves, it is the gift of God—not by works, so that no one can boast" (Ephesians 2:8-9 NIV). "The New Testament holds two seemingly paradoxical ideas in tension: first, that our works of righteousness do not earn our salvation, and second, that the life of faith includes doing the work God calls us to do."[52]

The problem comes when we make works the goal, not the natural outcome of our faith walk.

"Some of us don't fall prey to doing good works just to look good to others, but our good works are infected by another common virus: the hope that God will find us just a bit more acceptable if we do something good. A works-gospel is about the ought-to's."[53]

Do you sometimes live by the "ought-to's"—and, if so, which ones?

Steve is a self-proclaimed "recovering legalist" from Tennessee:

> When I was steeped in legalism, struggling was a way of life
> for me. I was extremely critical of myself and others, and I just
> could not seem to help myself. I remember telling this to a
> trusted counselor who said, "You've got to learn how to apply

grace in your life." Well, I didn't know about all this namby-pamby grace and love stuff. . . . Thank God he opened my eyes enough that I took a chance on living by grace. I haven't been the same since I took the first step![54]

Wouldn't you rather depend on grace than works? See if any of these describe your situation now:

1. Do I believe that God's love for me depends on what I *do*?

2. Is my most important goal meeting the expectations of others?

3. Because I try hard to obey God, does it irritate me when others don't?

4. Do I believe my failings are due to lack of faith or not enough prayer?

5. Is my main goal in life to gain God's favor by trying to impress Him?

6. Is my sense of spiritual well-being linked to a person in leadership rather than God?

If you can identify with any of these, it's time to receive God's grace gifts and live in freedom.

─────────────────────────

൭൙ඌ

My child, stop striving. Life in Me is all about grace, plus nothing. You don't need to rack up points in good works. However, as you begin to "live loved," I suspect you will find yourself pouring out to others in many varied ways. Good things. Let go of legalism and embrace life.

22. Love

*If we **love** each other, God lives in us, and his **love** is brought to full expression in us.*

~ 1 John 4:12 NLT

"Mama, I got somethin' to tell ya," said four-year-old Maggie as she knocked on my door during naptime.

"What is it, hon?" I casually replied as I closed my notebook.

"Mama, I cut off all my hair!"

And she had. Her shoulder-length bob had been turned punk-like with several bangs—only one-eighth inch long. For once in my life, I was speechless. But I distinctly heard a voice in my head: "Be careful, Cindy. She will always remember how you handle this one!"

After studying grace for so long, I was now faced with the lab exam.

As I held her close, her words tumbled out. "Mama, can you make my hair long again? Mama, am I still pretty? Mama, *do you still love me?*"

My actions-have-consequences sermon could wait. What she needed now was an assurance of love, an offering of grace.

Do you ever feeling like you're running out of love? You've simply used up your allotment for the day, the week, the whole month.

If so, isn't it great to be reminded in today's verse that when God lives inside us, it's "his love" that fills and releases through us?

But love was "brought to full expression" in me that snowy day as I was writing a presentation on grace.

On my own, I would have flipped out—horrified that she had found and used scissors. Chagrined that the next day was picture day at preschool, and I had, of course, preordered a gazillion photos. But with God's love inside me, I was able to wash her hair, trim it and tell her no matter what she did or looked like, I would always love her.

For Maggie, at that time, it was enough.

Who hasn't stumbled into the heavenly Father's presence with a similar confession: "Lord, I have somethin' to tell Ya. I blew it again. *Do You still love me?*"

How grateful I am that He, too, gathers me in His arms of love and grace.

Because God's very nature is love, He cannot be other than what He is.

We can refuse the love of God. In fact, most of us have at one point in our lives found a reason to do just that. But we can never stop God loving us. We can reject His love, which may prevent its flow into us, but we can do nothing to stop its outflow from Him. Grace is God's unconditional love freely given to the sinful, the imperfect, and the totally undeserving.

Are you having a hard time loving someone today? Would it help to remember how very much you have been loved, even at your lowest point of failure?

"Christianity is not primarily a moral code, but a grace-laden mystery; it is not essentially a philosophy of love, but a love affair; it is not keeping rules with clenched fists, but receiving a gift with open hands."[55]

Open the gift. Take the love deep into your heart.

My child, there is nothing you can do to make Me love you more. And there is nothing you can do to make Me love you less. So, when you come running in with regrets and apologies, know that My arms are waiting. We will move forward together. In love. Which covers a multitude of sins. There is always enough to go 'round.

23. *Righteous*

So, since we have been made **righteous** *by his grace, we can inherit the hope for eternal life.*

~ Titus 3:7

He didn't have to do it. Switch places so we could become "righteous by his grace."

This is how I best understand how such a miracle gift happens: Imagine there are two empty journals. On the cover of one is my full name: "Lucinda Secrest McDowell." The inside of this journal is filled with lists of all my sins—pages and pages of them. The other journal has "Jesus Christ" written on its cover. What's inside is not a list of sins, but empty white pages representing the sinless purity of Christ.

The work of Jesus Christ on the cross is sort of like reversing the covers of these two journals. When you open the book with His name on the cover, you find a long list of all my sins. But when you open the book with my name on the cover, the clean white pages reveal my new and redeemed life.

The righteousness of God.

"God caused the one who didn't know sin to be sin for our sake so that through him we could become the righteousness of God" (2 Corinthians 5:21).

> The gospel is simple. And huge. God the Father showed us his grace not by overlooking our sin but by demanding a payment. . . . Now we are able and deserve to enjoy all of the benefits of sonship. The penalty for our misdeeds was fully paid by the sacrifice of Jesus Christ and affected the great switch: our sin for his righteousness. The record of our sins for the record of his accomplishments. It's an unfair deal from the start.[56]

Sound too good to be true?

A few years ago, one baking company came out with a new instant cake mix where water was the only added ingredient. It was an instant flop—people couldn't believe that making a cake could be that easy. So, the manufacturer revamped their mix so both water and an egg had to be added. Sales jumped rapidly and the cake was a success.

Some people feel this way about salvation and righteousness—is it really the gift of God?

Yes, the Bible clearly states we are saved "not by works of righteousness which we have done, but according to His mercy" (Titus 3:5 NKJV). And God does not need to make this more marketable or complicated.

We just need to receive this grace gift.

"Mercy is *not* getting what you deserve. Grace is getting what you *don't* deserve—the righteousness of Christ. Everything you've done wrong is forgiven and forgotten. And then God calls it even. . . . It's not just good news. It's the best news."[57]

And a perfect recipe.

───────────────────

My child, you can never do enough. I arranged all the payment for sin so that you could now live free. My righteousness is now yours. A gift, not a reward for right living. But you can honor Me by seeking to live in holiness and hope from now on. The journal has empty pages—write a good life story.

24. Lavished

In him we have redemption through his blood, the forgiveness
of sins, in accordance with the riches of God's grace that he
lavished on us.

~ Ephesians 1:7-8 NIV

The lavender-scented lotion squirted from the bottle way too freely, and I found myself covered in more of the soothing silkiness than my skin could possibly absorb. I spread it and still had plenty of fragrance to spare.

Grace is like my lavender lotion—God offers more of it than I can possibly use.

My friend Kathy says it is "abundant, overflows our lives, and spills out all over. God has lavished us with His grace so we can freely and generously share it."[58]

Lavished. This rich word evokes luxury, excess, and generosity.

When it appears in Scripture, the New Testament Greek word *perisseuo* is translated "to super abound, be superfluous, have abundance, to remain over and above."

These are the kind of words used to describe God's many gifts: the riches of Christ, the riches of grace, the riches of mercy, the riches of glory.

We hear the word *immeasurable* and think there is no way to measure the riches of God's grace. We hear the word *unsearchable* and know that there is no way for the mind to comprehend or absorb intellectually the grace of God. More than any other epistle, the book of Ephesians pulsates with Paul's feelings of euphoria, exhilaration, and elation.

This same lavishness of God is expressed in other places in the Bible.

Do you remember the first miracle of Jesus in the Gospel of John (turning water into wine)? There were six vats of wine, each holding thirty gallons. There were 180 gallons of wine for that wedding—and a whole lot left over. Excessive. Extravagant. Exuberant. In other words, lavish.

Have you ever experienced something lavish in your life? A party, a meal, an evening gown, a tuxedo? How did it make you feel about yourself, and about the giver of such things?

For one follower, thinking about God this way was a whole new paradigm: "As I thought about God lavishing His love on me I realized how radical that was. Too often I act as if He parcels out his love, trickle by trickle, drip by drip, definitely sparingly, without waste. Oh no! He lavishes. Contemplating this fact changed my entire day!"[59]

Friend, God has lavishly provided more than you need, more than you can possibly even use.

"Think about this: God doesn't give us just enough grace to get by. He doesn't even give us a generous amount. He gives us grace in such abundance we cannot hold it all. It overflows our ability to contain it. Praise God! What are we to do with this lavish abundance of grace?"[60]

Spread it around.

***

My child, I am rich but not merely in the material ways of the world. It's all Mine, but the parts I want to share with you are those intangible gifts—the mercy, the forgiveness, the power, the wisdom. Indeed, I long to give lavishly from this great storehouse of grace gifts. So don't be surprised when you begin to overflow with excess.

25. Communication

*Let no corrupt **communication** proceed out of your mouth, but
that which is good to the use of edifying, that it may minister
grace unto the hearers.*

~ Ephesians 4:29 KJV

The word escaped my lips before I could hold my tongue. It wasn't a
curse word or an evil word, but my tone was biting and I could tell the
damage was inflicted immediately. My friend stood before me. Crushed in
spirit.

Does your mouth ever get you in trouble? Words released before mind
is engaged.

Just as it is impossible to retrieve the seeds blown off the feathery heads
of a snowy dandelion, it is also impossible to take back hurtful words, once
uttered. Instead, they sink into the heart and soul.

I can remember words hurled at me more than fifty years ago: *Chubby!
Bossy! Stubborn!*

Are you still dealing with the damage of someone's words from long
ago? Sometimes those wounds are the hardest to heal.

In the area of communication, I can relate to Paul: "I don't do what I
want to do. Instead, I do the thing that I hate" (Romans 7:15).

Still, Paul is also the one who cautions us in today's verse to "minister
grace." And he used three different Greek terms to describe communication in making his point:

> *Sapros*—"corrupt communication." This word was
> used to refer to rotting fruit, foul and dirty.
> *Agathos*—"good." This word is considered beneficial
> and helpful to those who hear them.
> *Oikodome*—"edifying." This term is used figuratively
> for words that build up and encourage.

Which category do your words usually fit into—corrupt, good, or edifying? How can we communicate grace to a world that prefers to spew hate and engage in quarreling?

We could start by living this proverb: "A gentle answer deflects anger, but harsh words make tempers flare" (Proverbs 15:1 NLT).

A book with the great title of *Listen, Love, Repeat* suggests:

> Scripture calls us to be thoughtful when we are speaking to someone, especially when we answer them. This means we stop and think. We pause and pray. We don't just bark out something mindlessly, but we give careful attention to what it is we are about to say, striving our best to make sure it is appropriate and helpful.
>
> . . . I sure have seen this to be true, especially when I react properly to someone's question. You know, even those annoying questions. . . . When I make an effort to really think through what I'm going to say and then say it in a tone that is soft and gentle, wrath is often deterred. If I don't, the interaction can escalate into a full-blown argument.[61]

My mother said, "Think before you speak." My teenage daughter urged me, "Mama. Self-edit!" And Jesus would probably say, "Pray before you speak."

May all our words be grace gifts.

❦

My child, it's virtually impossible to retrieve words once they've been released. That's why I urge you to pray and consider your gentle, grace-filled answer. Even when you're attacked. Or put down. Allow Me to help you defuse a potentially volatile situation with kindness.

26. Belong

*I always thank my God for you and for the gracious gifts he has
given you, now that you **belong** to Christ Jesus.*

~ 1 Corinthians 1:4 NLT

I read the word several times before investigating its meaning—FOMO.
When I discovered the definition, the widespread use made sense to me.

Fear of Missing Out.

Added to the Oxford English Dictionary in 2013, *FOMO* is defined as
"anxiety that an exciting or interesting event may currently be happening
elsewhere, often aroused by posts seen on social media."[62]

Basically, it is the twenty-first-century equivalent of keeping up with
the Joneses. *Where is everyone, and what are they doing, and why don't I belong
there too?*

> Thanks to social media and digital technology, we're faced
> with constant comparisons of our vacations, our clothes, our
> relationships, our social lives, even our life choices, with those
> of others. Naturally, that ever-present stream of perfection
> leaves us feeling sub-par. You start to question and doubt
> yourself, thinking things like: *Where does she get those amazing
> power outfits? My desk looks like a disaster, not a pretty Pinterest
> board. I wish I could afford a week in the Mediterranean on the
> salary I make.*[63]

We have a need to feel that we actually belong. Somewhere.

But too often the social media posts, rather than bringing us into a place
of belonging, only exacerbate our sense of lack. There is always someone
who has more—more invitations, more grandchildren, and more beautiful
home decor.

Where do we belong in the scheme of things?

Thousands of women invested precious resources of both time and money to experience an event titled "Belong." The name alone drew many in, as one of the speakers elaborated on the appeal of the name. "Because you do. Your friends do. Your neighbors do. Your colleagues do. Your churchy church friends do. Your totally not churchy church friends do. We are setting a big table, girls. Come to us. You can trust us with the fragile hearts you love. We will hold your stories with tender hands. We are for you."[64]

I don't know if they all found what they were looking for.

But had these women asked, I would have said that our ultimate sense of belonging is only found in our union with Jesus Christ. In our verse today the apostle Paul writes to the new believers at Corinth and reminds them of the many gifts they have received "now that you belong to Christ Jesus."

What are some of those gifts? *Who* are some of those gifts?

As we begin to thank God for all He has given, a new sense of belonging seeps into our souls—that the reality of what we already possess in Christ is far better than the controlled posts on Facebook and elsewhere.

You already belong. Right here with Jesus.

My child, I know you want and need a tribe. A place that accepts and welcomes you. And on earth there are often glimpses of such things, which is precious. But remember that you will always find a place of belonging in My presence. My arms are always ready to embrace you. Count on it.

27. Glory

And as God's grace reaches more and more people, there will be
*great thanksgiving, and God will receive more and more **glory**.*

~ 2 Corinthians 4:15 NLT

Who gets the glory? Does it matter?

There's a dilemma in the publishing world today, at least from my point of view. Most authors love to write out of our passion and purpose. Many of us also enjoy speaking opportunities as well.

But self-promotion? Not so much.

And yet, today's public figures are required to have a robust online presence through social media, blogging, Tweeting, and more. Potential publishers are eager to know our digital reach. Especially when a new book comes out. And I get that. I know the importance of marketing. It's just that it's a delicate dance between "offering others an opportunity" and "tooting my own horn."

Kind of like "who gets the glory?"

One fellow author shared a time that this kind of pressure caused her to spend money on a business coach who told her to embark on his surefire method of getting speaking gigs. Even though resistant to formulas, she discovered her blind obedience cost her way too much for zero results. She felt the Lord taught her an important lesson—that if she relied on Him rather than a formula for success, then He would get the glory from the increase.

God is our ultimate agent. He can do whatever He pleases to promote our efforts that will bring Him glory.

Our part? Today's verse reminds us that it is "as God's grace reaches more and more people" that God is glorified.

I know, of course, that I must continue to have a generous and grace-filled presence in the world in order for my message to be heard and read.

But my goal is to do this with kindness, humility, and complete trust in my God, who is sovereign over all.

The New Testament Greek word used here is *doxon*, which is translated "glory," "honor," "inherent worth." The corresponding Old Testament Hebrew word for glory is *kabo*, often translated "weight" or "significance."

A weight and an inherent worth that belongs only to the Creator and Sustainer of the universe. Not to us be any glory.

"What is the chief end of man?" *The Westminster Shorter Catechism* answers this question with the following mandate: "To glorify God, and enjoy him forever."

"God made us in His image so that we can reveal His glory through our transformed lives. We can live in a way that brings change—not only within us, but in our relationships, our communities, our country, and our world."[65]

Our lives glorify God whenever we allow Him to do things through us that could never have been done by our own efforts. Then all credit and honor goes to the One who indwells and empowers us.

Living so that ordinary graces are not only noticed and appreciated, but passed along to others. That is our call.

Bringing thanksgiving to all and glory to the ultimate Grace-Giver.

My child, I find great pleasure in lifting you up. In commending and confirming your efforts for the kingdom. But I will not share My glory. I will, however, be glorified every single time you use My power and presence in your efforts. And that makes us all shine.

28. Striving

*"Cease **striving** and know that I am God. I will be exalted
among the nations, I will be exalted in the earth."*

~ Psalm 46:10 NASB

Did you know that Ernest Hemingway once wrote a six-word story?

"For sale. Baby shoes. Never worn."

From that, a magazine editor chose to run a "Six-Word Memoir" contest that is still ongoing.

The challenge? "Describe your life in six words."

I was stumped. How had I spent my early days? What changed? How am I living now? Finally, the six words came to me—the bare essence of my life story so far.

"Tried hard. Embraced grace. Forever thankful."

Tried hard. That was me. Striving. To get it *right* (whatever that meant at the time). To be excellent. Striving to somehow orchestrate my life so that God might love me more. Ah, that was the problem.

I spent too many years striving for brownie points by which to earn God's love.

And yet God says, "Cease striving!"

I am so reminded of the iconic Bob Newhart comedy skit where the psychiatrist just tells his patient, "Stop it!" after hearing a great litany of struggles. Forgive me for comparing God to a twentieth-century comedian, but there you are. Plain words.

Just *stop* what you are doing. Of course, in most Bible translations the words here are the somewhat gentler "Be still."

Where in your life do you need to cease striving and be still? "All I know is that many of us need to stop. . . . When was the last time you breathed deeply, parked your busy brain for a moment, and took your body for a walk, then sat outside and closed your eyes and let the sunlight sit

on your face as you reveled in the holy love of God? Given the chance, our bodies themselves can actually refresh our relentless minds."[66]

And, once stopped, what will it take for you to "know that I am God"? That He is indeed enough? Trustworthy. Powerful. Loving. Forgiving. Handing out grace gifts to anyone who lingers long enough to touch his garment or hold out our open hands.

When you stop striving, what then? Will you rest in His love and acceptance? Will you converse with Him through prayer?

Words three and four of my six-word memoir are "Embraced grace." The pivotal change. The catalyst for the 180-degree turn to the final two words, "Forever thankful."

Andrew Murray does encourage *striving* in prayer: "Do not strive in your own strength; cast yourself at the feet of the Lord Jesus, and wait upon him in the sure confidence that he is with you, and works in you. . . . Strive in prayer; let faith fill your heart—so will you be strong in the Lord, and in the power of His might."[67]

May your own six words result from a certain experience of God's many ordinary graces showered upon you as you wait expectantly with open hands.

My child, remember I know your heart. I know how much you want to please Me. To serve Me. To get it right. But hear My heart now: all you have to do is receive the gift. Will you rest in My love? I'm offering grace to you with an open hand. Just reach out.

29. Least

*"Truly I tell you, whatever you did for one of the **least** of these
brothers and sisters of mine, you did for me."*

~ Matthew 25:40 NIV

My heart went out to this wife and mother. It really did.

After all, her brother had only sent a quick text message informing her
he was bringing a homeless man to their farm—a man who needed both
work and a place to stay. And now she was face-to-face with him at the
kitchen door. He was obviously dirty and thirsty.

She could certainly offer him a cup of cold water.

But her mind was spinning—would her young children be safe with
him around? Should she be cautious or leap into radical loving?

The New Testament Greek word for hospitality, *philoxenia*, is actually
made of two words: *philos*—"brotherly love," and *xenia*—the "stranger."

Why is it so hard for us to love the stranger in a tangible way? Especially since in giving to the least, we encounter Christ.

"The mystery of ministry is that the Lord is to be found where we minister. Our care for people thus becomes the way to meet the Lord. The
more we give, support, guide, counsel and visit, the more we receive, not
just similar gifts, but the Lord Himself. To go to the poor is to go to the
Lord."[68]

What can you do today?

Most of us don't have extra housing, but we can "do small things with
great love," as someone once encouraged. Fill backpacks with toiletries,
warm socks, T-shirts, nutrition bars, water bottles, gloves, fleece throws,
toothbrushes, cleansing wipes, pens and pads, and food gift cards. Keep
these filled backpacks in your car and pray for God to lead you to the indi-
viduals who need them most. Go through your stash of surplus coats and
professional clothing, donating them to an agency that arranges appoint-

ments for the unemployed. Volunteer to serve at a soup kitchen. Give a ride to someone who doesn't drive. Visit a senior center and offer your talents, even if those talents are just being friendly or reading aloud.

Why not come up with your own ideas for reaching out to the marginalized and the least?

That farm family not only opened their home, but they learned the joy of ordinary graces—broken people coming together and discovering Christ in their midst.

If we are too full of self, we may miss such opportunities—even if they arrive on our doorstep. "How many times have I missed Him? . . . What the world says is weak and small may be where Christ is offering Himself to you most of all. . . . You miss Jesus when you aren't looking for His two disguises: the smallest and the servant."[69]

May you and I reach out to the least and small today. Perhaps we will discover Jesus in the process.

My child, I know it's confusing to know how to help stop the ocean of pain surrounding you today. And that you build walls to insulate yourself from the feeling of helplessness. But you can do one thing today. For the least of these. And when you do, it will be for Me as well.

30. Treasure

*We now have this light shining in our hearts, but we ourselves are like fragile clay jars containing this great **treasure**. This makes it clear that our great power is from God, not from ourselves.*

~ 2 Corinthians 4:7 NLT

I always wanted to be a Ming vase for God.

Beautiful. Exotic. Perfect. Wouldn't that be a powerful witness to my great God? Think of the people who would flock to faith once they experienced me in all my loveliness—always being, saying, and doing the *right thing*!

Alas, it was not to be.

No Ming vases here. I saw in the mirror a clay pot—the gal next door.

Finally, I was where God wanted me to be.

Now He could pour His light and treasure into my simple vessel, and thus it would be noticed for what it was. God's power. God's glory. God's beauty. Manifested from the center of an ordinary life.

To "[make] it clear that our great power is from God, not from ourselves."

On a recent live radio interview, my host, Lynne, read my new one-word-a-day devotional, *Dwelling Places*, and was sharing about the words that most ministered to her. One was the word *return*, about returning to the Lord and what it can mean in our lives. Lynne said that just after she read those two pages, she encountered a prodigal—a woman who insisted she was now closer to the devil than to God. Since Lynne had just read all those words of hope and grace and mercy that Jesus extends to the wanderer, she passed along what she had learned.

"May I read your closing prayer from that day—'Return'—on the air right now?" she asked.

As I listened to words I had written only a year before, I began to weep quietly.

I was so deeply aware that *God* was the one who had put those words in me to share with others. He is the "Great Treasure" inside this ordinary person. And because I allowed Him to use me, He was glorified and perhaps a broken soul was encouraged.

In today's verse we are called "fragile clay jars." How easily we break! How utterly chipped and cracked, faded and fragile we are—particularly after a lifetime of pouring out. We wonder if we are too damaged to be used, too weak to fight the battles. But the more holes in our armor, the brighter the "light shining in our hearts."

Madeleine L'Engle observed, "If we are qualified, we tend to think we have done the job ourselves. If we are forced to accept our evident lack of qualification, then there's no danger that we will confuse God's work with our own or God's glory with our own."[70]

When we finally meet—and I sincerely hope we will one day—you will see an older woman with laugh lines, bling, extra pounds, and big hair. A woman who fails daily, but finally has enough sense to confess and receive forgiveness, tentatively moving forward in my favorite cowboy boots.

Actually, you might not even notice me. Well, except for the Light.

I sure hope on the day we meet, a glow just happens to be peeking through from where my heavenly Father dwells deep inside. Then you will know the truth about me.

It really *is* all about Him.

My child, there are no ordinary people. Each one is created in My image and is a true treasure. But the packaging—well, I intentionally make that simple so that you are approachable by all kinds of folks. Just remember to shine from within, and I will do the rest.

Strength

Lord, we would endure; O sift us
Clear of weakness; make us **strong**.
Lord, we would endure, O lift us
Into joy and conquering song.
Cause us in Thy peace to dwell
Seeing the invisible.

~ Amy Carmichael
"Endurance"

1. Strength

*The LORD gives **strength** to his people; the LORD blesses his people with peace.*

~ Psalm 29:11 NIV

"Pay no attention to that man behind the curtain!" the loud voice boomed.

This iconic movie quote are the words of a very ordinary man who has spent years pretending to be the Wizard of Oz, so those around him in the Emerald City will have confidence that he is a "wise and all-knowing leader." This "wizard" used tricks and imagery to exercise authority over others, rather than face up to his own helpless situation of being stranded.

His real name? Oscar Zoroaster Phadrig Isaac Norman Henkle Emmannuel Ambroise Diggs. When he is unmasked by Dorothy and her curious dog, Toto, his supposed power proves to be little more than wishful thinking played out in smoke and mirrors. Literally.

Throughout the Bible, God promises to give strength to His people. In our verse today, this word "strength" is translated from the Old Testament Hebrew word *'oz*, also meaning "force, security, majesty, might, and boldness." The Wizard of Oz was indeed on a search for true strength.

Do you long for this kind of strength and power in your life?

I know from my own failed experiences that all the machinations and amplification in the world—any false show of force—cannot make me strong. The Lord alone offers the gift of *'oz*.

In the Book of Numbers, a strong and brave young man name Caleb accompanied eleven other men to spy out the Promised Land. He and Joshua returned to the desert, reporting to Moses that they believed, with God on their side, the Israelites had strength to defeat Jericho. But the "ten faithless spies" drowned out all hopes with their own fear and weakness.

It took forty more years of wandering before the Israelites risked crossing the Jordan, and even then, only Joshua and Caleb were allowed to enter the Promised Land.

Eventually Joshua had the great task of dividing the land. Caleb, at eighty-five, claiming the same strength and energy he had when he spied for Moses and his people, asked Joshua to award him a land inside Judah.

"Give me the hill country!" (Joshua 14:12a NLT).

Caleb knew that Anaks (giants) still inhabited that particular land, but he was not asking for a comfortable dwelling in his old age. He didn't want to just coast. He was passionate and wholeheartedly devoted to the Lord—very much willing to do the hard things.

"If the Lord is with me, I will drive them out of the land" (Joshua 14:12b NLT).

Joshua blessed his old friend Caleb and gave him Hebron. And the result of Caleb counting on God's *promise* and *power*?

"There was *peace* in the land" (Joshua 14:15 CEV, emphasis added).

In this season of your life, where do you need strength? That is exactly where God's ordinary grace gifts will appear. What we need, when we need it. Promise. Power. Peace.

Let's discover how strength comes in many different packages in the days ahead.

My child, I know that sometimes you feel weak and weary. Demands override your ability to fill. It would be so easy to quit . . . or coast. Please don't. If you are willing to "do hard things," I will always give you my power and strength to accomplish them. Trust Me and count on it.

2. Broken

*A **broken** spirit is my sacrifice, God. You won't despise a heart, God, that is **broken** and crushed.*

~ Psalm 51:17

I learned about brokenness through an ancient Japanese practice called *wabi-sabi*.

Wabi-sabi is defined as "the art of finding beauty in imperfection by revering authenticity above all." The somewhat scary idea of shining light on the real and broken areas of my life.

While our natural tendency is to mend broken pottery with clear glue, hiding the imperfections, here gold-sprinkled lacquer *highlights* the cracks and imperfections. "Japanese culture sees *wabi-sabi* as beautiful because it is imperfect and broken. The gospel is like spiritual *wabi-sabi*. It is the story of how God redeems imperfect, broken people and uses them to bless a fractured world."[1]

My own default is to hide the broken parts of my life—losses and insecurities, inability to cope or control, fears and failures. Part of this is for self-preservation: *Once released, would I ever be able to hold myself together again?* Part of it is from pride: *No matter what has happened, I'm okay. I'm strong. Really, I got this.*

But today's verse says that God wants to embrace those places where my heart "is broken and crushed." To somehow piece me back together with gold that highlights the mended cracks. It is taken from King David's beautiful confessional prayer after he had sinned with Bathsheba. He was racked with shame and guilt. But as he poured out all this brokenness to God, he was healed to move forward.

Are you also hesitant to share broken places?

In a world where strength is valued over weakness, who doesn't want to at least appear whole? But our partnership in suffering with others can bear much fruit. Until we own our broken places as part of who we are, we can never fully experience the ordinary gifts of grace offered again and again with the goal of growing us into compassionate "wounded healers."

The week Ann Voskamp's best-selling book *The Broken Way* premiered, I made arrangements to be with her at an event in Boston called "The Deeper Life." Ready to worship, learn, listen, and experience going deeper with God as a participant after a busy season of work and ministry, I arrived open for whatever God would do.

Until life interrupted. One phone call. And I immediately drove back to Hartford, where my husband had been unexpectedly hospitalized with a stroke.

During that anxious, tearful drive, God spoke to me about clinging to Him during those seasons when all we have is our brokenness. Whether it comes through physical, chronic pain or diminished professional ability or lack of control over a loved one's suffering, it is the same. We stumble forward and hold out our hearts.

To receive the gold for the cracks.

"God's way is always the broken way. The fellowship of the broken believe that suffering is a gift He entrusts to us and He can be trusted to make this suffering into a gift."[2]

Will you embrace the gift of being broken today?

My child, I turn broken into beautiful. But first you must bring the shattered parts of your soul and lay them at My feet. As I pour the gold into your cracks, you will experience new strength to go beyond what you ever imagined. Shining with the grace of restoration and renewal. Beautiful.

3. Rescue

*"Go with the strength you have, and **rescue** Israel from the Midianites. I am sending you!"*

~ Judges 6:14 NLT

"If the Lord is with us, why then has all this happened? . . . The Lord has abandoned us" lamented newly appointed judge, Gideon, right after an angel had appeared and addressed him as "Valiant Hero" (Judges 6:13 NASB).

He felt like anything but a hero.

The cruel, evil Midianites were crushing Israel; what could one man possibly do? Rescue seemed like a long shot.

But our verse today is exactly the message the Lord gave Gideon then, and perhaps has for you and me today. "Go with the strength you have."

Even if it's just a little strength. Even if it seems like no strength at all.

The deciding factor for victory will be the words "I am sending you!" Not who we *are* or what we can *do*, but rather that we have been *sent by God*.

Gideon was quick to point out his lack of qualifications—he was from the weakest clan in Manasseh and was the least in his father's house (see v. 15). But he eventually allowed God to act on his behalf, even in seemingly impossible circumstances.

The Old Testament Hebrew word used here is *natsal*—often translated "to rescue, deliver, snatch away, or save." It can refer to God's rescue of people, or of one person's rescue of another. And often it refers to divine rescue, especially when part of a prayer.

Do you need to be rescued today?

"The word *rescue* in the Old Testament is a picture, again, of God's grace. It also is a prophetic theological concept, pointing toward the ultimate rescue from sin and its deadly consequences."[3]

Whatever you are facing today, it couldn't be any more implausible than

Gideon taking only three hundred men, armed with only rams' horns and clay jars, to attack thousands of ruthless soldiers.

But because God fought for them and sent them forward, "the Midianites rushed around in a panic, shouting as they ran to escape. When the 300 Israelites blew their rams' horns, the Lord caused the warriors in the camp to fight against each other with their swords" (Judges 7:21-22 NLT).

Panic turned to peace after the victory. "Throughout the rest of Gideon's lifetime—about forty years—there was peace in the land" (Judges 8:28 NLT).

One friend learned this lesson from Gideon: "Thankfully, God offers a principle—a secret—to help us overcome panic: resting in his deliverance. Gideon isn't much of a poster child for a less-panicked life. . . . But he learned a secret. God acts on our behalf when circumstances seem impossible."[4]

God wants to rescue you from panic and fill you with His peace. Will you follow, even when it seems impossible?

My child, I am the One who rescues you. But first you must respond in obedience, even if My way seems out-of-the-box peculiar. Trust Me. And go with the strength you already have. There are victories ahead.

4. Weakness

He said, "My grace is all you need. My power works best in
weakness. *" So now I am glad to boast about my* ***weaknesses,***
so that the power of Christ can work through me.

~ 2 Corinthians 12:9 NLT

Jesus and the early church turned the world upside down.

To find your life, you must first lose it; the smallest is the greatest; the last shall be first. All concepts totally opposite of what the world teaches.

And the apostle Paul continued in like manner when he stated, "The weakness of God is stronger than men" (1 Corinthians 1:25 NASB).

We often think of the apostle Paul as larger-than-life. But the reality is that he was all too human, just like us.

Once he told the believers at Corinth, "I came to you in weakness—timid and trembling. And my message and my preaching were very plain. Rather than using clever and persuasive speeches, I relied only on the power of the Holy Spirit" (1 Corinthians 2:3-4 NLT). He wanted people to know that it was God's power in him that gave him strength.

Did you know that frailty can become the pathway to God's power?

> Our weakness is the very place God does his most beautiful work. Paul knew this, most likely because he had been trained by weakness. He had learned to welcome it as a friend, knowing his weakened state would leave room for the power of God.[5]

Jesus imparted to us the greatest grace gift when He was at His weakest—on the cross. Frederick Buechner said this means we are never *safe.* "There is no place where we can hide from God, no place where we are safe from his power to break in two and recreate the human heart because it is just where he seems most helpless that he is most strong."[6]

Where are you feeling most helpless today?

Will you give that to Jesus and ask Him to use you in the midst of your weakness?

Suzanne felt totally inadequate when it came to being a speaker and being a mama. But because God had clearly called her to do both, she was willing to allow Jesus to take her beyond her strengths into that scary place of serving out of weakness. She realized that Jesus hadn't chosen His own disciples merely based on their talents and strengths. So why *not* her?

> I believe Jesus loved nothing more than watching one of the disciples discover what he was capable of. Just as much, I believe he delighted in watching his strength show up in their weaknesses. Get to know your strengths. Live them as much as you can, but don't underestimate how life-changing it is when God shows up in your weaknesses. If he leads us into our weaknesses, it teaches us to depend on him. It grows us in areas that we wouldn't go on our own.[7]

Perhaps we can all say with Paul, "When I am weak, then I am strong" (2 Corinthians 12:10 NLT).

My child, sometimes it's almost impossible to keep going, isn't it? To simply put one foot in front of the other, moving forward in faith. Don't you know this is the very place where I step in and work through you? In My power, you have total access to all I am and all I have. Be encouraged.

5. Sustain

*Cast your cares on the Lord and he will **sustain** you.*

~ Psalm 55:22 NIV

It is rare for three different ships from the same docks to be lost at sea in the short span of two weeks.

Yet that's exactly what happened to the *Cape Fear*, the *Adriatic*, and the *Beth Dee Bob* in January 1999. Ten men died, five never to be found.

Yes, commercial fishing can be a dangerous way to make a living. But investigations revealed that (1) none involved a hull breach; (2) all were piloted by veteran, experienced captains; (3) all were near the end of their journeys, fewer than fifteen miles from port.[8]

What happened?

They either carried way too much weight or carried the weight improperly. Unable to support its load, each boat eventually sank.

When asked what in the world made them think they could add an extra ten to fifteen *tons* of excess weight, the captains shrugged and indicated that such practices were the norm. Sadly, because "everybody did it," they never perceived their ships to be in danger.

Are you carrying more than you were designed to bear—people to care for, tasks to accomplish, responsibilities to cover?

You, too, may be in danger of sinking under the weight of it all.

We were simply not made to be constantly available to everyone for everything. And yet that's exactly how many of us find ourselves living today.

One of the ships wasn't actually overloaded; it was carrying its weight improperly. By stacking full crates on top of empty ones, the crew compromised the boat's center of gravity. Seaworthy vessels must be heavier below the waterline than above it. That weight is called *ballast*. It's vital but often unseen.

Look at your calendar. Is there any white space, or are all the little squares already filled in? Look at your living space. Is there some semblance of order, or is your suitcase from last week's trip still waiting to be unpacked? These sorts of things are the "red flares" that show us we need to cut back and organize all the cargo in our lives and our homes. The great thing is that this will also benefit those who are closest to us.

If you and I don't balance the part of our lives that lies deep in the soul, we can sink. All it might take is one more "care" combined with weather, pressure, and fatigue to send us to the bottom.

> The *Cape Fear*, the *Adriatic*, and the *Beth Dee Bob* all went down in heavy weather. . . . But even when dealing with a "normal" sized storm, when you enter the equation compromised by too great a load, you greatly increase your chance for disaster.
>
> According to *Seatrade Review* (Dec. 1994): "The accident rarely has a single overwhelming cause. Usually there are a number of elements, none necessarily of outstanding significance in isolation, whose combination proves fatal."[9]

Don't be a shipwreck waiting to happen!

Today's verse urges us to toss some of that extra load off our ships— "cast your cares on the Lord." God, your Creator, wants to also be your Sustainer—"he will sustain you."

─────────────────────────────

෧෩

My child, are you close to sinking under the incredible weight of all your responsibilities, concerns, and fears? I am here to sustain you, but first we may need to do some rearranging of your cargo. You were never meant to carry it all. I will help you bear the load. In all the right places.

6. Dignity

*She is a woman of strength and **dignity** and has no fear
of old age.*

~ Proverbs 31:25 TLB

I was disappointed when I saw the guest speaker.

It was College Life on Sunday night and our featured guest was a very old lady wearing a housecoat and a crown of braids. At only seventeen, I was hoping for a "jock for Jesus."

But that night I learned an important lesson about age. And dignity.

As she began speaking in a Dutch accent, the woman held up a cloth showing tangled thread, reciting a poem about her life being a "weaving between my Lord and me." She then turned over the tapestry to reveal the beautiful pattern. Evidently God knows what He's doing when He weaves both dark and bright threads in our lives.

By now I was completely spellbound as she continued. "My name is Corrie ten Boom, and I have spent my life telling people all over the world that there is no pit so deep that God's love is not deeper still. Let me tell you my story . . ."

I heard of her family hiding Jews in their cupboard, her experience in a Nazi concentration camp, and God's presence in that deep pit of hell. Corrie radiated dignity, strength, and God's love.

At that moment, I wanted what she had. I whispered, "God, make me a godly, courageous, strong woman like that."

Today *I* am often the older woman in the roomful of younger people— sharing my own stories of God's faithfulness through the painful and joyful experiences of life. And though I don't wear a housedress and bun, I can only hope I vaguely resemble the Corrie I met so very many years ago.

Her heart of dignity and strength.

Seasoned enough to be comfortable in my own skin. Grateful for any opportunity to invest in the next generation. Wise enough to accept my limitations and focus on the essentials.

Are you wasting time worrying about growing old?

Why not embrace your current season of life, making the most of your wisdom and strength? In our verse today, "dignity" is one way to translate the original Hebrew word *hadar*, also defined as "magnificence, beauty, excellence, glory, honor, and majesty."

Wouldn't you like to display that kind of dignity—at any age?

> We've seen how gorgeous God's woman can be. Her eyes shine with His love, her mouth smiles with His joy, her hands move at His bidding, and her feet follow where He leads. She exudes His peace, she offers His hope, she knows His Word, she speaks His truth, she embraces His people, she glorifies His name. She's the woman we all want to be when we grow up. God alone makes that possible.[10]

If you are younger, why not seek out an older believer and ask him or her "At what time in your life did you feel closest to God?" or "What would you say to your younger self today?" Inquire of that mentor's valuable life lessons, of his or her great successes and deepest failures.

And if you are the one who has lived longer, be present and listen. Ask younger friends about their biggest challenges and deepest desires. And if they seem open, prayerfully share your story.

Strength and dignity are for all ages at all times, God's gift when we show up and live fully.

───────── ❧ ─────────

My child, dignity is not a stuffy trait, but a regal one. Befitting a daughter or son of the King. And I want to imbue you with this character trait as you continue to be My representative. No matter what your age or season, you can shine for Me in strong and gracious ways.

7. Groaning

*O LORD, hear me as I pray; pay attention to my **groaning**.*
Listen to my cry for help, my King and my God, for I pray to no
one but you.

~ Psalm 5:1-2 NLT

Have you been there? Stretched prone on the floor, crying your eyes out; perhaps a bit of wailing or a deep gasp here and there. Your heart is pleading for someone, but there are no real words.

Only groaning.

Friend, God hears you, and He totally understands.

Even when we cannot put into words what we are experiencing, or asking, or wondering. Like the psalmist, we cry for help to our King and "pray to no one but you."

How well I remember crying out to God as a new wife and new mother of three small children, feeling so overwhelmed and like such a failure that I literally didn't have words to express either my prayers of confession or my prayers of petition. There were simply no words.

But I still went to Him. Like a child.

Perhaps similar to the little girl who was overheard kneeling by her bed, quietly saying prayers: "Dear God, a, b, c, d, e, f, g." When she reached *z*, she said, "Amen." Her mother asked why she was saying her alphabet, to which the little girl answered. "Mama, I didn't know what to say, so I just said the letters and decided God could put them together."

God understands our prayers.

> When you and I speak a ragged and imperfect prayer or have
> no words to express our groaning, heaven responds to it as if
> we had spoken flawlessly. . . . Our wordlessness is no hindrance
> to him because he reads our hearts.[11]

The precious gift we are given at such an extremely low point is the third person of the Trinity, the Holy Spirit. "And the Holy Spirit helps us in our weakness. For example, we don't know what God wants us to pray for. But the Holy Spirit prays for us with groanings that cannot be expressed in words" (Romans 8:26 NLT).

Groaning on our behalf. Right beside us.

This word in the New Testament Greek, *stenagmois*, is usually translated as "unspoken, never rising to the audible level at all." Sometimes our failure to know God's will makes us unable to petition Him specifically. Yet here the Holy Spirit steps in and expresses to God intercession that perfectly matches His will. He puts the words together as He sees fit, just as the little girl suggested.

Don't know how to pray? Ask the Spirit to pray for you.

The Holy Spirit knows exactly how to connect our needs with God's gifts. "Though we feel ignorant in our prayers, the Spirit does not. God is not so far off that we need to raise our voices to be heard. We need only groan."[12]

My child, I hear you. I know what is in your heart that is too deep for words. Prayer is simply our dialogue, and you can come to Me with anything and everything. I will always listen and respond. Even when you don't have the words. Especially when you don't have the words. Just come.

8. Carry

*They couldn't **carry** him through the crowd, so they tore off*
part of the roof above where Jesus was. When they had made an
opening, they lowered the mat on which the paralyzed man was
lying.

~ Mark 2:4

Kevan wasn't your typical twentysomething taking a backpacking trip to Europe.

He was actually *in* the backpack.

And his friends—Philip, Luke, Tom, and Ben—carried their sixty-five-pound friend because he has spinal muscular atrophy (SMA), a genetic disease that severely limits strength and mobility. The places he and his friends visited—catacombs, monasteries, and remote villages—would have otherwise been inaccessible for someone who uses a wheelchair.

So the guys designed a custom backpack. Not unlike the friends in our verse today who "couldn't carry him through the crowd, so they tore off part of the roof above where Jesus was."

Whatever it takes. To bring our friends to Jesus.

Before the trip Kevan felt both thrilled and nervous.

> "Each place we're visiting has a different element that both excites me and terrifies me. It's funny how those can often be one and the same." His friends had to train before the trip to build up the strength needed to carry [him]. . . .
>
> The group consisted of teachers, musicians, photographers, writers, and two who were filming the trip. "I think we're all broken and disabled in some way. It's just less obvious for some people. My message to people with extreme disabilities is if you have something you want to do, you can find a way to do it."[13]

Like the New Testament man lying on the cot, Kevan has limited mobility, through a degenerative disease with no known cure. But his philosophy is to keep moving and thus inspire people who feel limited to know they really aren't limited. He wants others to seek to live their dreams, even if that's a bit more difficult.

Do you know someone who could use a little help to meet his or her dream?

Offering to "carry" doesn't always mean physical burden-bearing—it may mean investing in a person's project, providing transportation, or mentoring in an area of your expertise. It can almost always mean interceding in prayer on someone else's behalf.

When I read about the men bringing their friend to Jesus for healing—using creative ways to get around a seemingly impossible obstacle (thus lowering him through the roof)—I thought of Philip, Luke, Tom, and Ben. Kevan's friends signed up to help him reach a special destination—the sixth-century monastery on the Irish island of Skellig Michael.

At the top of six hundred stone steps.

Not possible for a wheelchair-bound man. But a limitless possibility for a man with strong and faithful friends.

Reaching this particular peak was a spiritual victory for Kevan, who is a follower of Christ. "I convey to those who are not disabled the aspect of self-sacrifice, and carrying one another. Not just physically, but emotionally and spiritually through this life."[14]

His friends embodied what we are all called to do: "Carry each other's burdens and so you will fulfill the law of Christ" (Galatians 6:2).

My child, you are never too heavy for Me to carry. When your strength runs out, from illness or weariness, I will step in and gladly help. Sometimes in the form of friends. So receive this gift. And then one day you will carry someone else.

9. Evil One

*But the Lord is faithful, and he will strengthen you and protect you from the **evil one**.*

~ 2 Thessalonians 3:3 NIV

When Steve Brown was growing up, a bully moved into his neighborhood. Much older and bigger, the guy was frightening. But Steve, deciding that the only way to get the bully off his back was to stand up against him, stood his ground one day after being chased home from school.

"Much to my surprise, he became scared. He started to tremble all over. I said to myself, 'Man, I'm really something!' Then I heard a noise and turned around to notice my father, standing behind me on the front porch. I hadn't terrified that bully, but the presence of my father sure had."[15]

The evil one is more than just a bully. He is a powerful enemy of your soul.

But God is more powerful. Our verse today reminds us of His gift to both "strengthen you and protect you."

How? By standing, not just behind us, as Steve's father did, but right beside us. Always. We are never alone when the bullies come after us.

Evil's favorite lie? *You are all alone, and nothing will ever change.*

When I hear those whispers, I become most vulnerable. I believe the lies that I have ruined my life and others' lives so much that God can never love me again, never use me in His kingdom.

> The serpent, the enemy of your soul, his name means "prosecutor" and that's what he does—he tries to make you feel alone and on trial. . . . He poisons you endlessly with self-lies. And the first tactic of the enemy of your soul is always to distort your identity.[16]

Have you ever given in to the "fake news" the evil one broadcasts to you daily?

If so, then you too are ready to receive God's grace gifts offered freely to anyone targeted by evil. "Grace embraces you before you prove anything, and after you've done everything wrong. . . . Grace loves you when you are at your darkest worst, and wraps you in the best light."[17]

In addition to receiving the grace gift, we can turn to Scripture, which offers us a two-part strategy of defense: "Submit yourselves therefore to God. Resist the devil, and he will flee from you" (James 4:7 KJV). One way I resist is to shout into the darkness, "In the name of Jesus, be gone!"

Jesus intercedes for us in the same way He prayed for His disciples in the upper room: "My prayer is not that you take them out of the world but that you protect them from the evil one" (John 17:15 NIV).

To the evil one: "Be gone!" To us: "Be assured."

My child, there is one who lies to you. All the time. Who whispers taunts into your ear, words that have the ring of truth but are not true. That evil one cannot have you. I am here for you, to protect you and guard you from his ways. But you need to use My strength as a gift in the battle. And My courage.

10. Joy

*"Do not grieve, for the **joy** of the LORD is your strength."*

~ Nehemiah 8:10 NIV

C. S. Lewis spent his life marked by *Sehnsucht*. A longing for joy.

That longing led him to eventually renounce atheism and become one of the greatest Christian apologists of the twentieth century.

> In a sense the central story of my life is about nothing else. . . . It is that of an unsatisfied desire which is itself more desirable than any other satisfaction. I call it Joy, which is here a technical term and must be sharply distinguished both from Happiness and Pleasure. Joy (in my sense) has indeed one characteristic, and one only, in common with them: the fact that anyone who has experienced it will want it again.[18]

Have you ever experienced true joy? Do you want it again?

God's Word says that we can actually live in the middle of strength and joy. "Strength and joy are in his dwelling place" (1 Chronicles 16:27 NIV). In the Old Testament Hebrew the word *chadah* translates to "joy, rejoicing, gladness."

One man put it this way:

> Whenever things in my life leave me unhappy, joy can still be present because it comes from a different source. Joy is an attitude I adopt in spite of how things go; it's the deep assurance I have that the God who loves me is in control. Joy does not happen to me one day and avoid me the next. Joy is the result of a choice based on the knowledge that I belong to God, who is my Refuge. And nothing, not even death, can take God away from me.[19]

James, the brother of Jesus, certainly knew that joy wasn't contingent on circumstances as he sought to lead the early Christians in Jerusalem.

"My brothers and sisters, think of the various tests you encounter as occasions for joy" (James 1:2).

I have always gravitated to the word *joy*. In fact, I named my very first doll, who was really a person, Joy. Made of hard plastic, she had red hair and ugly joints that allowed her wrists and knees to move. But she was a grace gift from an understanding mama who took me the day after Christmas to find the one doll left over in our small-town department store. For months I had insisted I didn't want a doll for Christmas. But when I didn't get one, I realized that's *all* I wanted. Mama offered me grace. This Joy lives at my home to this day.

"Joy is strength. It has muscle. It's what can make you strong in this busted-up world of manifold heartbreak. When we are flattened under the curse of the world, joy is what will help us rise up again, fist in the air."[20]

Will you embrace joy today and become stronger than you are?

My child, joy really is a choice. To embrace something deeper than what is happening in outward circumstances. To realize that I am at work to orchestrate good things for you. I long to infuse your life with the kind of real joy that brings strength and trust. No matter what.

11. Resource

*In conclusion be strong—not in yourselves but in the Lord, in the power of his boundless **resource**.*

~ Ephesians 6:10 PHILLIPS

"We want to give your church three million dollars," said the man on the other end of the phone.

The pastor was speechless, as the donor said there were no strings attached and they wanted to remain anonymous.

"Pastor Mark, we love your vision and trust your leadership. There are some churches we wouldn't feel comfortable investing in because they wouldn't know what to do with the money, but *you have vision beyond your resources*," he concluded.

What does it mean to have a vision based on God's "boundless resource" instead of letting what we already have determine our vision?

It means praying through what you sense God is directing you to do and say. It means believing that the God who owns the cattle on a thousand hills has an unlimited supply. It means being smart and practicing sound financial management, but sometimes stepping out in big faith.

Pastor Mark had done just that when he began praying for two million dollars to pay off the mortgage on his church's outreach coffeehouse. His four prayer partners prayed for that two-million-dollar promise for four years. "I had no idea how God would do it, but I knew I needed to circle that promise in prayer. . . . Then one day at about three in the afternoon, I got the phone call. . . . The moment I heard those words, 'We want to give you three million dollars,' I knew it was a fulfillment of the promise God had given us."[21]

If my vision is truly God-given, it may very well be beyond my ability to fulfill it. Honestly, that scares me. Who wants to fail? But I also don't just want to invest my life in small endeavors that are easily accomplished. Why not Pray Big and be strong in the Lord of limitless resource?

Jennie Allen, who began the IF:Gathering, believes God has called His people to a huge vision—to gather women into discipleship, show them Jesus, see people transformed, feed the poor, bring hope to the sick, and love families through hard times.

> While sometimes we miss the wonder because we daily live out our calling in mundane ways, He has called us to an exciting and noble and awesome task, and if you are not a part of it, I can promise that is one reason that you feel like you are missing something—because you are.
> . . . We cannot accomplish any of the purposes of God unless we do them with the power and the resources and the energy of God.[22]

If you do the same thing in the same old way, you will continue to achieve the same results. What would you attempt today if you counted on the God of the universe to provide whatever was needed?

Pray for direction. But also be willing to step out in faith, as God guides you to do the next thing. His power and provision are boundless.

My child, perhaps your vision is too small. Or you are only pursuing that for which you can already see provision. Did you not know that I have boundless resource? Whatever you are called to do, you can be sure the provision will eventually come. Pray for it. Look for it. Then move forward as you are guided.

12. Surrounds

*As the mountains surround Jerusalem, so the LORD **surrounds**
his people both now and forevermore.*

~ Psalm 125:2 NIV

A missionary once told the story of biking for two days into the nearest African city to purchase supplies for his small field hospital. After treating the injuries of a man he encountered, he visited the bank and supply store, and then continued his bike journey home, camping one night in the jungle.

When he returned to that town several weeks later, the man he had bandaged confessed to him that he and some friends had planned to rob him at the campsite. They knew he had money and were going to take it and kill him. But they were frightened by twenty-six armed guards surrounding the sleeping man.

When the missionary said he had been all alone, the African vehemently declared that the protection of the guards was the only reason they had run away. The next year when the missionary shared this story at his home church while on furlough, one man asked him the date and time of this occurrence.

> After being told the date, the man explained, "At the time of this incident, I was on the golf course for some morning practice. I was about to putt when I was struck by a sudden urge to pray for you. It was so strong I left the course and called some men at our church to join me in praying for you. Would all you men who prayed that day stand up?" One by one the missionary counted the men.
>
> There were twenty-six—the exact number of "armed guards" the thwarted assailants had seen.[23]

One day the prophet Elisha and his servant awakened to discover they were surrounded by the enemy.

Though his servant panicked, Elisha could see that spiritual protection was also in place. "'Don't be afraid,' Elisha said, 'because there are more of us than there are of them.' Then Elisha prayed, 'Lord, please open his eyes that he may see.'

"Then the Lord opened the servant's eyes, and he saw that the mountain was full of horses and fiery chariots surrounding Elisha" (2 Kings 6:16-17). So then Elisha prayed that his enemies' eyes would be blinded. They were, and Elisha led them directly into the hands of the king of Israel.

You are surrounded today. Perhaps by distractions and duties and discouragement. But also surrounded by God's presence and power; even in the form of heavenly guard!

The psalmist compares this protection to the city of Jerusalem, and rightly so. "In ancient times there was no more militarily secure position for a city than to be behind encircling mountains. Trusting in God is like being in a mountain fastness. . . . How? . . . Trusting God is . . . the way to eventually get breathtaking sights of God himself. Most of all, trusting God means connecting yourself to the one person who will endure forever. And that means you will endure as well."[24]

In a world in which seemingly everything changes and nothing lasts, always remember that you are indeed surrounded.

My child, you are never alone. Always surrounded by angels sent from Me—to guard, to guide, to give. You may not see them or ever know they are there. But you can trust Me to surround you always.

13. Spirit

*I ask that he will strengthen you in your inner selves from the
riches of his glory through the **Spirit**.*

~ Ephesians 3:16

Americans are desperate to have strong bodies. In fact, "the global fitness and health club industry generates more than 80 billion U.S. dollars in revenue each year."[25]

But what about inner strength? How much time and resources are you investing in becoming a person with a strong heart and soul?

When we invest in our inner lives, God provides by "riches of his glory through the Spirit."

Just before His crucifixion, Jesus tried to prepare His disciples for His death and resurrection by promising them He would always be with them in spirit. When He later appeared to them, Jesus "breathed on them and said, 'Receive the Holy Spirit'" (John 20:22 NIV). Eugene Peterson says Jesus "replaced Himself with Himself."[26]

The New Testament Greek word used here is *pneuma*, which also means "breath" or "wind." "God breathes life into us through His Spirit. Just as a body can't live without air, a believer can't live without the Holy Spirit. "The spirit . . . bestowed on us shows the world we belong to Him. The Spirit is a gift—unearned and undeserved—from the One who knows that our wobbly faith will require constant proof of His love, His acceptance, His grace, His affection."[27]

I am reminded of the great wind that accompanied Pentecost—when the Holy Spirit was given to the group of disciples gathered together (Acts 2). Not only does this Spirit unify us with one another and with God, but that unity brings us great strength.

> It isn't up to you to grit your teeth and try harder. Instead,
> He's given you the full power of the Holy Spirit to enable you

to become the person He has created you to be. You can't do it alone. . . . When you depend on His Holy Spirit, you will experience His supernatural power and freedom.[28]

When Christ lives in us through His Spirit, our inner selves become strong. And the overflow of a healthy soul life contributes both to outer strength and unity. We are no longer seeking to live in our own power, which is limited, but in God's Holy Spirit power, which is limitless!

One young woman confessed to investing her prime energy and time in stuff that happens on the outside: "I was on a dangerous track, giving the best of myself to people and things 'out there,' while the tender inner core of my life and my home were increasingly stretched, pressurized, brittle. And now they're not."

She made the radical choice to step back and tend her inner life with proactive soul care. "Now the most beautiful, well-tended, truly nurtured and nourished parts of my life are the innermost ones, not the flashy public ones. That's just as it should be."[29]

How will you invest in your inner self today?

My child, you will come to the end of your own strength. Possibly sooner than you hoped. But that's the very reason for the third person of the Trinity—the Holy Spirit. Filling you with divine strength and counsel. Helping you to accomplish more than you could ever do on your own. Indwelled.

14. *Abandon*

Be strong! Be fearless! Don't be afraid and don't be scared by
your enemies, because the LORD your God is the one who marches
*with you. He won't let you down, and he won't **abandon** you.*

~ Deuteronomy 31:6

Perhaps there are no more haunting words than those of Jesus on the cross when He cried out, "My God, my God, why did you abandon me?" (Matthew 27:46 GNT).

It was the ultimate desertion.

Yet God had a purpose. "If he was to be really a man, if he was to know in its fullness what it means to live out a human life, if he was to understand that final suffering and humiliation of which men are capable, then he had to know this: the sense of abandonment by God."[30]

Because all of us will feel abandoned at some time.

And while Jesus had this momentary sense of abandonment on the cross, because of His victory over death, He is the last person who need ever feel forsaken by God. Through the Trinity, God can always be near to us today.

One mother who adopted internationally once visited the Asian dump where her now daughter had been abandoned as a disabled baby. Can you imagine anything more tragic than an abandoned child?

Agonizing over all this represented in her precious daughter's early life, she journaled a fresh way to view the story:

> You weren't abandoned in this place to be forgotten—you were placed in this place to be found.
>
> That place that may feel like *abandonment*—is *placement*.
>
> And what may feel like being thrown away—*is about being placed because a way is coming always.*[31]

Someone shows up.

Mary showed up at the cross when her Son was dying in agony. Perhaps she was recalling His words, "A time is coming . . . when . . . you will leave me all alone. Yet I am not alone, for the Father is with me" (John 16:32 NIV). Her silent presence testified to the truth that though she could not keep Him for herself, His true Sonship was with the Father, who would never leave Him alone. Even if it *seemed* He was alone. Placement.

Who has God placed in your life to alleviate your sense of abandonment?

> Mary encouraged Jesus to move beyond his experience of abandonment and to surrender himself into the embrace of his Father. She was there to strengthen his faith that, even in the midst of darkness, . . . he remains the beloved Son of God, who will never leave him alone. It was this motherly care that finally allowed Jesus to win the battle against the demonic powers of rejection, to ward off the temptation of abandonment, and to surrender his whole being to God, with the words, "Father into your hands I commend my Spirit" (Luke 23:46).[32]

In today's verse, we are reminded that "God is the one who marches with you." We never fight the battles alone. He will never let us down.

Draw near to the One who knows firsthand exactly how you feel. He is here.

My child, perhaps the greatest fear of all is to be abandoned. Alone. Lost. Deserted. I know how that feels, and it's excruciating. But with Me, you never need worry. I will always be at your side. Just a breath prayer away.

15. Confess

*If we **confess** our sins, he will forgive our sins, because we can
trust God to do what is right. He will cleanse us.*

~ 1 John 1:9 NCV

I've learned a lot about confession from my husband, who regularly
journals his confessional prayers to God.

Mike says that being specific and intentional helps him complete the
process described in our verse today: confess sins, receive forgiveness from
God, and be cleansed to move forward.

Each completed cycle brings more strength and grace because we can
"trust God to do what is right" with our vulnerable revelations.

In some church traditions, there is a communal service of confession,
modeled after the ancient church. "Many of the believers began to confess
openly and tell all the evil things they had done," with the result that "in
a powerful way the word of the Lord kept spreading and growing" (Acts
19:18, 20 NCV).

Whether private or public, we need to understand that confession is not
telling God something He doesn't already know, nor is it complaining or
blaming.

"Confession is a radical reliance on grace. A proclamation of our trust in
God's goodness. 'What I did was bad,' we acknowledge, 'but your grace is
greater than my sin, so I confess it.' If our understanding of grace is small,
our confession will be small, reluctant, hesitant, hedged with excuses and
qualifications, full of fear of punishment. But great grace creates an honest
confession."[33]

Ephraim, who lived in Syria in AD 306–373, offers a prayer of confession still appropriate today:

> Lord, I am utterly bowed down. I have despised Your com-
> mandments; I have in various ways soiled my soul, created in

Your image; I have wasted my life in sins. But, O Master, look mercifully from Your holy high place, behold my incorrigible soul and with the means and ways You know correct me by Your mercy. As if standing before You, O Christ King, as if touching Your immaculate feet, so I implore You with a broken heart. Have mercy on me, O merciful One. Amen.[34]

What do you need to confess today?

If you're not sure, why not take a "spiritual MRI" using this verse: "Search me, O God, and know my heart; try me, and know my anxieties; and see if there is any wicked way in me, and lead me in the way everlasting" (Psalm 139:23-24 NKJV).

In a posture of prayer and receptivity, ask God to call to mind past shame, bitterness, and guilt. Even after a whole year of denying His sin with Bathsheba, David finally came to God and pleaded, "God, be merciful to me because you are loving. Because you are always ready to be merciful, wipe out all my wrongs. . . . You are the only one I have sinned against; I have done what you say is wrong" (Psalm 51:1, 4 NCV).

Confess and receive forgiveness. Then move forward in fresh strength.

My child, I know it's hard to face the sin in your life. How much easier just to cover it with modern words or masks. And yet, I ask for You to bring Your sincere repentance to Me so that I might forgive. Then You will be free to move forward in hope.

16. Weary

*"Come to me, all you who are **weary** and burdened, and I will give you rest."*

~ Matthew 11:28 NIV

What load are you trying to carry today?

- A chronic health problem that doesn't appear to be getting any better?
- A challenging financial requirement for which no funds are available?
- A wandering child or a wandering spouse?
- Unemployment or underemployment?
- Confusion as to which path to take in the future?
- Fears about terrorism or prejudice or culture wars?

No wonder you are weary!

Weary is different from just plain tired or sleepy. Weary is soul deep, and usually cannot be cured by a good night's sleep (though that most certainly helps).

In our verse today, Jesus uses the Greek word *kopiao*, which means "to grow tired with burdens or grief." This is the kind of emotional fatigue that penetrates every point of the body.

The psalmist prayed, "My soul is weary with sorrow; strengthen me according to your word" (Psalm 119:28 NIV). The prophet Isaiah sought to address this real need in his people: "The Sovereign Lord has given me a well-instructed tongue, to know the word that sustains the weary" (Isaiah 50:4 NIV).

Both turned to God and His Word for their strength.

Even God rested (see Genesis 2). Why would a God who "will not grow tired or weary" (Isaiah 40:28 NIV) choose to rest? He knew the importance of rest for His children, emphasizing this message after He finished His work of creation. "He rested. And He gave His shiny new people His gift of rest. . . . Their needs were met, they lived in a garden paradise, and they had perfect connection with God and each other. . . . They lived in the present: the gift of God's rest."[35]

But we are not God.

It seems we are never finished with work, with family, with living our unique kingdom story. It is only in our believing in Jesus' finished work on the cross that we can rest from our own striving. Much of our sense of being "burdened" is self-inflicted—we feel as if everything is all up to us, when in reality we can now "rest in dependence upon the activity of Another who dwells within."[36]

Don't try to live the Christian life on your own strength. Or even for your own self-validation. For you will always be weary. "When we are living in Jesus, having come to Him, sitting with Him, staying with Him and in Him—then we are always resting, even when we're working."[37]

All you have to do is take Jesus up on His invitation to "come." Now is the time to send Him that RSVP—yes!

My child, bring your weary body and soul to Me. I offer you the gift of rest in the midst of a quiet peace that will envelop you as you draw near to the One who created you. With limits. You are not meant to keep going constantly. So come apart and rest beside your weary road.

17. Everlasting Arms

"The eternal God is your dwelling place, and underneath are the everlasting arms."

~ Deuteronomy 33:27 ESV

In a single day, I thought about arms in two totally different ways.

Holding my toddler grandgirl in my arms, I never wanted to let her go. I felt protective and loving and strong. In that moment I silently promised her that Granny's arms would always be there for her, however she might need them.

To welcome her with a hug, to prod her further in pursuing a dream, or to support her in disappointment.

But that evening I had to write a friend who had experienced the heart-breaking loss of his wife, and I wrote him what would be my deep desire were I in his place: "May God wrap you in His arms of compassion, comfort, and peace." Arms reminiscent of the *Pietà*—that beautiful imagery of Mary holding the broken Jesus in her arms.

The same arms that hold me close when I'm at the end of myself.

Isaiah provides another picture of this: "He tends his flock like a shepherd: He gathers the lambs in his arms and carries them close to his heart; he gently leads those that have young" (Isaiah 40:11 NIV).

I find these words comforting, as my own daughter is currently mothering two babies in a faraway country, where she has yet to make many friends. Sometimes there just aren't enough arms to get around everyone.

Have you ever felt that way? I suspect every parent or teacher or pastor feels that way at one time or another. Too many people need you—to lift them up, to keep them steady, or to hold them close.

This is when God takes over—with a power that doesn't overwhelm or smother.

> This was no weak arm, but a powerful and mighty one. It takes great strength for One so strong to show gentleness. Did

we not see this in the life of Jesus, our Lord, when it was said of him, "He took the children in his arms, put his hands on them and blessed them" (Mark 10:16)? I have known what it is like to be upheld by these everlasting arms. Those arms have been instantly available to us when we have been in the crucible of life's experiences. It's hard to express to others what it's like: you simply know that someone is holding you up when everything inside of you feels like giving way.[38]

Are you falling? Do you know that God is here to catch you?

Our verse today reminds us that our "dwelling place"—where we live, where we focus—is God and God alone. He is our home. He is our shelter. He is our strength.

Both eternal and everlasting.

My child, arms are for holding, for carrying or even catching. Mine are here for you. Anytime. All the time. Do you need to be enveloped in compassion and security? I am strong enough for both of us—lean on Me. Know that your hug may just be what someone else needs today too.

18. Endurance

After all, you know that the testing of your faith produces
endurance. *Let this **endurance** complete its work so that you*
may be fully mature, complete, and lacking in nothing.

~ James 1:3-4

While watching the Olympics, I was greatly impressed by the endurance of the athletes. Whether it was running long distances, lifting heavy weights, or defying gravity in gymnastics, clearly these world-class athletes endured the challenge and emerged as victors.

It didn't just happen—many of them had been training for a lifetime.

In sports, "endurance" refers to an ability to exert yourself or remain active over time. It also refers to the ability to withstand fatigue, stress, or pain. Endurance training not only enhances your performance while working out, but also contributes to overall health, providing you with energy, improved heart function, and increased metabolism.

But what about endurance in life itself—far more important than any sports competition? Oswald Chambers suggests believers embrace endurance through tenacity:

> Tenacity is endurance combined with the absolute certainty that what we are looking for is going to transpire. Tenacity is more than hanging on, which may be but the weakness of too afraid to fall off. Tenacity is the supreme effort of a man refusing to believe that his hero is going to be conquered. The call to spiritual tenacity is not to hang on and do nothing, but to work deliberately on the certainty that God is not going to be worsted.[39]

In our verse today, James urges endurance, a quality that would serve him to the end. As bishop of Jerusalem, he angered the Jewish teachers, who eventually threw him off the southwest pinnacle of the temple in Jerusalem. After surviving the one-hundred-foot fall, he was stoned to death by a mob, even as he prayed for them. He and other faithful followers of Christ, including the other James (sometimes called James the Greater, who was killed by the sword), endured to the end.

> In AD 44, King Herod ordered that James, son of Zebedee, be thrust through with a sword. . . . Luke was hung by the neck from an olive tree in Greece. Doubting Thomas was pierced with a pine spear, tortured with red-hot plates, and burned alive in India. In AD 54, the proconsul of Hierapolis had Philip tortured and crucified because his wife converted to Christianity while listening to Philip preach. . . . Matthew was stabbed in the back in Ethiopia. Bartholomew was flogged to death in Armenia. Simon the Zealot was crucified by a governor of Syria in AD 74. Judas Thaddeus was beaten to death with sticks in Mesopotamia. Matthias, who replaced Judas Iscariot, was stoned to death and then beheaded. And Peter was crucified upside down at his own request. John the Beloved is the only disciple to die of natural causes. . . . When a cauldron of boiling oil could not kill John, Emperor Diocletian exiled him to the island of Patmos, where he lived until his death in AD 95.[40]

Though we most probably will not need to endure such persecution, every day may we dig deep for that which makes us stronger in Christ.

My child, how do you keep going when everything in you screams, "I can't go on"? You turn to Me and claim the gift of both My presence and My power. In you. For you. All around you. Many before you have endured much more. You can do this. With My help.

19. Uphold

*"So do not fear, for I am with you; do not be dismayed, for I am your God. I will strengthen you and help you; I will **uphold** you with my righteous right hand."*

~ Isaiah 41:10 NIV

The new playground at Camp of the Woods was dedicated on July 4.

Bright orange, blue, and yellow tunnels, swaying bridges, wavy slides, bars and swings! As more than a hundred children joined in the celebration, Mike and I occasionally caught sight of our daughter's American flag hair bow.

Five-year-old Maggie was delighting in a world of discovery when she came upon it—the fireman's pole. We watched as she looked down from the landing, carefully calculating whether or not she really wanted to leap out and slide down on her own. I felt it coming long before I heard the word.

"DAADDY!" Her shriek was lost in the cacophony of play, but one man certainly heard it.

Mike rushed quickly to her side and supported her little body as she bravely attempted to slide down the pole. With fear gone, Maggie explored each piece of equipment, but every time she reached the fireman's pole platform, she hollered, *"DAADDY!"* and Mike rushed to her rescue. She couldn't see us, but she knew if she called out, we would come.

I marveled at this vivid picture of my own life being played out by my youngest child. For I am also the child of an attentive and caring Father. While enjoying life, health, discovery, all too often I find myself perched on a precipice, ready to risk it all in one giant leap of faith. As I utter, "Dear Lord . . ." it sounds a whole lot like *"DAADDY!"*

I am frightened at the size and scope of the task ahead. Or I am weary from exerting too much and resting too little.

Can't you just imagine Jesus running to the playground of my life and supporting me as I slide down the pole? He indeed is always there to *uphold* me with His righteous right hand.

This can happen even to those who are strong. Moses was an incredible man, the consummate leader. But Exodus 17 reveals to us another aspect of Moses' leadership: the willingness to accept the assistance of others.

In fact, he actually needed friends to hold up his arms.

Some nomadic raiders, the Amalekites, had attacked the people of Israel in the desert. While Joshua led the troops into battle, Moses, along with Aaron and Hur, watched the battle from a nearby hill. "So it came about when Moses held his hand up, that Israel prevailed, and when he let his hand down, Amalek prevailed" (Exodus 17:11 NASB). Eventually, Moses became weary, so Aaron and Hur responded by holding up his arms until the Israelites were able to finally defeat the Amalekites.

Are you willing to depend on others (including God) to uphold you in the tough times?

> We may be tempted to hide our fears and weaknesses, feeling that we need to be strong for others. We may find it difficult to trust others with our insecurities and doubts. . . . Such tendencies are rooted in our cultural ethic of self-reliance, and they can lead to feelings of loneliness and isolation that will ultimately handicap our effectiveness in ministry. To truly grow, we must, like Moses, be willing to embrace the support of trusted friends and advisors.[41]

My child, I hear your cry. Whether it's a shriek or a whispered summons in prayer. I know your voice and I'm quick to respond. Before you know it, My arms are underneath to uphold. Until you find your strength. And begin to give it away to others.

20. *Seek*

Look to the LORD *and his strength;* **seek** *his face always.*

~ 1 Chronicles 16:11 NIV

As passengers debarked our plane and began moving into the airport terminal, I noticed a startling phenomenon.

No one—*no one*—was looking where they were going. *Everyone* was looking down at their cell phones.

Now bumping into folks at a terminal is merely an inconvenience. But statistics are showing that more and more pedestrian accidents, often fatal, are occurring simply because people are not looking up.

"When texting, you're not as in control with the complex actions of walking," said Dr. Dietrich Jehle, a professor of emergency medicine at the University of Buffalo. "While talking on the phone is a distraction, texting is much more dangerous because you can't see the path in front of you."

The Academy of Orthopedic Surgeons recently launched a campaign called "Digital Deadwalkers" to encourage safety in this area. The problem is that even though a survey revealed that 78 percent of adults in the United States feel distracted walking is a "serious" issue, only 29 percent admitted they are part of the problem.[42]

When was the last time you looked up?

Because far more important even than watching where you are walking, is keeping your eyes on the Lord—seeking His face.

The Bible tells us to draw strength in the search for Him. The truth is, what we often discover as we come close to the living God, is that He is the One who has been seeking us all this time.

And maybe we didn't even realize it. Maybe we were busy looking else-where.

I sought the Lord, and afterward I knew
He moved my soul to seek Him, seeking me.
It was not I that found, O Savior true;
No, I was found of Thee.
Thou didst reach forth Thy hand and mine enfold;
I walked and sank not on the storm-vexed sea.
'Twas not so much that I on Thee took hold,
As Thou, dear Lord, on me.[43]

Jesus calls us to "seek first his kingdom and his righteousness, and all these things will be given to you as well" (Matthew 6:33 NIV). This New Testament Greek word for seek is *zeteo*, meaning "to worship God," but also to seek knowledge or meaning by asking questions.

Seeking is a lifelong process. While we may find new life in Jesus, we must daily decide to follow him and seek to know him more fully. The Bible says we should seek God, but also that he seeks us out. A beautiful interplay exists, where God seeks us, stirring and whispering in a voice we may not yet recognize.[44]

Look up. Find the One you have been seeking all your life.

My child, when I look at the masses, it's your face that comes clearly into focus. I am always seeking you. But what about you; are you looking for Me? Please don't consult everyone and everything else first. I have the words of life—the gifts of life. You will find so much when you seek Me.

21. Pilgrimage

Blessed are those whose strength is in you, whose hearts are set on
pilgrimage. . . . They go from strength to strength.
~ Psalm 84:5, 7 NIV

I made a pilgrimage of sorts when I returned to my university forty years after I had graduated. My full life had previously prevented me from going to reunions. But I wanted to revisit the place where four years of growing and discovery had launched me into the person I am today.

And, of course, see the people.

So, a handful of women friends and I made plans for a slumber party before the official reunion began. A time to reconnect and remember. A time to look back and look forward.

> A pilgrimage is a ritual journey with a hallowed purpose. Every step along the way has meaning. The pilgrim knows that life giving challenges will emerge. A pilgrimage is not a vacation; it is a transformational journey during which significant change takes place. New insights are given. Deeper understanding is attained. New and old places in the heart are visited. Blessings are received and healing takes place. On return from the pilgrimage, life is seen with different eyes. Nothing will ever be quite the same again.[45]

I wanted to thank these special people for being my friends. I wanted to rejoice with them about doors that had opened since our student days, and to weep with them over unexpected tragedies. Beth gave me a priceless gift when she deposited into my hand a manila envelope full of my lengthy letters to her—all written when I was between the ages of eighteen and twenty-six. Back then, this was how we communicated! And my words to a close friend were as complete as a journal.

Connie offered her home to us on the top of a Blue Ridge mountain. Truly it was a sacred spot. Coming together after so many years and soaking in the beauty and the peace conjured up so many feelings of gratitude and grace.

Our time on campus that weekend was filled with laughter and reminiscences, for every corner of the campus held a memory. Yet I had a purpose far greater than the afternoon homecoming football game—an appointment with my favorite professor, Albert.

Simply to thank him for changing my life.

He was my first Renaissance man, arriving on campus fresh out of Harvard with his young wife and baby in tow. Brilliant. Musical. Biblical. And he prodded me to learn, and search, and question, and believe, and read. And write. He set the bar high. And that helped me not "settle" for someone less than a lifetime kindred-spirit partner.

As we sat in folding chairs on the lawn overlooking the hilly campus and glistening lake, I thought of today's Scripture and especially the phrase "they go from strength to strength."

Albert is in his eighties, and I, his former student, am a grandmother. In the span of a lifetime, both of us have continued to simply put one foot in front of the other, counting on God's strength as we journey forth as pilgrims. Was it prophetic that this esteemed professor had gifted me at graduation with the then-new Annie Dillard book *Pilgrim at Tinker Creek*? Perhaps he knew even then that I would continue in the pilgrim way . . .

May you always keep walking, friend. In His strength alone.

My child, yes, the road is long. The journey is hard. Did you really think you could live an adventurous life in safety? But your companions are many. And I'm in the lead. Keep going from strength to strength, but stop along the way and learn from all I send you. This is your legacy.

22. *Sleep*

*I lie down and **sleep**; I wake again, because the LORD sustains me.*
~ Psalm 3:5 NIV

Do you have a hard time sleeping?

If so, you are in good company. Studies say that a high percentage of Americans are sleep-deprived. Before we had artificial light, most Americans slept ten hours a night, but now the average is six hours. Now there's too much to do and too little time to do it. We cram more than is possible into a mere twenty-four hours a day.

The first place to steal those needed extra hours? Sleep.

But there is a price to pay. "Experts estimate that sleep deprivation and sleep disorders account for $100 billion in lost productivity, medical expenses, and property damage per year."[46]

Our lack of sleep isn't just because we are doing too much.

Fear, anxiety, and worry keep many of us awake at night.

With so many challenges and concerns in our world today, it's no wonder that scenarios continue to spin around in our minds long after our bodies have shut down. We recall news stories or replay arguments. We know there is a stack of unpaid bills on our desk downstairs and we aren't sure where the money will come from. A loved one is out wandering the world, and we cannot get that person off our minds, knowing he or she could be doing anything. Anywhere.

Or perhaps we feel miles away from the person who is lying only inches from us—a lonely place to be.

This aspect of sleeplessness isn't new. Hundreds of years ago, the great British preacher Charles Spurgeon admitted that the only way he could find true sleep was after a time of entrusting all to God.

> I have lain awake at night, wondering whatever should I do in certain cases. And at last I have come to the conclusion that

I could not do anything and that I must leave it all with the Lord. When I have left everything with Him and submitted myself absolutely to His sweet will, and had full fellowship with Christ, I have wondered what I could fret about if I tried. There is peace for me everywhere.[47]

Some people need continuous positive airway pressure (CPAP) in order to get full rest at night. A CPAP machine increases air pressure in your throat so that your airway doesn't collapse when you breathe in. It helps those with obstructive sleep apnea to breathe more easily during sleep.

Perhaps "the Lord sustains me" is the way many of us receive spiritual airway pressure therapy, helping us breathe out the concerns of our day and breathe in God's peace.

King David experienced this. "I will lie down and fall asleep in peace because you alone, Lord, let me live in safety" (Psalm 4:8). And he passed down this grace gift to his own son, King Solomon, who proclaimed, "He gives to his beloved sleep" (Psalm 127:2 ESV)

Rest well. God's got it.

My child, is it hard to turn off your mind at night and get much-needed sleep? Do the images replay over and over again until your worries keep you awake? Come to Me. I long to give you rest, deep sleep for your soul and body. Close your eyes.

23. Patiently

*You also must wait **patiently**, strengthening your resolve,
because the coming of the Lord is near.*

~ James 5:8

I had only been waiting seven days past the due date for my new grandchild to be born, but I confess, I did not do it patiently.

The fact that my daughter lives on the other side of the world in a totally different time zone is the only thing that keeps this granny from obnoxiously texting or Facetiming for updates about her grandchildren!

Perhaps you are struggling today with waiting for something a lot more challenging—a biopsy report, a lost child, or that check in the mail that you desperately need for rent.

If so, you may be tempted to join me in saying, "Hurry up, God!" instead of "Be still, my soul."

But our verse today reminds us that waiting patiently is a gift that strengthens us in the process. The New Testament Greek word here is *makrothumeo,* which means "to be of a long spirit, not to lose heart, to persevere patiently."

Two things help me as I seek to be patient. The first is remembering God's patience with me. "The Lord isn't slow to keep his promise, as some think of slowness, but he is patient toward you" (2 Peter 3:9). My goal is to be as patient with others as He is with me.

But the second thing is I must remember that what may seem like slowness in keeping promises is actually a plan of preparation for those eventualities. In other words, the time of waiting is not empty time; it is a time of growth and nurturing.

There was a very good reason my grandbaby had not yet been born. And it had absolutely nothing to do with me and everything to do with the child and mother. When I am impatient I need to remember that my sense of timing is not all there is to the story.

Sometimes God is busy working a miracle for someone else.

> I hear God saying to me, "Sometimes, child, it's not about you.
> It's about what I'm doing in someone you love. It's about the
> big picture." And I am reminded that I don't have to know
> everything. . . . I am called to faith in the dark. . . . When you
> have no control, when you don't know what's going on with
> the ones you love, remember, God is making a way.[48]

The apostle Paul named patience as one of the fruits of the Spirit (see Galatians 5:22) and how often have I prayed "Lord, give me patience, and give it to me *now!*" But I realize that fruit is the by-product of a healthy plant or tree. So rather than praying for patience, I pray to become more and more like Jesus, who was never in a hurry and never overlooked anyone on His path. As I begin to gradually take on bits and pieces of His likeness, then fruit will appear.

As we learn to live patiently, may we have more to offer others. In Jesus' name.

My child, this may just be a lifelong struggle for you—patience. But I see progress as you remember My intervening in the past. At what was just the right time. That's because I'm sovereign and see the total picture that you don't. So, calm down and trust Me. I've got it all under control.

24. Heart

*My health may fail, and my spirit may grow weak, but God remains the strength of my **heart**; he is mine forever.*

~ Psalm 73:26 NLT

Every Valentine's Day as a single woman, I would recite words found in the middle of Psalm 73, crying out to God, "Whom have I in heaven but you? I desire you more than anything on earth" (v. 25 NLT).

I always felt wistful on that holiday, which celebrated love.

And I thought that if I practiced trusting God with my fragile heart, then perhaps the reality of true belief would settle into my soul.

It did. I became stronger and proactive with my life, because of God filling my heart first with His love. No one else could satisfy fully.

Then, after a decade of Psalm 73 Valentine Days, my thirtysomething heart found true love. At an appointment in my office, of all places.

Ordinary graces indeed!

"At the heart of the universe, there is a heart of grace. It's the heart of one Jesus described as a loving Father, one who find joy in bringing good gifts into the lives of his children. . . . The heart of grace is also a heart of truth, as eternal and unchanging as the God who has revealed it."[49]

Our hearts almost always contain two seemingly opposite qualities, like grace and truth. In fact, when the psalmist spoke of his heart, he meant both what he felt and what he thought.

The original Hebrew word here is *lebab*, usually translated "heart, mind, or midst." Though this often refers to the inner person, with a focus on the psychological aspects of both heart and mind, it can also translate to "mind, understanding, or courage."

In King David's time, the goal of life and faith was to bring the inner and outer self into alignment. The heart represented the seat of both emotions and intellectual understanding. And since the Hebrews believed that one's actions flowed from the heart, any true transformation would begin there.

That's why the psalmist often prays for God to touch his heart with renewal and strength and hope. "Create in me a clean heart, O God. Renew a loyal spirit within me" (Psalm 51:10 NLT).

In Psalm 73, Asaph shares his struggle when the wicked appear to prosper. After identifying the bitterness that threatens to take hold of his heart, he then reminds himself of the great gift of strength, found in today's verse.

> Without grace and truth together, we don't have the God of the Bible. Without compassion and righteousness together, we don't have Jesus of the Gospels. Without love and holiness together, we don't have the good news. The Christian faith is not one instead of the other or one more than the other but both together in equal measure because this is the nature of our God.[50]

Everything else may fail, but God is the one who will forever keep our hearts strong.

※

My child, your heart is fragile. Words and actions can crush and disappoint you to the core. But your heart is also strong. It can withstand a battering, a loss, and rebuild from brokenness. I love your heart. May it always balance both truth and grace. To give away to other hearts.

25. Hope

*Be strong and take heart, all you who **hope** in the LORD.*

~ Psalm 31:24 NIV

May I confess something? I had *hoped* our country would be in a vastly different place by now.

I had *hoped* there would be more unity, kindness, wisdom, and compassion for all people.

I still hope for these things. But everywhere I turn, people seem to have lost hope.

As her husband's presidency neared an end, even First Lady Michelle Obama expressed this in an interview: "We are feeling what not having hope feels like."

She recalled moving to Washington, full of hope. "Hope is necessary. It's a necessary concept," Obama continued. "What else do you have if you don't have hope? What do you give your kids if you can't give them hope?"[51]

Are you feeling a lack of hope today as well?

My response to you (and the former First Lady) is that we *can* have hope and we *can* pass it along to our kids.

But hope doesn't come through any political system, cultural mandate, or religious or educational institution—*as good as all those things can be*. These values must be personally embodied through people living from a place of grace, selflessness, courage, respect, wisdom, and compassion.

And the only hope for that to ever happen? God.

> Hope, in the biblical sense, is not a vague longing, but a confident assurance that things will turn out the way they should in the end—even if they may not seem to in this life. To truly have hope in God requires putting all our eggs into one basket. That is frightening, or would be, were the basket

not firmly in the grasp of Jesus, who conquered, among other things, death—a very hopeful thing indeed.[52]

Unfortunately, many people in the world don't put their "eggs" in the basket of God. Faith is essential, the basis for all hope. In fact, those two words often appear together in God's Word: "Faith is the reality of what we hope for, the proof of what we don't see" (Hebrews 11:1); "Now faith, hope, and love remain—these three things . . ." (1 Corinthians 13:13); "We eagerly wait for the hope of righteousness through the Spirit by faith" (Galatians 5:5).

What can we do to become people of hope?

Wait with confident expectation. Trust God. "Be strong," as today's verse suggests. Things may actually get worse before they get better.

The psalmist's word for hope is the Old Testament Hebrew word *yachal*, calling us to be patient. Because hope connects what's going on now to what will be in the future. Hope doesn't ignore today's struggles, but acknowledges them.

Pray with King David, no stranger to hopeless situations, "Guide me in your truth and teach me, for you are God my Savior, and *my hope is in you* all day long" (Psalm 25:5 NIV, emphasis added).

Then pray today for all those who seem hopeless. Even if you are one of them.

My child, many surrounding you have no hope left. And they don't know where to go to find it. Even if you are struggling with hopelessness on any given day, at least you realize that in placing your hope in Me, you will never be disappointed. Help others see that everything else will let them down, but I created them and remain forever their Source.

26. Renew

*"I will strengthen the weary and **renew** those who are weak."*

~ Jeremiah 31:25

When Rachel and I were praying about and searching for a new name for a writing retreat we codirect here in New England, we must have tried on dozens of words for size.

Words that captured our sense of calling as communicators of the good news. Words that reflected the creativity of believers who write and speak for the kingdom. Words that offer the experience of going deeper with God in our power and purpose. Several worked; some were even good. But after a few weeks we both agreed on Rachel's original choice.

Renew.

And thus, "reNEW—retreat for New England Writing" was christened, founded on the biblical promise that we can be "renewed in knowledge after the image of him" (Colossians 3:10 KJV).[53]

None of us want to stay the same. We desire to be continually made new, to grow, to be strengthened and redirected. To reflect the image of Jesus.

And many of us can totally relate to those mentioned in today's verse—we are "weary" and "weak." Thus, the actual Old Testament Hebrew word used here—*mala*— applies to us. It is translated "renew, fulfill, complete, gratify, refresh, overflow, satisfy."

What does it take to move us out of a spiritual comfort zone into a more daring life of fulfillment and renewal?

Turning to God. If we pray for Him to shine light into our dark places, He often reveals to us both seemingly impossible dreams as well as possible damaging choices that have prevented our pursuit of them thus far.

The Oxford dictionary defines renewal as "the replacing or repair of something that is worn out, run-down, or broken."

Do you feel worn-out, run-down, or broken?

Then grab hold of another grace gift: "He gives power to the faint, and to him who has no might he increases strength. Even youths shall faint and be weary, and young men shall fall exhausted; but they who wait for the LORD shall *renew* their strength; they shall mount up with wings like eagles; they shall run and not be weary; they shall walk and not faint" (Isaiah 40:29-31 ESV).

What are you doing when you most feel "this is who God made me and why I'm here"? It brings you joy and a settled sense of fulfillment. It's something that uses your unique gifting and desires. These endeavors—instead of draining you, they fill you. Instead of depleting your energy, they spark new force and fervor.

Perhaps it is as Frederick Buechner says, "The place God calls you to is the place where your deep gladness and the world's deep hunger meet."[54]

When God renews you, He helps you awaken and rediscover your true identity as the beloved; then He moves to galvanize your sense of mission and purpose for His kingdom.

This kind of strength can be yours today. Just come close to the One who made you. And called you. And will use you.

Yes, *you*!

My child, is it starting to feel old and tattered—that dream? That faith? I am the One who makes all things new again. I will take your worn-out spirit and refresh the vision, the beliefs, even the body. But you simply must come near for renewal. Let all subside and seek Me alone. Then walk in resurrected purpose and power.

27. Light

*"If you are filled with **light**, with no dark corners, then your whole life will be radiant, as though a floodlight were filling you with **light**."*

~ Luke 11:36 NLT

There is a lot of darkness in the world.

But Jesus came to bring light. To make us "radiant, as though a floodlight were filling you with light."

According to the Bible, He is the light of the world (John 8:12) and we also are the light of the world (see Matthew 5:14). How can that be?

He's the floodlight inside us.

The New Testament Greek word used here is *phos*, a word related to light and shine. These words evoke such symbols as strength, glory, and knowledge. Today we sometimes use them in like manner, such as "they saw the light" when someone finally understands.

What is our role in helping to light up a dark world?

We go forward into the darkness. We shine.

Oliver Wendell Holmes expressed it well in this hymn:

> Lord of all life, below, above,
> whose light is truth, whose warmth is love,
> before Thy ever-blazing throne
> we ask no luster of our own.[55]

Light travels fast (nearly 671 million miles an hour). It travels far. It never stays where it starts. It doesn't retreat from darkness. It keeps shining, wherever it is.

Is there a "dark corner" in your community?

> Jesus wants us to get out of tidy Christian ghettos and, rather than spending every spare moment in church activities, find

time to hang out with people who are far from God. Not to judge them. Not to demand some Christian standard of behavior from them. Not to look down our noses at them or use them as object lessons or sermon illustrations, but to truly and genuinely be their friends, accepting them, relating to them, expressing interest in what they think and what they enjoy, and not trying to squeeze them into our mold.[56]

"Shine! Keep open house; be generous with your lives. By opening up to others, you'll prompt people to open up with God, this generous Father in heaven" (Matthew 5:14-16 MSG).

Where are you to bring light today? What "dark corners" will you help eliminate?

I believe we are to spend our days and hours, our love and our work, our presence and our hopes punching holes in the darkness rather than hunkering down and trying to protect ourselves from the darkness that seems all around us. Where there is Light, we are to celebrate. Where there is darkness, we are to raise our fist and punch a hole in it—as hard as we can, as often as we can. Evidently, that is how the Light of the world sneaks in.[57]

Turn on the light!

My child, I see that flicker. Your little light that has never gone out completely, though many have tried to blow disapproval or discouragement on your tiny flame. You are a light that will keep shining. Why? Simply because I am the fuel—that never ends. I will pour into you. You will light the darkness of this world. One candle at a time.

28. Share

*For as we **share** abundantly in Christ's sufferings, so through*
*Christ we **share** abundantly in comfort too.*

~ 2 Corinthians 1:5 ESV.

On December 7, 2016, Dr. Helen Roseveare, British missionary doctor to the Congo, died at the age of ninety-one.

When I heard, a vivid memory crossed my mind.

At the "Urbana '76" student convention, I sat among seventeen thousand young people and watched as she slowly stripped an artificial tree of its leaves while speaking on "the cost of declaring his glory."

Dr. Roseveare was telling us her story of serving as a medical doctor in the Belgian Congo during the 1964 Mau Mau rebellion. With each new "cost" of sharing in Christ's suffering, she removed another limb from the tree.

A powerful word picture.

And one I never forgot. (I still encounter many attendees who were also deeply affected.)

The entire stadium was silent as she explained how she was captured, savagely beaten, and repeatedly raped. Recalling those events, she said she knew someone back home must have been praying for her because she was past praying in the midst of the terror.

Then suddenly she experienced God's majesty and power surrounding her with His love and whispering, "Twenty years ago you asked Me for the privilege of being a missionary. This is it. Don't you want it?"

Dr. Roseveare elaborated:

> Fantastic, the privilege of being identified with our Savior. . . .
> He clearly said to me, "These are not your sufferings. They are
> not beating you. These are my sufferings. All I ask of you is the
> loan of your body." And an enormous relief swept through me.

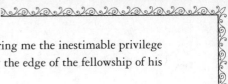

> . . . He was actually offering me the inestimable privilege of sharing in some little way the edge of the fellowship of his suffering.
>
> In the weeks of imprisonment that followed and in the subsequent years of continued service, looking back, one has tried to "count the cost," but I find it all swallowed up in privilege.[58]

This was the first time Paul's words rang clear not only in my head but in my heart. It became something of a mandate to desire: "That I may *know him* and the *power of his resurrection*, and may *share his sufferings*, *becoming like him* in his death" (Philippians 3:10 ESV, emphasis added).

Because if we know Him and share His sufferings, then we become like Him.

But we also share in His comfort. The New Testament Greek word here is *paraklesis*, which means "calling to one's side; an exhortation, or consolation, comfort."

Those who have suffered understand. They are the ones most likely to offer comfort by just sitting with us. Being present. Knowing exactly what is needed because they, too, were once struggling as we are.

This is the life of a wounded healer. The life Helen Roseveare was called to for ninety-one years.

Are you called to both suffer and share?

The cost is great. The privilege is even greater.

My child, if you really want to follow Me, you must know there are sufferings to share. You will be ridiculed, rejected, perhaps even falsely accused or physically attacked. I walked that path too. And that's why I know the hearts of those who suffer. As you persevere, your heart will grow so very tender toward the broken. Sharing is redemptive.

29. Kindness

Your own glorious power makes us strong and because of your
kindness, *our strength increases.*

~ Psalm 89:17 CEV

I bought the little wooden sign impulsively—in fact, it seemed to jump off the shelf into my hands—*Be Kinder than Necessary.*

A few days later I understood why.

I was unkind to someone I care about. Not intentionally, of course. Just a careless word blurted out in a too-harsh tone. But the damage was done.

Fortunately, because the person is full of grace, we were reconciled when I reached out and asked forgiveness. But I was left with a deep, deep desire to somehow pursue kindness as my default reaction to . . . well, *everything*!

So kindness became my word for the year. I determined to explore every aspect of the word and incorporate every dimension into my soul.

First, I gave the Author of kindness praise and gratitude: "I will tell of the *kindnesses* of the Lord, the deeds for which he is to be praised, according to all the Lord has done for us" (Isaiah 63:7 NIV, emphasis added).

Secondly, I clothed myself in kindness: "We put no stumbling block in anyone's path, so that our ministry will not be discredited. Rather, as servants of God we commend ourselves in every way . . . in purity, understanding, patience and *kindness*" (2 Corinthians 6:3-4, 6 NIV, emphasis added).

Finally, I chose to receive the Lord's kindness offered to me: "I led them with cords of human *kindness*, with ties of love. To them I was like one who lifts a little child to the cheek, and I bent down to feed them" (Hosea 11:4 NIV, emphasis added).

That year is long gone, and I confess I haven't totally mastered kindness, within or without. But it was a pivotal focus for me, and it changed my life.

Soon after, *Parade magazine* observed, "Seems like we're in a bit of a kindness crisis these days," and sported a full-color cover that read, "Throw

Kindness Around Like Confetti!" Evidently, half the people in a recent survey said that the practice of kindness had deteriorated in the past ten years.

"There is less kindness in public life, which trickles down and invites people to be less kind in our personal lives," says psychologist Harriet Lerner. "But kindness is not an 'extra.' It's at the heart of intimacy, connection, self-respect and respect for others."[59]

Nineteenth-century Scottish pastor John Watson, writing under the pen name Ian Maclaren, once wisely wrote, "Be kind. Everyone you meet is fighting a hard battle."

What hard battles are you facing today? Will you receive the Lord's great kindness extended to you? And then pass it along?

> Living a life of radical kindness, a life that others are watching, means owning up to the fact that our lives are messy and uncertain, our roads are crooked. We don't have it all together. The life of kindness is the authentic life—not the perfect life, and not the predictable life, and hardly the buttoned-up life. To lean into kindness means embracing an honest acknowledgement of our limitations and fears, that we do not have this road trip all figured out.[60]

I'm an imperfect person who sometimes gets it all wrong. But when I make a deliberate decision to seek kindness, I know God strengthens me.

May I extend that strength to others.

My child, I have drawn you in a loving-kindness embrace (see Jeremiah 31:3) so that you might know how powerful kindness is. Will you now spread kindness widely as you live your life? The world is desperate for simple, kind words and deeds. I will fill you so you can overflow.

30. Battle

*By faith these people overthrew kingdoms, ruled with justice, and received what God had promised them. They shut the mouths of lions, quenched the flames of fire, and escaped death by the edge of the sword. Their weakness was turned to strength. They became strong in **battle** and put whole armies to flight.*

~ Hebrews 11:33-34 NLT

Do you have heroes of the faith?

What about Corrie ten Boom, whose family hid Jews during the Nazi occupation and were sent to concentration camps? Or William Wilberforce, who used his influence in British government to finally abolish the slave trade in England?

Perhaps your hero is not a famous name. Your own single mother, who prayed and worked to raise you? Your neighbor who gave up his career to lovingly take care of his wife with early onset Alzheimer's?

If no one comes to mind immediately, may I direct you to our verse today, taken from the amazing eleventh chapter of Hebrews? You will review stories of many recognizable biblical names, but also stories not listed by name but by the battles they waged through faith: "There were others who were tortured, refusing to be released so that they might gain an even better resurrection. Some faced jeers and flogging, and even chains and imprisonment. They were put to death by stoning; they were sawed in two; they were killed by the sword. They went about in sheepskins and goatskins, destitute, persecuted and mistreated" (Hebrews 11:35-37 NIV).

These were ordinary people who had placed their faith in an extraordinary God.

Our text today says that "Their weakness was turned to strength. They became strong in battle." I doubt they began life thinking they were hero material; in fact, they were probably just as weak and frightened as we are.

Yet these were the very ones God used to stand strong against the enemy of our souls.

How will you approach your own battles today?

When the shepherd boy David volunteered to go up against the giant Goliath, King Saul offered his own armor. But the size and weight of the armor hindered this young man from using the God-given strength he already had. David needed to go to battle in what God had provided for *him*, not what was appropriate for Saul.

The world wanted a certain image of a hero fighter—one with glistening metal and sharp sword. But God can use anyone and anything He chooses to fight battles. When Goliath faced a small boy with a slingshot and a few stones, his moments were already numbered because David knew "the battle is the LORD's, and he will give you into our hand" (1 Samuel 17:47 ESV).

> David knew himself and trusted God. Although David was often overlooked as the runt of the litter, his quiet obedience in the pastures merited closeness to God. In that crucible of aloneness, he learned he didn't need a mask to impress God, didn't need to be anyone but himself. Be you. And once you are chosen, don't try to wear battle armor tailored to someone else. Remember, God is your deliverer.[61]

I don't know what battles you will be called to fight today. I do know you can rely on God's strength in your weakness, His guidance in your confusion, and His armor for the fight.

My child, I wish I could say that life would be easy as you pursue faithfulness and truth. But it is hard. And no more so than when you don't get the answers until the other side of heaven. There is a battle between good and evil, and you are on the frontlines as My warrior. But I provide armor that fits beautifully. I am with you. And we are ultimately victorious.

Gratitude

---

*How often, Lord, our **grateful** eyes*
Have seen what Thou hast done;
How often does Thy love surprise
From dawn to set of sun.

~ Amy Carmichael
"Surprising Love"

1. Gratitude

*Therefore, since we are receiving a kingdom that cannot be shaken, let's continue to express our **gratitude**. With this **gratitude**, let's serve in a way that is pleasing to God with respect and awe.*

~ Hebrews 12:28

They are the first words I see.

The moment my eyes open from a night's sleep. Stenciled on the gable directly across from my bed—"Each day is a gift from God."

Prompting me to thank God even before my feet hit the floor. Before the world inevitably begins to invade my posture of praise. The morning news is violent. Icy roads disrupt my schedule. And I'm still waiting on medical tests results.

But today's verse reminds me that because of my ultimate dwelling place—"a kingdom that cannot be shaken"—I am called to "express" my gratitude and to "serve" others.

Do you sometimes find it difficult to muster up feelings of gratitude?

Jonathan Edwards suggested we live "gracious gratitude—being thankful not just for God's gifts and blessings but for God Himself and who He is."[1] So in those moments when we cannot think of one thing to thank God for, we can thank Him for who He is.

Nothing sparks gratitude like perspective. What if you awakened each day only to remember you had been diagnosed with ALS, a highly degenerative disease with no cause and no cure?

When this happened to pastor Ed Dobson, he sought to face each diminishing of his body and mind with a deep abiding gratitude. Though much had been lost, he chose to focus on what he *could* do: "Lord, thank You for waking me up this morning. Lord, thank You that I can turn over in my bed. . . . Lord, thank You that I can still eat breakfast. . . . Lord, thank

You that I can still talk." This man's conclusion and choice? "I have learned in my journey with ALS to be grateful for the small things in my life."[2]

Thanksgiving and praise to God run throughout the pages of the Old Testament even in the midst of violent and horrific circumstances. And they continue through the New Testament, despite persecution and danger. In the next days we will unpack many words that call us to live with hearts full of gratitude, not just when we awaken to a sunny sky, but when we face a day of darkness and despair.

"On your best day, gratitude reminds you that your gifts are not your own. And on your worst day, gratitude reminds you that you are not alone."[3]

"Gratitude flows from the ability to see all you have and all you are as a gift. This means you insist that persons are more valuable than things. Ultimately the opposite of gratitude is not ingratitude, but chaos. If we are to be human in the truest sense of this word, it will be as we tenaciously insist that we live life grateful."[4]

I am so very grateful. First for God. Then for His gifts.

Will you join me in unwrapping them?

My child, it is My deepest joy to offer you gifts—of grace, mercy, and hope. As you unpack their worth and usefulness, may your own heart be filled to overflowing with gratitude. For opportunities that come your way. For people you can bless. And yes, for Me, the Lover of your soul.

2. Blessing

*"I will make of you a great nation and will bless you. I will
make your name respected, and you will be a **blessing**."*

~ Genesis 12:2

It took me a moment to recognize this holy moment, occurring in the midst of ordinary.

I had just settled my first newborn grandchild into my eldest son's lap when Uncle Justin did the unexpected. He gently laid his hand on top of his niece's little head and prayed aloud: "Lord, we give this child to You and pray that one day she will know You and follow You. Jesus, bless little Saoirse. Protect her. And help her grow up to be a strong woman of God. Amen."

A blessing.

His father (the pastor) and his mother (the Christian author) had not yet performed such an act. But Justin, known his whole life as one with differing abilities, proved to be wiser than us all.

To welcome the newest member of the family, he chose to impart on her a blessing.

In the Old Testament a blessing *(barak)* often indicated a declaration of favor. Used more than four hundred times in the Bible, a blessing is something that God is, does, or says that glorifies Him and edifies His people. God gave blessings freely to people, land, animals, and more. As those blessings were received, a natural response was to choose to then bless others.

We are blessed to be a blessing. How does that look in your life?

First we have to recognize and receive God's blessings as gifts He bestows to us.

Always due to His love. Gifts of promise and of prophecy. Gifts of land or meaningful work. Gifts of people, such as children and friends. Doing as the hymnist suggests: "Count your blessings, name them one by one. Count your many blessings, see what God hath done."[5]

Next, we must ask how we can turn these gifts into acts of blessing others. Throughout God's Word we see countless incidents of fathers blessing their children or grandchildren. But uncles and aunts, teachers and mentors can also offer a kind of blessing that is much more than just sentimental well-wishing. Biblical blessings named both character strengths and weaknesses and sometimes even had a prophetic element foretelling how those traits might ultimately play out.

My son blessed his niece from a simple faith that wanted to lift her up before God. If you would like to do something similar today, here are five elements that often accompany such a blessing:

- Meaningful and appropriate touch—such as laying your hand on the person's head.
- A spoken message—indicating your commitment and love to that loved one.
- Attaching high value to the one being blessed—pointing out his or her worth as one created in God's image.
- Picturing a special future for him or her—since we aren't actual prophets, it's best to be generic here, as with Justin's "strong woman of God."
- An active commitment to fulfill the blessing—continued investment in the person's life through prayer, guidance, and presence.[6]

Anyone can give a blessing. Pray about opportunities; ask God to guide you and give you the words and the gracious manner. He will do the rest.

My child, you are indeed a blessing to Me. And I have called you to go forth and bless others, lifting up to them what they could be and do through My power. Offer gentle words of encouragement and hope as you touch lives. In My name.

3. Soul

Let them thank the LORD for his steadfast love,
for his wondrous works to the children of man!
*For he satisfies the longing **soul**,*
*and the hungry **soul** he fills with good things.*

~ Psalm 107:8-9 ESV

"I did not know then what I would learn over many years—that he was a healer of souls." John reflected upon his first visit with Dallas Willard.

He later asked his mentor, "What do I need to do in order to stay spiritually healthy?"

Dallas responded with the unexpected. "You must ruthlessly eliminate hurry from your life."

After writing down that point, John continued. "Okay, Dallas, I've got that one. Now what other spiritual nuggets do you have for me? I don't have a lot of time and I want to get all the spiritual wisdom from you that I can."

"There *is* nothing else," Dallas replied. "Hurry is the great enemy of spiritual life in our day. You must ruthlessly eliminate hurry from your life."[7]

Are you in a hurry today?

And, if so, what gets "left behind" as you zoom past people? What is neglected in order to attend to the most pressing need?

Your soul?

"Someone starts talking about things like grace and rest and peace, and the soul feeling its worth, and that language feels so foreign and so beautiful, like water in a desert, like one bright bud pushing up in an otherwise arid landscape. And like a song you used to love but haven't heard for years, something breaks through: that's what I've been missing. That's it. My soul."[8]

When we are hurried, it is because we are more preoccupied with *doing* than with *being*. Let's face it: all of us are busy. But when our busyness squeezes God completely out of our lives (or relegates Him to leftovers), then our inner condition becomes hurried. Our souls are empty, longing to be filled "with good things."

And one of the first things to go when our souls are weary is gratitude. Who has time to count our blessings when we are counting minutes? If we slow down long enough to notice the many ordinary grace gifts right in front of us, our souls are nourished by that recognition.

"We feel better when we are grateful because the fundamental mind-set of the life of the soul is gratitude. The Hebrew word for gratitude is *hikarat hatov*, which means literally 'recognizing the good.' That's what sustains your soul. That's what lifts you beyond yourself and into God's presence."[9]

Will you thank God today for the fact that He "satisfies the longing soul"?

And then will you make space for this to happen? The psalmist knew that "He makes me lie down in green pastures, he leads me beside quiet waters, he refreshes my soul" (Psalm 23:3 NIV).

"Where are your green pastures? Where are your still waters? The space where we find rest and healing for our souls is solitude. The world, culture, society—all of this—exerts a relentless, ceaseless, lethal pressure on your soul, and without relief from all of this chaotic interference, the soul dies. We withdraw so our souls can rest in God."[10]

Slow down. Receive grace, peace, and restoration deep into your soul.

My child, are you taking care of your soul? Since it is the source of your strength and devotion, perhaps it is time to make soul care a priority. Draw near to Me in silence and seeking. I will meet you whenever and however you come. Just come.

4. Promises

The LORD *is trustworthy in all he **promises** and faithful in all he does.*

~ Psalm 145:13 NIV

What if you were promised your heart's deepest desire—a child?

God said to Abraham, " 'Look up at the sky and count the stars if you think you can count them.' He continued, 'This is how many children you will have' " (Genesis 15:5).

But then a quarter of a century passed, and still God's promise remained unfulfilled.

For Sarah, this reality was three hundred months of *not* becoming pregnant. Dying a little each month. Finding it almost impossible to hold on to the promise of God to Abraham that their children would outnumber the stars in the heavens. And yet, now they were ages ninety and one hundred and still without a child together. How could God possibly be trusted to keep this promise?

Are you still waiting for a promise to be fulfilled in your life?

God has His own timing. When He announced that Sarah would give birth within the year, she burst out laughing. After all, she was way past childbearing years, an old woman.

But the Lord thundered out His response to such doubt and scoffing: "Why did Sarah laugh and say, 'Me give birth? At my age?' Is anything too difficult for the LORD?" (Genesis 18:13-14).

The word here that we translate into "difficult" is the original Hebrew word *pala,* which means "to be surpassing or extraordinary"—in other words, something difficult beyond all human effort.

Which is nothing if we trust God. Even in the face of the impossible. Our verse today reminds us that the Lord is both trustworthy and faithful.

God waited until there was no way other than a miracle. The chances were gone, the conniving ended. There was nothing left but him and the last call to believe anyway, hope anyway, trust anyway. But it was hard. So hard. But Sarah's laugh of doubt didn't disqualify her from receiving what God had promised. God didn't take back the promise . . . Our God knows us in our hidden hearts where laughter is colored with the strain of the long wait. He knows us and doesn't condemn. Instead, he calls us deeper.[11]

"God's promises are unchanging and not dependent on us. . . . We don't just have the promise *of* Jesus, we have Jesus who *is* the promise."[12]

When your neighbor invites you over for tea, it's important you show up, sit down, and drink the tea. The promise of this delicious drink is there, but does you no good until you follow through and receive it.

"Your promise gives me life" (Psalm 119:50 ESV).

The promise is on its way. Unclench your fists and open your hands wide. To receive it.

My child, it's hard to wait for a promise to be fulfilled. And yet I urge you not only to trust Me in this matter, but to relinquish any semblance of control you have over how and when the promise will come. I may surprise you in delightful ways.

5. Burdens

Praise be to the Lord, to God our Savior, who daily bears our
burdens.

~ Psalm 68:19 NIV

As hard as it is to hear your young husband's brain cancer diagnosed with "no cure," my friend Jennifer Kennedy Dean would tell you that in that moment a divine blanket of peace descended on them both, and the Source of comfort entered into their lives in a fresh way.

"God is not a burden giver," Jennifer recalls, "testing you to see just how much he can pile on you and still leave you standing. He is the burden bearer. When we learn to hand over burdens in the daily issues of life, we'll be ready when the big ones come along."[13]

What is your heaviest burden today?

One of the most challenging can be exhibiting godliness, like Jesus. Impossible. Except for today's promise—He "daily bears our burdens." Whatever they are, we do not carry them alone.

"Give your burdens to the Lord, and he will take care of you. He will not permit the godly to slip and fall" (Psalm 55:22 NLT).

Tim Keller says, "To bear someone else's burdens is to sympathize, identify with, and become involved in the person's life so they do not have to face it alone. In Christ, God literally identified with us, becoming human, bearing not only the sufferings of mortality but also the judgment we deserve for the sin."[14]

The ultimate role of the church is to be Christ to one another—"Bear one another's burdens, and so fulfill the law of Christ" (Galatians 6:2 ESV). The New Testament Greek word here is *baras*—"a heavy weight pressing down on another person."

Here are some answers when I asked a group of women to name some of their burdens:

- being in a loveless or abusive marriage,
- raising a child with disabilities,
- never having enough money for basic needs,
- gaining weight because food is their (legal) addiction,
- carrying bitterness from an unjust accusation . . . years ago,
- failing their own expectations of being a super-woman, or
- holding onto guilt from an abortion or immoral act in their youth.

Into the middle of all this comes Jesus. The One who offers to walk beside us and carry all this stuff. He says, "My yoke is easy and my burden is light" (Matthew 11:30 NIV).

Will you offload your burden(s) to Him today?

Why not visualize your own list piled into a large backpack. Okay, a large suitcase. Now stand up, wheel that suitcase over to the cross, and kneel down. Unzip it and begin to take out each item. In an act of complete surrender, offer that burden back to God.

> *Dear Lord, I have been carrying this {name the person, situation, or emotion} for so long. I am utterly broken under the weight, and need to be yoked to you for strength. So I surrender to You now, and pray that I might understand how to continue this journey with You and in full healing. Amen.*

Don't pick it up again. Go forth with praise on your lips and a spring in your step, knowing that you are free.

My child, I know it is unspeakably heavy, this burden you have been bearing for way too long. And my desire is to not only lift it off you, but to lay it down forever. Will you come and relinquish it to Me? I can bear anything. And now you can walk freely.

6. *Chose*

*"You didn't choose me. I **chose** you. I appointed you to go and
produce lasting fruit."*

~ John 15:16 NLT

I was usually the last one chosen for sports teams during elementary
school recess. Back in the day, the captain of each team would take turns
choosing players. Raised hands and shouts of "Me!" echoed until they
grudgingly accepted the final leftover people.

Kids like me. Chubby. Nonathletic. Slow runners.

Is it any wonder I spent much of my life silently pleading, *Choose me?*

And then one day I realized that Jesus had. He'd chosen me. A gift for
all to see—*"I chose you."*

Choose in the New Testament Greek is *eklego*, which means to "pick out
or select, especially with the motivation of love and kindness." God's grace
is a gift to all and, as we embrace it, we each become a chosen one—spe-
cially selected. The question becomes, will we choose to accept this gift?

Do you realize you have been chosen? Or are you still raising your hand
and trying to get His attention by doing stuff to make yourself worthy?

Mary struggled with trying to be like someone else in order to be chosen: "Being rejected means we have no worth. Being chosen means we have
it all. So we contort ourselves in whatever impossible positions we can to
make ourselves chooseable. We let go of our will, conform our lives to make
others approve, and lose our personalities at the altar of being picked."[15]

Another's success does not mean my failure.

It is only when we know ourselves as beloved that we can settle down as
fully desired and chosen members of the Jesus Team. Secure. Serene. Loved.

> When I write to you that, as the Beloved, we are God's chosen
> ones, I mean that we have been seen by God from all eternity
> . . . long before you were born and became a part of history

you existed in God's heart. Long before your parents admired you or your friends acknowledged your gifts or your teachers, colleagues, and employers encouraged you, you were already chosen. The eyes of love had seen you as precious, as of infinite beauty, as of eternal value. When love chooses, it chooses with a perfect sensitivity for the unique beauty of the chosen one, and it chooses without making anyone else feel excluded.[16]

God says to you today, "I took you from the ends of the earth, from its farthest corners I called you. I said, 'You are my servant'; I have chosen you and have not rejected you" (Isaiah 41:9).

My child, you are My first choice! Not a consolation prize, but a treasure. Because I know the you deep inside, I can see all your potential and possibilities. Will you rest in that knowledge today? Stop looking to everyone else. I'm calling you forth.

7. Peace

*"I am leaving you with a gift—**peace** of mind and heart. And the **peace** I give is a gift the world cannot give. So don't be troubled or afraid."*

~ John 14:27 NLT

"I am a pacifist who yells at her husband," wrote the young author.

Needless to say, I read on . . . "Though I profess big ideas about the beauty of shalom and Christ's ministry of peace crashing into our world, I often find myself squabbling and quarreling my way through the day—with those I love the most."[17]

Frankly, I can identify.

I've already admitted earlier in this book that my deepest prayer is still for world peace. But some days I don't even do my part for peace at our little "Sunnyside" cottage here in New England. Why is that?

Because first, we must receive the gift. Before we can live it.

What rituals or disciplines invite peace to enter your chaotic life?

For me, it often helps to be out in nature. Inevitably, it's finding a comfortable spot to be still and silent, sitting with open hands and breathing quiet, simple prayers, like, "Lord, have mercy," or "Here I am, Father," or "I trust You, Jesus." There might be tears. Even groans. Music is occasionally playing or coming from my own mouth. But I try to wait for peace to permeate my soul.

In today's text, Jesus is speaking final words to those He loves most. He knows their world has caused them to be troubled and afraid. There is only one gift that will suffice—peace.

But this peace from Jesus is "a gift the world cannot give."

Marlo discovered this kind of peace one day when the demands of five children, one with special medical needs, totally overwhelmed and prompted an avalanche of tears and relinquishment.

I can't undo past mistakes. I can't control what happens to me or my kids today. I am not God. He is God of yesterday. There's nothing in my past that can't be forgiven, nothing I've done he can't redeem. He's God of today. Whatever happens is in his hands. And he's God of tomorrow, of my hopes and dreams, and my fears. I can leave all that in his hands. I just need to trust the one who promises impossible peace, the one who holds all my days in his hands.[18]

What do we do with such a valuable and precious gift?

We pass the peace.

You may recognize this phrase from your church's liturgy—that time in the middle of the service when the congregation gets up and mingles, saying, "Peace be with you." But how can we "pass the peace" every day?

"Mostly in small, unseen moments as we live together, seeking to love those people who are the constants, the furniture in our lives—parents, spouses, kids, friends, enemies, the barista we chat with each week as we wait for coffee, the people in the pew behind us with the noisy toddler, the old man next door who doesn't get out much."[19]

"Then the peace of God that exceeds all understanding will keep your hearts and minds safe in Christ Jesus" (Philippians 4:7).

*My child, I'm sure you've discovered by now that there is no peace to be found on this earth except through Me. So draw near for the kind of peace that passes all understanding. No matter what is going on in your world—or **the** world.*

8. *Where*

*Jesus replied, "Weren't ten cleansed? **Where** are the other nine?
No one returned to praise God except this foreigner?"*

~ Luke 17:17-18

Leprosy is a horrific disease.

It's easy to recognize lepers. They're the ones missing noses, fingers, and toes.

Because they can't feel pain, injuries aren't treated. Not only does this infection spread to other people, but it carries with it a huge social stigma. In biblical times, leprosy was considered a punishment from God for sin and bad morals.

But Jesus didn't see a scaly disease. He saw the soul deep inside.

The pain, the loneliness, the despair. And with a gentle touch, He healed ten lepers and offered them a whole new future.

Can you imagine how they felt—the relief, the joy, and the hope? The gratitude? With this encounter with a seemingly ordinary man, their lives had been extraordinarily transformed.

But only one person thanked Jesus.

Where were the other nine?

Running to look in the mirror? Chatting up all those other people who had kept their distance? Making plans and moving forward? Instantly forgetting the One who took time to really see them and meet their deepest need.

It was, in fact, the foreigner among them—the refugee—who recognized that this gift of healing had come from a Giver. As he fell on his face at Jesus' feet and thanked Him with loud praises, Jesus had a further word for him. "Get up and go. Your faith has healed you" (v. 19). Not only was the man's body whole, but his heart was also now faith-filled.

I can't help but wonder what the story would be if we revisited all ten men twenty years after their healing. Physical healing is one thing, but deep inner healing (the kind that prompts gratitude and faith) is what lasts for the long haul.

"All ten lepers had reason to be happy. But only the one who offered gratitude experienced a more potent kind of happiness. When we stop to say thank you, we bring delight to the Giver. Our thankfulness is more than the polite response for a gift. It's the heart-moving response that stretches all the way to the Giver."[20]

Do you utter a prayer of thanksgiving as soon as your prayer request is granted? Just as quickly and automatically as you shouted out your desperate need to God?

Probably not. We always default to *Help*, but not always to *Thank You* for the help.

Yesterday a young mommy blogger asked for prayer on social media because she was going to be hearing the results of cancer testing at a doctor's appointment. I don't know her, but I uttered up a prayer for God's presence and provision in the situation. A few hours later she graciously praised God for good test results and thanked those who stood with her.

When Jesus healed ten men with leprosy, it was a Big Deal. People who were once doomed were now suddenly delivered from this fate. Their whole lives changed. Now there was hope and a future.

I hope Jesus doesn't have to search for me when it's time for gratitude.

My child, you are always on My mind. I know those places of pain—where you need healing. And I delight in helping to make you whole. I also delight when you share your joy with Me and others. Gifts are to be celebrated—don't be left behind.

9. *Answers*

Don't worry about anything; instead, pray about everything; tell
*God your needs, and don't forget to thank him for his **answers**.*

~ Philippians 4:6 TLB

I hung up the phone and cried.

The answer was not the one I had hoped for. Prayed for.

I wanted "yes." Would have settled for "wait." But what I got was "no."

And now it was time for the hardest step of all, to "thank him for his answers." Yes, even if it wasn't the answer I wanted. The one I needed.

You see, I have lived my entire life on these words from God's Word. In fact, I recorded them here in the same translation I memorized as a teenager with my brand-new dark green Living Bible. "Don't worry about anything; instead, pray about everything."

What are you worried about today?

Okay, go ahead and write down three of your current concerns.

_____

_____

_____

Now, what would happen if you chose, instead of worrying, to pray about them? Go ahead—do it. Offer each one to God in prayer.

A great model for life.

But only if we always end our prayers with "Thy will be done." After all, that's how Jesus taught us to pray (see Matthew 6:10 KJV). After being very specific about our wants, our needs, our great concerns, we then relinquish all that into the powerful and worthy hands of our Savior, allowing Him to answer in His way and His timing.

Because we really do want His will to be done. And even if we think we know exactly the path that should take, we must hold our expectations very loosely.

When I was much younger, Elisabeth Elliot once encouraged me to tell God everything I was feeling about His answers to my prayers. She pointed out that He already knew anyway. But she warned me to share with others discreetly; "God can take it—others sometimes can't."

From what she had shared, I knew that even this strong woman of God occasionally struggled with getting a disappointing answer to prayer.

> I have often asked why. Many things have happened which I didn't plan on and which human rationality could not explain. In the darkness of my perplexity and sorrow I have heard Him say quietly, *Trust Me.* He knew that my question was not the challenge of unbelief or resentment. I have never doubted that He loves me, but I have sometimes felt like St. Teresa of Avila who, when she was dumped out of a carriage into a ditch, said, "If this is the way You treat Your friends, no wonder You have so few!"[21]

In the Old Testament, God, through the prophet Jeremiah, not only encouraged us to cry out to Him but also assured us that He would always answer. "Call to me and I will answer and reveal to you wondrous secrets that you haven't known" (Jeremiah 33:3).

That answer? The one you didn't want? It may just contain a "wondrous secret" later to be revealed. Trust Him and keep praying. Always with thanksgiving.

My child, when you call upon Me, I will always answer. Do you believe that? Then you must wait quietly and openly to recognize when My answers come. They may not look exactly as you expected. Perhaps they will even be better.

10. Though

*Even **though** the fig trees have no blossoms, and there are no grapes on the vines; even **though** the olive crop fails, and the fields lie empty and barren; even **though** the flocks die in the fields, and the cattle barns are empty, yet I will rejoice in the LORD! I will be joyful in the God of my salvation!*

~ Habakkuk 3:18 NLT

The news tonight was horrific. And frightening. Seemingly hopeless. And the news last night was the same.

So, I must admit, I'm tempted to feel a bit like the Old Testament prophet Habakkuk, who cried out to God as the Babylonians were overtaking Israel:

> "Violence is everywhere!" . . .
> Must I forever see these evil deeds?
> Why must I watch all this misery?
> Wherever I look, I see destruction and violence.
> I am surrounded by people who love to argue and
>   fight.
> The law has become paralyzed and there is no justice in
>   the courts.
> The wicked far outnumber the righteous. (Habakkuk
>   1:2-4 NLT)

What in the world was happening to them (and why does it sound so much like today)?

"The crisis internationally was serious. But of even greater concern was the national corruption. . . . No wonder Habakkuk looked at all the corruption and asked, 'Why doesn't God do something?' Godly men and women continue to ask similar 'whys' in a world of increasing international crises and corruption. Nation rises up against nation . . . and sin abounds at home."[22]

What can we do at such times?

Habakkuk decided to "be joyful in the God of my salvation."

He knew how important it was to take the long view, to realize that God is sovereign. To know that God's timing is perfect.

Even if we, too, say, "How long, O LORD, must I call for help?" (Habakkuk 1:2 NIV). Can we handle slow?

> Above all, trust in the slow work of God. We are quite naturally impatient in everything to reach the end without delay. We should like to skip the intermediate stages. We are impatient of being on the way to something unknown, something new. And yet it is the law of all progress that it is made by passing through some stages of instability—and that it may take a very long time . . . Give our Lord the benefit of believing that his hand is leading you.[23]

Habakkuk looked around and all he saw was emptiness—no fruit, no animals, no wheat. But he knew God.

And so he chose to trust, praying, "I have heard all about you, Lord. I am filled with awe by your amazing works. In this time of our deep need, help us again as you did in years gone by. And in your anger, remember your mercy" (Habakkuk 3:2 NLT).

At first I thought that I would just fast from the evening news. But, alas, curiosity and concern caused me to realize that I have to live in reality. For one thing, news headlines make a prayer list all by themselves. For another, I am called to live in this world.

As I make my own list of "though . . .yet," I shall trust in the slow work of God.

My child, there is much to be concerned for in the world today. But I am always at work—in the hearts and minds of those open to My leading. Can you trust the slow process of transformation? Lift up your worries and concerns to Me in prayer, and then trust.

11. Story

Give thanks to the LORD, for he is good, his love endures forever.
*Let the redeemed of the LORD tell their **story**.*

~ Psalm 107:1-2 NIV

"I was crushed, so crushed I didn't even want to face the public. And yet, I didn't have a choice . . ."

Carol was a professional speaker who was used to sharing her story.

Until that day her only son was arrested for murder. While reeling from the unimaginable crime that would change all their lives forever, Carol knew she had to speak to a large crowd that weekend—people unaware of the recent event.

> I gave my message of hope based on biblical truth that I had always known to be true. When I began it was the most empowering thing I had ever experienced because I suddenly realized in the middle of speaking truth, that in the dark shadows of my mind I was probably questioning, but I had that sense, as I spoke from God's Word, of stomping on the head of the enemy, saying "You loser. You meant to wipe the parents out with the son, and you lose!" And it gave me the courage to do it again and again.[24]

Is God calling you, as one of "the redeemed," to share your own unique story?

Even if the story is a hard one—one that you would rather keep hidden?

"God is able to take the mess of our past and turn it into a message. He takes the trials and tests and turns them into a testimony."[25]

New York Times best-selling author Ann Voskamp found that writing her second book was even harder than telling the story of the first book. "It was slower because I was afraid. After *One Thousand Gifts*, I bear scars and wounds, so I wrote slower, tried to be more careful. Not very brave sometimes, paralyzed a lot of times. . . . [But] Christ is in the broken and hurting places where it looks like all ashes."[26]

If you speak to a world in pain, you will always have an audience.

"When we share our stories, we give people around us an opportunity to speak of their own unexpected challenges. We develop a bond with others and a risk-free environment for people to say 'This is what happened to me.' And God can use those times to bring about much good. I've discovered the benefits of telling our story far outweigh the liabilities, if we can just find the courage to move forward," says Carol Kent, who invests in teaching speakers.[27]

Long ago, Jill Briscoe shared this prayer with me and some other young speakers; I still use it today: "Give my words wings, Lord. May they alight gently on the branches of men's minds, bending them to the winds of Your will. May they fly high enough to touch the lofty, low enough to breathe the breath of sweet encouragement upon the downcast soul."[28]

God promises that He will bring beauty from ashes.

Share your story.

My child, your unique unfolding story is phenomenal because I am the Author. And you are the redeemed. So, I urge you to explore both small and large avenues of sharing how My grace gifts are transforming your life. Even when it's risky. You may just affect another's life story in the process.

12. Good Things

*"And you know in all your hearts and in all your souls that not one thing has failed of all the **good things** which the LORD your God spoke concerning you. All have come to pass for you—not one word of them has failed."*

~ Joshua 23:14 NKJV

God keeps His promises. Even when all seems bleak.

I'm sure when Joshua and Caleb were sent (along with ten other "faithless" men) to spy out the land and see if God's chosen people would be able to conquer it, they were full of hope. But the nay-saying of their companions won out. Thus, the Israelites wandered in the desert for forty more years!

They already *owned* the land of Canaan because of God's promise to Abraham way back in Genesis 13:15, "All the land that you see I will give to you and your offspring forever" (NIV). But Joshua ended up being the man God called to actually usher them into crossing the Jordan and *possessing* their great gift.

And then he had to believe another impossible promise—"I have given you Jericho" (Joshua 6:2 NLT).

But the fortified city of Jericho was surrounded by two substantial walls. Yet even though they were afraid and even though God's strategy seemed unorthodox, Joshua and his men obeyed the Lord's commands. "It was by faith that the people of Israel marched around Jericho for seven days, and the walls came crashing down" (Hebrews 11:30 NLT).

At long last!

Joshua spent a lifetime heeding God's words not to fear because God would accompany Joshua through any situation, including almost impossible battles: "The LORD your God fights for you, just as he promised" (Joshua 23:10 NIV).

What good things are you asking God for in your own life?

Perhaps they aren't even things as much as circumstances—provisions, blessings, relationships. If you've ever thought He is holding back because He is stingy or mean, then consider this promise: "The LORD gives—doesn't withhold!—good things to those who walk with integrity" (Psalm 84:11).

He longs to shower us with good things—even as we long to live with integrity for Him!

By the time Joshua reached old age, it was time to divide the land between the twelve tribes of Israel. Each time a new group of people was settled, a promise was fulfilled. Many had waited a lifetime for the "good things" to arrive in their lives.

You may be looking at a Jericho today.

> Maybe something in your life looks too big. Your enemy might be pointing out all the reasons why your obstacle will win the day. If so, remember this: when God calls you to battle, he has already won the victory. The only way your Jericho will stand is if you believe your limited perceptions instead of God's Word and slink away, missing the opportunity to see God's power in action.[29]

"Not one of all the good things that the LORD promised to the house of Israel failed. Every promise was fulfilled" (Joshua 21:45).

Do you know "in all your hearts and in all your souls" that God will never fail you? Count on His promises today, and have courage to obey wherever He leads.

My child, sometimes what at first appears impossible is merely improbable. And that's what I do best. Enlist my servants to do incredible feats with My unlimited creativity and power. I did it with Joshua, and I will do it again. All you have to do is obey.

13. Circumstance

*In any and every **circumstance** I have learned the secret of
being filled and going hungry, both of having abundance and
suffering need.*

~ Philippians 4:12 NASB

When was the last time you complained about life?

A recent scientific study showed that only 10 percent of our happiness is dictated by life's circumstances. The rest is up to us.

How's your attitude today?

Paul aimed for the positive when he "rejoiced in the Lord greatly" (v. 10 NASB) and learned how "to be content in whatever circumstances I am" (v. 11 NASB)

That same research revealed that in contrast to our circumstances having little power to dictate our demeanor, a full 40 percent of our happiness is due to our intentional choices—what we do and what we think.

No matter what life hands us, our response is within our control.

Researcher Sylvia Lyubomirsky explains how to live beyond circumstances: "Genuinely happy people do not just sit around being contented. They make things happen. They pursue new understandings, seek new achievements, and control their thoughts and feelings. In sum, our intentional, effortful activities have a powerful effect on how happy we are, over and above the effects of our circumstances."[30]

"But," you may say, "*my* circumstances are horrific—there's no way I can live gratefully in the midst of them!"

And Paul's weren't? Allow him to remind us of challenging circumstances:

> I've worked much harder, been jailed more often, beaten up
> more times than I can count, and at death's door time after
> time. I've been flogged five times with the Jews' thirty-nine

lashes, beaten by Roman rods three times, pummeled with rocks once. I've been shipwrecked three times, and immersed in the open sea for a night and a day. In hard traveling year in and year out, I've had to ford rivers, fend off robbers, struggle with friends, struggle with foes. I've been at risk in the city, at risk in the country, endangered by desert sun and sea storm, and betrayed by those I thought were my brothers. I've known drudgery and hard labor, many a long and lonely night without sleep, many a missed meal, blasted by the cold, naked to the weather. And that's not the half of it, when you throw in the daily pressures and anxieties of all the churches.

(2 Corinthians 11:23-28 MSG)

What are your circumstances today? "Whether our circumstances put us in the brightness of sunshine or in the darkness of shadow, we are to bring our thanks to God and proclaim His unfailing love and mercy."[31]

Dallas Willard says that God has yet to bless anyone except where they actually are. "First, we must accept the circumstances we constantly find ourselves in as the place of God's kingdom and blessing."[32]

Learn the secret of living in your circumstances.

My child, where do you find yourself today—physically, spiritually, emotionally, vocationally, and relationally? Those unique circumstances have all been carefully orchestrated by My wisdom. Some circumstances are there to help you grow, others to help you influence others. Just be exactly where I've placed you and look for opportunity to thrive.

14. Selah

*Blessed be the LORD, who daily loads us with benefits, the God of our salvation! **Selah**.*

~ Psalm 68:19 NKJV

"Whoa! You're talking way too fast. You must stop long enough to breathe. Pauses are also important in a speech."

How well I remember some of my early training as a public speaker. My instructor was telling me to vary the rhythm—inserting pauses, rather than continually spouting information.

Our word today is just that—a command to pause. *Selah*.

How often do you deliberately step back from your own life and just allow God's goodness and blessing to soak over you?

King David practiced this frequently, as in today's verse. After expressing gratitude and praise, he sits back and absorbs the grace gifts of benefits and salvation.

> Selah helps us remember who we are; it's a place to be still, to know God. It's a place where we can deal with choices and changes. In these pauses, we're reminded that we have a certain number of days, and we can ask ourselves, Do I want to spend the rest of my life doing what I'm doing? In these places, we see things we need to add or to let go.[33]

What question do you need to ask yourself today? And is there any space in which to do that?

Experts disagree on the actual meaning of *Selah*. Some Bible translations use the word *Interlude,* identifying it with the world of music. Others suggest it comes from the same root as the Hebrew word *Calah*, which means "to weigh, to measure," indicating that Selah could mean a time to weigh and evaluate.

Whatever the true meaning, Selah calls out to us as a boundary—a place to be still and perhaps do absolutely nothing. A fence around our thoughts, our bodies, and our souls.

My friend Nancie, who wrote an entire book on this word, explains some of the benefits. "I need Selah in my life more than ever, and I suspect you do too. We live in a world of information coming at us. A lot of information. Some of it is trivial, some of it important. But we need these pauses in the presence of God to examine our priorities—to pursue what matters most."[34]

And though the Hebrew word *Selah* is not used in the New Testament, one look at Jesus and we will find that he lived it. And if the Son of God needed to pause and focus every now and then, then those of us who are Christ-followers would be wise to follow his ways.

"What activities did Jesus practice? Such things as solitude and silence, prayer, simple and sacrificial living, intense study and meditation upon God's Word and God's ways, and service to others. . . . So, if we wish to follow Christ—and to walk in the easy yoke with him—we will have to accept his overall way of life as our way of life totally."[35]

How can you incorporate pauses in your own life? You will never find time; you must simply *make* time.

Thanks be to God. Selah.

My child, breathe. That's right; take in a deep breath, and now let it out slowly. See? You need pauses in life. They are what help to fill you up for the busy times. Praise Me and serve Me just as the psalmist did. But then pause and let it all soak in. Selah.

15. Sacrifice

*Offer God a **sacrifice** of thanksgiving! Fulfill the promises you
made to the Most High!*

~ Psalm 50:14

Today Jen blogged, "I was pregnant and now I'm not."

My young friend shared the loss of her baby of nine weeks in the womb:
"I'm still in the thick of this one, so I have less than half figured out. Some
days, grief hangs heavy around my neck and other times, it's a smelly onion
I thought I'd gotten rid of until another painful layer peels away."

On the eve of what should have been glorious occasions for celebration—the launch of her first book and anticipation of a new baby—Jen
finds herself in a quandary. How to "offer God a sacrifice of thanksgiving."

A sacrifice is the surrendering of one valuable thing for the sake of something else considered even more valuable.

"I need to instruct my heart. So I'm processing. Many moments and
even hours are good and full of peace. And then sometimes, I hit these
tough spots where my thoughts go crazy and feelings start flooding. I remind myself of what I know to be true and anchor myself there."[36]

The truth is that God is still loving, still in control, and still able to
bring about His ultimate plan for good in our lives. Yet each of us must
decide whether we believe this enough to trust Him—with our hearts, our
hopes, and those in our homes.

"Therefore, let us offer through Jesus a continual sacrifice of praise to
God, proclaiming our allegiance to his name" (Hebrews 13:15 NLT).

"When we offer a sacrifice of praise, we may not be killing a snow-white
lamb, but we are laying our personal hopes and plans on the altar. We are
agreeing with God that He is worthy of praise and thanksgiving regardless
of our circumstances. We are admitting that God's greatness has nothing to
do with how we feel at the moment and everything to do with who He is."[37]

How do you praise God in the midst of pain?

The New Testament Greek word *thusia* means "sacrifice" and is derived from the root *thuo*, a verb meaning "to kill or slaughter for a purpose." Our praise and thanksgiving often come about fully after we have "killed" our fear, pride, or laziness—anything that interferes with worshipping God.

Perhaps every time we choose God over our default emotions, we are sacrificing. Jen is doing this in the midst of grief. Others are choosing to do this in the middle of anger or confusion. "The gospel tells us we'll know we are Christians by our love, which doesn't mean agreement with someone. God says it's sacrifice. God so loved that He gave His only Son. Love is sacrifice, so how do we love in this world? It means we live surrendered, sacrificial lives."[38]

Lay it down, and God will lift you up.

My child, when you lay down a dream or a person on the altar of your heart, I know the sacrifice is great. And yet, what better way to entrust that loved one to Me than giving back? And yes, it hurts. But the pain and the loss are ultimately redemptive. Remember My Son.

16. Rhythms

*"Walk with me and work with me—watch how I do it. Learn the unforced **rhythms** of grace."*

~ Matthew 11:30 MSG

Sometimes I feel like that girl who always claps at the wrong time.

You know what I mean. You are singing or worshiping in a large group and there is someone who is clapping to the offbeat? And it drives you crazy.

Do not blame that person! He or she may just have what is known as "beat deafness."

Scientists have discovered that a small percentage of people literally cannot bring into sync normal rhythm functions. Seems that their "internal oscillating function" is out of whack, no matter how many metronomes you try to use to bring them up to speed.

"Think of it as traveling over a cyclic pattern of peaks and valleys on a mountain. Humans can synchronize their rhythmic activities, like the pace of walking or jogging, to a beat by adapting their internal oscillators to the rate of 'highs and lows' in things like music."[39]

Some people either overshoot or undershoot the tempo but can't regulate the beat.

When it comes to rhythms of life, I sometimes feel "beat deaf."

Either I'm moving at a fast pace, accomplishing everything; or I'm catatonic on the couch, doing nothing. Not balanced.

Is Jesus saying to you today, "Learn the unforced rhythms of grace"?

We are all hardwired with an internal clock, a rhythm indicator that helps us thrive in healthy, balanced ways—eat, sleep, breathe. But when we ignore it and push ourselves to the limit, everyone suffers.

It's also true with our emotional and spiritual rhythms. "If I neglect my relationship with God, if I go beyond my people limits, if I don't nurture delight and joy, my soul begins to die."

Rhythm has to do with timing—when it's time to engage or disengage, to remain or to transition, to be with people or be apart, to work or to rest, to play or to be serious. Jesus paid attention and honored his rhythms. He knew when it was time to move to another town. He knew when he needed to be alone. He knew when it was time to preach and when it was time to pray.[40]

But what if my personal rhythm is in conflict with yours? Then we must respect and negotiate needs and preferences.

Our model for all this is Christ, who encourages us today to "walk with me and work with me—watch how I do it."

But we also have to live and work in community. God knew all about such things when He commanded the people of Israel to set aside certain days for celebration and rejoicing. Everyone—young and old, slaves and free, aliens, orphans, and widows—observed the ebb and flow of community.

The rhythm of life is one of God's mercies. We are called away from our personal inclination by the dawning of each new day, by the sun's going down so that we may cease from work, by the changing seasons, and by the regular occurrences of "feasts" when, without reference to how we happen to feel, we may join with others in purposeful rejoicing. We may choose to be glad.[41]

Start clapping!

My child, there is an ebb and flow in nature and also in your life. At least there should be. These rhythms are established so that there is time for all that must be accomplished. When you ignore such things, there is fallout—for body and soul. Rest in My grace and proceed gently.

17. Thrill

*You **thrill** me, LORD, with all you have done for me! I sing for*
joy because of what you have done.

~ Psalm 92:4 NLT

"Susan," exclaimed Nellie as she welcomed her guest to breakfast, "a miracle has occurred."

"What?" Susan responded, expecting some huge event.

"Why, I woke up!" her host replied, smiling from ear to ear.

Nellie and her husband, Bishop Julius, lived in a rural village in Muranga, Kenya, a place where the roads were dangerous, unpaved, dusty, and filled with potholes. Where shacks were taped together, with children playing in the dirt and men sitting on cans, swatting flies.

Susan and John Yates had been invited to speak to pastors in that remote region. African women in vivid colors had walked many miles to welcome them with food. They had also been given the best sleeping quarters, complete with mosquito netting.

And now, breakfast was served by a host who was clearly thrilled with God and His goodness.

Susan later reflected, "Nellie's attitude shamed me. From the world's perspective she had so little. But in true reality she had so much—a spirit that noticed the ordinary and called it a miracle! She had a truly grateful heart. Oh how I long to be like Nellie."[42]

Do you sometimes feel like that classic blues song "The Thrill Is Gone"?

How do we recapture the sense of wonder and gratitude we once felt upon first understanding all God's grace gifts to us?

We make a choice. Like King David in today's psalm: "You thrill me, LORD, with all you have done for me!"

And what had God done? In Psalm 92, David recounts that God had made him strong, put his enemies to defeat, helped him flourish and even remain vital enough to bear fruit in old age. No wonder David gives thanks—proclaiming God's love in the morning and His faithfulness every evening.

I want to be a believer who is simply thrilled with my Lord and Savior.

And I want that to show through my countenance, my words, and my actions.

Andrew Murray suggests that joy is the proof that Christ satisfies every need of the soul. "Be happy. Cultivate gladness. If there are times when it comes of itself, and the heart feels the unutterable joy of the Saviour's presence, praise God for it, and seek to maintain it. If at other times feelings are dull, and the experience of the joy not such as you could wish it, still praise God for the life of unutterable blessedness to which you have been redeemed."[43]

Think about how you view your life today. Do you awaken with a sense that just with merely opening your eyes, you have received a miracle? When you encounter that annoying colleague, do you thank God that you have a job? Instead of watching the news tonight, why not roll around on the floor with the littles and give them your full attention?

Show that you are literally thrilled to be their mama, or their grandfather.

Recapture the wonder of God's grace gifts—all around.

My child, sometimes responsibility gets in the way of rejoicing. When was the last time you felt thrilled? You may need to learn how to relax and recreate, to stop and notice little things. Hurry will not bring joy. But delighting in My presence and My presents most certainly will.

18. Mind

Do not conform to the pattern of this world, but be transformed
*by the renewing of your **mind**. Then you will be able to test and*
approve what God's will is—his good, pleasing and perfect will.
~ Romans 12:2 NIV

"A mind is a terrible thing to waste."

This phrase was one of the most successful public service marketing slogans ever. In the setting of 1972, it was an appropriate way for the United Negro College Fund to point out that there were many bright and capable African American students whose potential would be lost if they couldn't afford college.

Let's face it: our minds are crucial.

Mark Buchanan says, "What happens in our minds affects everything. As we think, so we are. Thinking is destiny, at least as far as a Christ-like life is concerned. The main work of discipleship is transformation through the renewing of our minds. Our mind changes as we walk with Jesus, talk with Jesus, look to Jesus. And then—without hardly trying—everything else about us starts to change too."[44]

Did you know your mind could be totally changed?

The key is a word I heard for the very first time last night—*neuroplasticity*. This is defined as the brain's ability to reorganize itself by forming new neural connections. In other words, this is the process where my thinking can actually physically shape my brain.

Switch On Your Brain is the popular book by Dr. Caroline Leaf, a cognitive neuroscientist with a PhD in communication pathology, specializing in neuropsychology.

> In it she reveals that because we are constantly reacting to circumstances and events, our brains become shaped by the process of thoughts and reactions. If we think positively, the

physiological aspects of our brains change in healthy ways that help us move toward a positive quality of life. Yet if we think negatively, our brains are changed in unhealthy ways, causing us to feel and act negatively. . . . This cycle shapes and designs our brains and, consequently, affects the health of our minds and bodies. Leaf also found that people who regularly meditate on Scripture and have developed a disciplined and focused thought life have increased intelligence, wisdom, and a feeling of peace.[45]

In today's text, Paul is saying that total change begins in our minds. When we submit our toxic thinking patterns to Christ, He can help "rewire" our whole system. Dr. Leaf says, "Thoughts occupy mental 'real estate.' Thoughts are active; they grow and change. Every time you have a thought, it is actively changing your brain and your body—for better or for worse."[46]

This strategy reminds me of another directive from Paul: "Take every thought captive to obey Christ" (2 Corinthians 10:5 ESV). This implies continuous, ongoing action.

"Taking thoughts captive means controlling them instead of allowing them to control you. It means actively replacing the enemy's thinking with God's thinking at every opportunity. Resist the urge to agree with or rehearse the negative thought. Instead replace it—repeatedly, diligently, and verbally—until eventually that brick in our stronghold comes tumbling down."[47]

If you are looking for lasting change, friend, it really is all in your head.

My child, this is not just the power of positive thinking. It is all about setting your mind on things above, that which is life-giving and hopeful. When you do such things deliberately, your physiology follows with a healthy response. So yes, be transformed, beginning with your thoughts and your mind. The rest will follow.

19. Generous

*"Keep open house; be **generous** with your lives. By opening up to others, you'll prompt people to open up with God, this **generous** Father in heaven."*

~ Matthew 5:16 MSG

"Oh, dear. Here comes the church crowd. Don't expect a big tip," my daughter's colleague warned.

At the time, she was in college, waitressing at a local restaurant. And it saddened her that Christians dining out for Sunday dinner didn't have a reputation for being generous.

Why do we withhold resources from those in need? What are we afraid we will lose?

When Jesus was among us, He not only challenged people to give generously to others, but He actually took it a step further—"be generous with your lives." In other words, make your whole life an "open house," welcoming others into your circle, your church, your heart, your home.

Be Jesus-with-skin-on. If others discover that opening up to you is safe, then just maybe they will "open up to God, this generous Father in heaven."

There was a time when followers of Christ had a reputation as truly generous.

"The believers devoted themselves to the apostles' teaching, to the community, to their shared meals, and to their prayers, . . . All the believers were united and shared everything. They would sell pieces of property and possessions and distribute the proceeds to everyone who needed them" (Acts 2:42, 44-45). The giving continued: "There were no needy persons among them. Those who owned properties or houses would sell them, bring the proceeds from the sales, and place them in the care and under the authority of the apostles. Then it was distributed to anyone who was in need" (Acts 4:34-35).

Out of gratitude for what Christ had done in their own lives, these early Christians naturally wanted to give back. And their countercultural behavior did not go unnoticed by the world.

A number of disasters overtook the Roman Empire in the first three centuries after Christ, prompting citizens to look out for number one—to protect themselves, ignore the less fortunate, or simply run. But the response of the early Christians was quite different: "To stay behind and nurse the sick, dispose of the dead, feed the hungry, and take in the orphan. Full-life generosity. No wonder the Christian movement expanded . . . The early Christians offered the world far more than just words. They offered a daily compassion that was full-life generous."[48]

Are you keeping "open house" with your life—among your work colleagues, your neighbors, even strangers?

And I'm not just talking about money here. There are many ways we can live generous lives. Offering kindness, doing something totally unexpected, like paying for the order of the person behind you in the drive-through. Offering advice or wise counsel to someone trying to navigate the complicated language of a government application. Secretly cleaning up the home of a church member who is returning from a long stay in the hospital.

This week, when I went to pay at the coffee shop counter, I was informed that someone had already covered it for me. This had never happened to me before. After recovering from my shock, I responded by doing the same for a future patron.

Full-life generosity. Blessed to be a blessing.

My child, it has always been risky to give away everything you have. But those who follow Me know that I will always provide—sometimes through you to someone in greater need. Live with generosity of time, energy, and resources. This is so counterintuitive to the rest of the world that your light will shine for Me.

20. Silence

*It's good to wait in **silence** for the LORD's deliverance. It's good for a man to carry a yoke in his youth. He should sit alone and be silent when God lays it on him.*

~ Lamentations 3:26-28

When prompted to add the spiritual discipline of silence to my daily prayers, I fought it. Sustained periods of silence do not come naturally to me.

But in sheer obedience to God's Word, I began to sit in silence. At first, a few minutes seemed excruciatingly long. But as the days increased, so did my longing for that quiet place.

It was a solace. A time and place to hear from my heavenly Father.

I then spent two years choosing silence every time I was alone in my car. No desire for radio or books on tape. Just soaking in the silence of my motorized womb.

Noise and busyness are all too often the scaffolding holding up our lives. But true strength is to be found in silence.

> Yes, silence and solitude invite me to gradually let go of the outer voices that give me a sense of well-being among my fellow humans, to trust the inner voice that reveals to me my true name. Silence and solitude call me to detach myself from the scaffolding of daily life and to discover if anything there can stand on its own when the traditional support systems have been pulled away.[49]

When was the last time you sat in silence?

Many Beautiful Things is a new film of the incredible life of Lilias Trotter, an English artist who spent her life serving the people of Algeria. It pleases me that more people are now exposed to the story of Lilias, whom I wrote about in my book *Live These Words*. A North African once spoke of her. "She was still and created stillness. She is beautiful to feel near. I love the quiet of her."[50]

When the Israelites wandered far from God and sought to replace Him with noise and idols, He spoke through the prophet Isaiah: "In return and rest you will be saved, quietness and trust will be your strength, but you refused" (Isaiah 30:15).

Please don't refuse the silence and quietness God is calling you to experience.

We must *be* before we can *do*. "Inner strength rekindled or sharpened before attempting exterior activity is part of Christ being formed in us. He did it; we follow in his steps. In order to draw and give the life-giving water to others, we must first drink deeply of the springs of life ourselves. We must 'come apart' in order to actively listen to God's inner whisper."[51]

In today's Scripture, we are told twice that silence is good. The reason is that we are finally able to hear the voice of God when our voice stops. The whisper that comes through His Word or hymns or grace gifts when all else is quieted.

"More than all things love silence. In the beginning we have to force ourselves to be silent. But then there is born something that draws us to silence. If only you practice this, untold light will dawn on you in consequence. . . . After a while a certain sweetness is born in the heart of this exercise and the body is drawn almost by force to remain in silence."[52]

Hush. And hear . . .

My child, sometimes I speak loudest in the silence. But you simply cannot hear if you are always chattering. Or if you are keeping your life full of noise. Please try the exercise of silence and learn how it will minister beauty and grace to your very soul. And you might just get a word from Me.

21. *Praise*

*Declare God's glory among the nations; declare his wondrous
works among all people because the LORD is great and so worthy
of praise.*

~ 1 Chronicles 16:24-25

In my green hymnal, it's the very first song.

> Praise, my soul, the King of heaven; to his feet your
> tribute bring.
> Ransomed, healed, restored, forgiven, evermore his
> praises sing.
> Alleluia, alleluia! Praise the everlasting king!
> Praise him for his grace and favor to his people in
> distress.
> Praise him, still the same forever, Slow to chide, and
> swift to bless.
> Alleluia, alleluia! Glorious in his faithfulness![53]

There are at least two things worth noting about this hymn:

1. Once I begin singing it, my body automatically
   reacts by standing up and lifting my hands (this
   from a cradle Presbyterian).
2. The rich lyrics in just these two stanzas are power-
   packed theology and definitely worth offering to
   Him through worship.

Frankly, I just love to "declare God's glory" through singing hymns.

And it will probably not surprise you that back in the day I was in a
singing group called the Joyful Noises. We may not have always sung on
key, but honey, we sure sang with joy!

How do you like to praise the Lord who is "so worthy of praise"?

Praise ushers us into joy as we focus on the perfection of God instead of our own concerns. To live in continual praise is to develop a second nature of our thoughts immediately turning to God with a litany of all He is and all He has done. He becomes the beautiful thought that exists just below the surface of my every thought. In this way, I am enjoying the "with God" life—experiencing His presence and pausing often to tell Him how grateful I am and how much I love Him.

Which, of course, infuriates the enemy of our soul.

"Because thanking God is pure worship. And in worship the power of the Holy Spirit is unleashed. When we choose to praise God something powerful takes place. His supernatural comfort and peace are poured out within our hearts, even the most broken. The Scriptures say 'the praise of children silences the enemy' (Psalm 8:2). When we praise Him, the enemy's power is broken."[54]

But the best part of offering praise is that the whole process changes us, helping us refocus on that which truly matters.

> Turn your eyes upon Jesus,
> Look full in His wonderful face.
> And the things of earth will grow strangely dim,
> In the light of His glory and grace.[55]

Will you make a joyful noise today—praise to the Almighty?

My child, the very best way to silence the enemy without and the depression within is by singing praises to Me. I don't care how your voice sounds—to me you are a joyful noise! And if you can't bring the energy to sing, then play hymns or praise songs. I inhabit each praise from your lips. And you will feel closer to the One who loves you most.

22. Prime Example

I thank Christ Jesus. . . . {who} "came into the world to save
sinners"—and I am the worst of them all. But God had mercy
*on me so that Christ Jesus could use me as a **prime example** of*
his great patience with even the worst of sinners. Then others will
realize that they, too, can believe in him and receive eternal life.

~ 1 Timothy 1:12, 15-16 NLT

No one wants to be the poster child for bad behavior.

Unless, of course, that was in the person's past. And sharing it might have a purpose.

I'll never forget the first time I heard a cassette tape of Kay Arthur teaching the Bible. After an excellent time of opening the Word, Kay closed the session with her own personal testimony.

Oh my! She detailed abuse in her first marriage to a bipolar man, her divorce, and going from man to man, "like the song says, 'Looking for love in all the wrong places.'" Kay continued, "I became what I thought I would never become—an immoral woman. . . . What happens is I have an affair with a married man. . . . [Sin will take you] farther than you ever wanted to go; it will keep you longer than you ever intended to stay; it will cost you far more than you expected to pay."[56]

Eventually, Kay did a complete 180-degree turnaround and committed her life to Christ. She confessed her sin, was forgiven, and began to grow in Christ and serve Him all of her days.

Like Paul in today's Scripture, Kay was perfectly honest about being "a prime example of his great patience with even the worst of sinners." Not because she loves to reveal her sordid past. Not because she feels superior in her present ministry. But for the goal that "others will realize that they, too, can believe in him and receive eternal life."

On January 9, 2017, Kay's husband of fifty-one years, Jack Arthur, died at age ninety from Alzheimer's disease, leaving a legacy of grace and mercy not only through Precept Ministries, but through a lifetime of faithfulness with his wife, Kay.

Prime examples of sin can become prime examples of faithfulness! The apostle Paul knew this better than anyone and was quick to share that he, too, had followed the wrong path until God got ahold of him.

Are you worried that because of your past, God cannot change your future? Friend, God is all about changing our lives, one grace gift at a time.

God doesn't call us to be perfect, only willing.

> Peter had a big problem with his mouth and was a bundle of contradictions. Andrew was quiet and behind the scenes. James and John were given the name "sons of thunder" because they were aggressive, hot-headed, ambitious and intolerant. Philip was skeptical and negative. He had limited vision. Nathaniel Bartholomew was prejudiced and opinionated. Matthew was the most hated person in Capernaum, working in a profession that abused innocent people. Thomas was melancholy, mildly depressive and pessimistic. James, son of Alphaeus, and Judas, son of James, were nobodies. Simon was a freedom fighter and terrorist in his day. Judas, the treasurer, was a thief and a loner.[57]

And yet these twelve men were the ones Jesus chose to share His life, to spread His message.

Are you willing to leave one life for another? God is so willing to receive you and use you.

ଚ୧୨୯

My child, I know you have regrets. But I see beyond what you once were to all that you can be as you continue to grow in godliness. Repentance and restoration go a long way in helping to form my choicest servants. You are in good company. All I ask is that you are willing and obedient.

23. Real

*As a face is reflected in water, so the heart reflects the **real** person.*
~ Proverbs 27:19 NLT

It's a dream—that seems like a nightmare.

The TV announcer on *To Tell the Truth* is ready for the reveal. All three on the panel have introduced themselves, each saying, "My name is Lucinda McDowell."

But two are imposters. Only one is the real me. As contestants ask each panel member certain questions, they narrow it down and vote for the most authentic. Then it comes.

"Will the *real* Lucinda McDowell please stand up?"

At this point I awaken—confused and worried.

This TV game show from my childhood has entered my subconscious thoughts, uninvited. Is it because I'm wearing too many hats? Am I having an identity crisis? Is the persona I offer the public out of line with what's going on inside?

The heart—what's inside—will always "reflect the real person."

Are you hiding behind a mask?

People do this for a variety of reasons—insecurity, shame, or confusion. But Christ-followers have no reason to fall into this trap. "God's Spirit touches our spirits and *confirms who we really are*. We know who he is, and we know who we are: Father and children" (Romans 8:16 MSG, emphasis added).

Why is it so hard to embrace the real me?

> My entire life has been a struggle to get out from behind the faces I put on: I want to be perceived as having it all together, as being the perfect wife, as being an intelligent Christian woman, as being compassionate . . . and inspirational. Authenticity can only be had in Christ. Because authenticity does not . . . rest in our natural selves, our only option for being truly

authentic people is to lose ourselves, . . . joyfully acknowl-
edging that Christ's power is made perfect in weakness. The
more we realize our desperate state and need of God's grace,
the more authentically human we will be.[58]

Are you ready to live your own life—not someone else's? It's a process,
but God will help.

Pursuing authenticity can sometimes feel like being a salmon swimming against the current.

When salmon prepare to mate, they swim upstream, up water-
falls, seeming to defy gravity. Salmon somehow know how to
turn their undersides—from center to tail—into the powerful
current coming at them. It hits them squarely and the impact
then launches them out and farther up the waterfall. They do
this over and over again until they actually climb over the
waterfall. From a distance it seems as if these fish are actually
flying. When you discover your integrity, listen to your inner
rhythms, set boundaries, and let go, like the salmon you push
against the strong currents in yourself and in our culture. And
you enter the joy of your own God-given life.[59]

This journey is valuable because God's best plan for us is to live trans-
parent lives that reflect His creation in our individuality.

"Your old life is dead. Your new life, which is your *real* life—even though
invisible to spectators—is with Christ in God. *He* is your life. When Christ
(your real life, remember) shows up again on this earth, you'll show up,
too—the real you, the glorious you" (Colossians 3:3 MSG).

❧

*My child, it's you I love. And I know you from the inside out. Even the parts
no one else sees. If I accept you and love you, then why not begin a path toward
more authenticity by loving yourself? Recognize all the grace gifts you have been
given and use them for others. Reject the lies and temptation to conform to lesser
standards. I am your Maker.*

24. List

*Who can **list** the glorious miracles of the LORD? Who can ever*
praise him enough?

~ Psalm 106:2 NLT

"I tell you I'm going crazy," the woman shouted to her mentor.

He gently replied, "Here is a yellow pad and here is a ballpoint pen. I want you to write down your blessings."

She refused, overcome by the despair that had seized her soul.

But he didn't give up.

"Think of the millions of people all over the world who cannot hear a choir, or a symphony, or their own babies crying. Write down, *I can hear—Thank God.* Then write down that you can see this yellow pad, and think of all the millions of people around the world who cannot see a waterfall, or flowers blooming, or their lover's face. Write *I can see—Thank God.*"

And so she began to make her list. As she reached the last line of that yellow notepad, clearly, "the madness was routed."

From then on, Maya Angelou wrote all of her books and poems on yellow notepads, saying, "As I approach the clean page, I think of how blessed I am."[60]

Ann, a Canadian pig farmer's wife, began listing her blessings on a dare. Pretty soon her entire life and outlook changed as she kept lists of her one thousand gifts. Ann Voskamp began blogging and writing books to encourage others to do the same. And in just a few short years, countless readers have seen their lives transformed by the spiritual practice of thanking God for all that is given.

Even science has shown that practicing gratitude is good for you. According to one study, those who keep gratitude journals:

- exercised more regularly,
- reported fewer physical symptoms,

- felt better about their lives as a whole, and
- were more optimistic about the upcoming week.

They were also more likely to make progress on their personal and professional goals if their gratitude was recorded in some manner, like on a list.[61]

The hymnist Frances Ridley Havergal kept what she called a "journal of mercies." She crowded it with remembrances of God's goodness. She was always on the lookout for tokens of the Lord's grace and bounty, and she found them everywhere. She believed that many a complaining life would be changed into music and song by a journal of mercies.[62]

Do you have a gratitude list? Why not?

The daily planner I ordered online this year includes a space each day to list gratitudes. My husband keeps one of those small pocket calendars solely dedicated to writing his everyday thanksgivings. Some people put them on slips of paper in a Mason jar.

You could even start right here:

I am grateful for _____

I am grateful for _____

I am grateful for _____

But however you choose to record God's goodness and faithfulness to you, my prayer is that it will enrich your life, bubbling over to all those you encounter.

⸙

My child, lists are good as reminders—of what to do, and also of what I have already done. When you begin counting your blessings, I think you will see a pattern of My mercies. Never ending. Always fresh. And as the list grows, so will your faith.

25. Near

*We thank you, O God! We give thanks because you are **near**.*
People everywhere tell of your wonderful deeds.

~ Psalm 75:1 NLT

Nicholas was a poor, uneducated house servant.

Until God took hold of his heart. Then he entered a monastic community and spent his life serving in the kitchen while devoting every moment of his time to being near to God.

When he died, his friends gathered together some of his letters and made them into the book *The Practice of the Presence of God*. This seventeenth-century volume is now considered the most widely read book of all time, next to the Bible.

Brother Lawrence (as Nicholas later became known) discovered that when one's soul was near God, it didn't matter whether one was a dishwasher or a king.

How can you and I learn to live near God every moment?

We can deliberately practice His presence.

> Brother Lawrence shows us that pursuing God doesn't need to be complicated. When he awoke, he purposed to think of God's love and greatness, then went about what he called his common business . . . Eventually this prayer-filled life can become instinctive rather than practiced.[63]

How can you live near God, in His presence, at all times?

Take the first step. "Draw near to God, and he will draw near to you" (James 4:8 ESV). Make a deliberate choice to acknowledge Him throughout the day—everywhere and in everything. And He will most certainly meet you there.

I love the old hymn that confirms this:

> There is a place of quiet rest,
> near to the heart of God.
> A place where sin cannot molest,
> near to the heart of God.
> O Jesus, blest Redeemer,
> sent from the heart of God.
> Hold us, who wait before thee,
> near to the heart of God.[64]

Will you draw near and allow God to hold you?

> Any virtually continual relationship requires . . . grace. The more we pray, the greater our awareness of God's grace in our lives. We slip up and he takes us back into his arms again. Brother Lawrence wrote that grace allows us to repair the lost time, and with that grace we're enabled to do anything God would set before us. Practicing God's presence primes the grace pump.[65]

He is near. Give thanks!

My child, yes, I am here. Near. In fact, literally next to you at this very moment. So we can dialogue through prayer and fellowship together even while you accomplish other tasks in your life. I'm always listening. Always caring. Always grateful that you have chosen to draw near. Never leave.

26. Forgives

*Let my whole being bless the LORD and never forget all his good deeds: how God **forgives** all your sins, heals all your sickness.*

~ Psalm 103:2-3

Why is it sometimes hardest to forgive those nearest to us?

Anne Lamott knows how supremely important forgiveness is at all levels. She says, "Earth is Forgiveness School. You might as well start at the dinner table. That way, you can do this work in comfortable pants."[66]

We are all broken people, called to "never forget all his good deeds." Those deeds include forgiveness for our many sins, which might definitely prompt us to say with the psalmist, "Let my whole being bless the Lord!"

Instead, we sound more like "Let my whole being whine and complain. Let my whole being point out what's wrong with *those* people and what they did. Let my whole being keep the argument going . . . on social media, in our church meeting, at the dinner table."

Because it's hard to forgive.

To forgive means to release. To give up the right to make the other person pay for what he or she did or said. Forgiveness costs us.

"We have to struggle long and hard for it, through time and tears. It will cost us something to be about the ministry of reconciliation. . . . When we have been wounded by those around us, extending forgiveness is giving up our right to recompense, to resentment, to self-righteousness."[67]

But unforgiveness and bitterness cost us more. So much more.

"When you refuse to forgive, you are giving the person who walloped you once the privilege of hurting you all over again—in your memory. . . . Forgiving is, first of all, a way of helping yourself to get free of the unfair pain somebody caused you."[68]

Some acts of forgiveness don't end in reconciliation; perhaps the person you forgive has died or, for necessity, needs to not be approached. Here we would offer "subjective forgiveness" which "includes both a disposition to forgive and an experience of forgiving: release of anger, hatred, and resentment—ending the internal recycling of the offense."[69]

But the other avenue—where people actually face each other in the process—is "objective forgiveness," which "refers to the elimination of the offense in the relationship, that is, it refers to reconciliation."[70]

Both kinds of forgiveness are grace gifts. "Be kind, compassionate, and forgiving to each other, in the same way God forgave you in Christ" (Ephesians 4:32).

The New Testament Greek word here is *charizomai*—translated "forgiving." Amazingly enough, it is a derivative of the word for grace—*charis.*

Who do you need to forgive today? Why not start close to home? How about . . . yourself?

ᕱᕤᕲ

My child, forgiveness has to be one of the hardest things in the world to do. And yet, as you are able to take that courageous step to forgive someone who has wronged you, then you are the one who is released into freedom. Whether "they" know it or not. I have forgiven you as a gift; now pass it along. You will be a whole new person.

27. Unfailing Love

*It is good to give thanks to the LORD, to sing praises to the Most High. It is good to proclaim your **unfailing love** in the morning, your faithfulness in the evening.*

~ Psalm 92:1-2 NLT

I awakened to the radio news report that Princess Diana had been killed in an accident.

Unbelievable.

To add to the sorrow that descended upon the world that day was the realization that this "people's princess" spent her whole life looking for love. One of her final statements indicates such: "I don't want expensive gifts; I don't want to be bought. I have everything I want. I just want someone to be there for me, to make me feel safe and secure."[71]

Are you just looking to be loved?

Then you are not alone. One psychologist points out that many experiments prove that the need to be loved is one of the most basic and fundamental needs.

> All of us have an intense desire to be loved and nurtured. . . .
>
> Given the importance of the need to be loved, it isn't surprising that most of us believe that a significant determinant of our happiness is whether we feel loved and cared for.[72]

But we also have a need to express love. "In our pursuit of the need to be loved, however, most of us fail to recognize that we have a parallel need: *the need to love and care for others*. This desire, it turns out, is just as strong as the need to be loved and nurtured."[73]

Is there a source of love both for you and for me? For all the Princess Dianas of the world?

Yes, it is God's "unfailing love."

The Hebrew word here is *hesed*, which is translated "unfailing love" or "loving-kindness." It quite simply means a love given freely—a grace gift.

"It means God's loyal, covenantal love. It's based on his steady and faithful character, not our flighty ways. It's the kind of love that makes a married couple stay together through pain and loss and betrayal. It's the pursuing kind of love that welcomes home prodigals. It's higher, wider, deeper, and stronger than anything we can conjure up."[74]

Our Scripture today extols the wisdom of giving thanks and praise every day for this kind of unfailing love. The one that reaches out to us at our lowest point and draws us in. The one that so fills and heals us that we are able to reach out and extend love to others.

The Bible is full of passages and promises about God's unfailing love. But perhaps my own favorite is Jeremiah 31:3, where *hesed* is used twice. "I have loved you with an everlasting love; I have drawn you with loving-kindness" (NIV).

This love is a grace gift for you today. All you have to do is receive it. And say thank You.

∾♥∾

My child, love is part of My very nature. So when I say I love you, I mean the kind of love that is unending, undeserved, unfailing, and undeniably complete! You cannot stop my love toward you. You can refuse to receive it, but I will always consider you my beloved. Always.

28. Knees

*Three times a day he got down on his **knees** and prayed, giving thanks to his God, just as he had done before. Then these men went as a group and found Daniel praying and asking God for help.*

~ Daniel 6:10-11 NIV

Immediately after her introduction, our guest speaker fell to her knees on the floor of the church platform and began to pray.

It was a powerful statement to me and everyone gathered there. A recognition of the holiness of God, His presence in that place, and the humility of the servant who was about to speak and teach His Word.

That was two decades ago, and Beth Moore has continued to begin each of her presentations in the same way—on her knees.

Beth says people need to believe in Christ, bend their knees, and receive His grace. "We must remember that bending the knee is ultimately a matter of pure obedience. . . . You may never feel like giving your circumstance, hurt, or loss to Him; but you can choose to submit to His authority out of belief and obedience rather than emotion. . . . You can begin a life of authentic peace today. The path to peace is paved with kneeprints."[75]

Daniel knew all about knee prints, and God's authority as well.

He and many fellow Jews had been deported to Babylon. But King Nebuchadnezzar, recognizing Daniel's leadership abilities, had elevated him as a high administrator. When this angered other officials, they began searching for ways to discredit him professionally, only he was above reproach. So they went after his personal life—"Our only chance of finding grounds for accusing Daniel will be in connection with the rules of his religion" (Daniel 6:5 NLT).

The officials tricked the king into signing an edict that one could only pray to the king. Prayers lifted to anyone else would amount to that person being thrown into a den of lions.

Daniel continued to pray to God regardless of the threat: "Three times a day he got down on his knees and prayed, giving thanks to his God, just as he had done before" (Daniel 6:10-11 NIV). He knew the potential consequence was death, yet he thanked God. Daniel's obedience to God was more important than his relationship to the king.

The schemers came in and took Daniel to the king, who had to comply with the law he had signed, even though he was "deeply troubled, and he tried to think of a way to save Daniel" (v. 14 NLT). As he regretfully sent Daniel to his fate, the king said, "May your God, whom you serve so faithfully, rescue you" (v. 16 NLT).

And God did.

The king was overjoyed to see that Daniel was released the next morning without even a scratch on him. Daniel's enemies did not prevail, and King Nebuchadnezzar became convinced that Daniel's was "the living God, and he will endure forever. His kingdom will never be destroyed, and his rule will never end" (v. 26 NLT).

What about you today? Do you need courage as you speak up? Do you need wisdom in making an important decision at work? Can you pray with a thankful heart, even while in danger?

Then fall to your knees in both obedience and prayer. And God will lift you up.

My child, to whom do you bend your knee today? If your ultimate allegiance is to the God who created you and redeemed you, then you will always be on the winning team. Stand up for what is true and right. But always kneel to My will and My way. I am honored by your allegiance.

29. Sunset

*From sunrise to **sunset**, let the LORD's name be praised!*
                                        ~ Psalm 113:3

Mike calls me out on the porch to watch the sunset.

It is glorious—fiery red and dazzling orange with a bit of purple mixed in. We are in awe and enjoy the companioned silence.

Six years ago we decided to downsize—give away or throw away pretty much half our life's "stuff." After living for twenty years in a beautiful, large, colonial parsonage, we were eager to settle into our own little nest. The fact that this cottage was high on a hill was a great determining factor for our future home. It was christened "Sunnyside," and we looked forward to such things as sunsets and vistas of the surrounding New England village.

It seemed appropriate that for the "sunset" time of life, we chose this verse for our home: "May God be gracious to us and bless us and make his face to shine upon us" (Psalm 67:1 ESV).

He is and He does. All the time. So I endeavor to thank Him "from sunrise to sunset."

And now it's time for bed. I set the alarm, turn on my sound machine (ocean waves), and snuggle deep into the warm fleece sheets. As my mind settles over the story of my day, I ask the only truly important question.

"Did my life today please you, Lord—have I loved well?"

St. John of the Cross once said that "at the evening of our day we shall be judged by our loving." Perhaps that means that my list of what was done and what was left undone is not as important as how I attempted each task, each encounter.

We can do no great things, only small things with great love. What small things did I do today—and were they done with love?

I usually go to sleep quickly once my head hits the pillow, but I linger a bit for three final rituals: pray through the names on my family list, ask forgiveness for today's sin, and begin my litany of praise for every single blessing. Sleep often overtakes me before I can even finish . . . "let the LORD's name be praised."

Have I loved well?

Ken Gire says that if we can answer yes to that sunset question, it is enough. "It may not be enough for our employer. It may not be enough for our fellow workers. It may not be enough for all the carpools and committees and other things on our calendars. It may not even be enough for us. But it is enough for God. And that should make it enough for us."[76]

Live with a grateful heart. Love well. And sleep in peace.

My child, a peaceful night of rest is My gift to you at the end of another hard day. One in which you tried to be salt and light in the world. One where you turned to Me in prayer and asked, "What do I say?" or "Show me the way." And now, I bring you to a quiet moment to simply give thanks. You did love well today. And tomorrow will be another fresh opportunity.

30. Rejoice

Rejoice *always.*

~ 1 Thessalonians 5:16

"I've been living without the use of my hands and legs for fifty years!" Joni Eareckson Tada recently wrote.

When she first broke her neck as a teenager, she met a guy who had been in a wheelchair for eight years—unimaginable to her at the time. And yet today this vibrant woman remains full of joy.

How has she been able to "rejoice always"?

Joni answers, "I shake my head in amazement, look back and wonder, how did I make it to this point? And how have I done it, for the most part, with a smile? It's all because of God, His grace, and loving Christians. The grace-filled believers that God brought into my life made all the difference."[77]

Do you find it hard to rejoice in hard times?

In today's verse Paul is writing to people in distress. After the Romans overtook Thessalonica, they stripped the people and the territory of everything valuable. They pillaged resources, then set into place a prohibition for trade between districts, which totally impoverished the Thessalonians.

Can you imagine how a command to "rejoice always" went over?

But Paul was able to empathize with them because he, too, had been there. "Over the course of his life, Paul is tossed into prison and brutally beaten on multiple occasions, shipwrecked, and nearly drowned. His life is marked by affliction and controversy, his body shaped by exhaustion, thirst, and hunger. Yet even in the midst of life's heaviest blows, he still says give thanks. If Paul lives a safe, comfortable life, his words could easily be dismissed. But Paul embodied his message."[78]

I have no problem rejoicing at the good things in life. But the test comes when we realize we are invited to rejoice also in the midst of bad things.

> Gratitude invites us to trust God in all things. Thankfulness is the acknowledgement that God can redeem every situation and make us more than triumphant in any circumstance. Whether we're facing a season of absence or abundance, barrenness or bounty, turmoil or tranquility, the command to give thanks remains. To the outsider, such an act is undeserved; but for those who place their faith in God, thankfulness is a powerful confession that God's purpose is being worked out in all things.[79]

What things in your life need to be worked out by God? Can you rejoice today that God is able?

In her book *Radical Gratitude,* Ellen Vaughn explores how the simple habit of constantly giving thanks connects us to God, creating a "rhythm of divine renewal in grateful hearts. As we keep thanking him, we more and more see from His perspective."[80]

Could radical gratitude reorient your own life toward God?

Begin not by looking at your circumstances. Look up—to God, the Giver of all good gifts. Rejoice!

My child, gratitude is really a lifestyle. One in which you gravitate to what has been given, rather than immediately seeing what is lacking. A lifestyle of noticing all the ordinary gifts that abound. If you can do this, then you will find yourself rejoicing, even in the tough times. And I will keep giving.

Life

For sunrise hope and sunset calm,
And all that lies between,
For all the sweetness and the balm
That is and that has been,
For comradeship, for peace in strife,
And light on darkened days,
*For work to do, and strength for **Life** –*
We sing our hymn of praise.

~ Amy Carmichael
"Sunrise Hope"

1. Life

*"I came that they may have **life** and have it abundantly."*
~ John 10:10 ESV

"Here lies another day, during which I have had eyes, ears, hands, and the great world 'round me; and with tomorrow begins another. Why am I allowed two?"[1]

These words by G. K. Chesterton remind us that life is precious. And fragile.

Today, as I write, three friends are facing their final days of life. And I'm just trying to figure out what to say in the last note I will probably ever write them.

Sometimes we don't treasure the gift of life until we almost lose it.

All it takes is a medical diagnosis, a near-miss wreck, or someone's sudden death to jolt us into asking, "Am I truly living my life to the fullest?"

Jesus' very purpose was to give us life "abundantly," but what does that look like?

Perhaps it's easier to know what it *doesn't* look like. Abundant life is not personified in busyness, tasks, image, accumulation of possessions, followers, or fame.

Life is made of moments. Passion for what matters most. Sacrifice and generosity. Creativity and discovery. Holding close and letting go. Being fully present and engaged with those in our path.

So very hard to do, isn't it?

One busy man confesses he divides his minutes into living and waiting to live. "Most of my life is spent in transit: trying to get somewhere, waiting to begin, driving someplace, standing in line, waiting for a meeting to end, trying to get a task completed, worrying about something bad that might happen, or being angry about something that did happen. . . . I am, almost literally, killing time."[2]

Jesus used three different words for life—*bios*, *psuche*, and *zoë* (New Testament Greek).

Bios refers to our physical life and is the root word for biology.

Psuche refers to the life of the soul—mind, emotion, and will—and is the root word for psychology.

Zoë refers to the divine life uniquely possessed by God.

Recently Ken Boa, president of Reflections Ministries, spoke at our church and pointed out that Christ "is offering not biological life that we are all born with, but *Zoë*, or spiritual life. He is saying that He is going to give us life, but also an '*abundance*,' a quality of life, and He is going to be the wellspring of life that flows in us and through us."[3]

> We're starved for a life that not only senses the sacred in the world around us but savors it. We're famished for experiences that are real, relationships that are deep, work that is meaningful. I think what we're longing for is not "the good life" as it has been advertised to us in the American dream, but life in its fullness, its abundance. The reflective life is a life that is attentive, receptive, and responsive to what God is doing in us and around us.[4]

I want this kind of life. In fact, I have already received it as a gift.

The question becomes, as poet Mary Oliver so beautifully said, "What is it you plan to do with your one wild and precious life?"[5]

Join me in exploring the many grace gifts of life.

My child, your waking breath is a grace gift from Me. Life is the opportunity to share My many gifts with others. Who will you visit and encourage today? To whom will you give sacrificially? What endeavor will demand your strength and wisdom to accomplish? This is why you are here today. Live fully.

2. Full

*Stephen, a man **full** of God's grace and power, performed amaz-*
ing miracles and signs among the people.

~ Acts 6:8 NLT

When they needed a good man, he was the first one chosen.

As he began to both serve others and speak up about Jesus Christ, those in authority spread lies about him, inciting crowds and violence.

So they stoned him to death.

But he prayed for them until his last breath. This was Stephen, "full of God's grace and power."

The first martyr. This man was chosen by God as a bridge between Peter's testimony to the Jews and Paul's ministry to the Gentiles. Stephen was chosen by Peter and killed with the consent of Paul, known then as Saul.

Imagine the controversial countercultural movement that we now refer to as the early church—comprising people of all ages, ethnicities, and backgrounds—united with one common purpose: the Messiah had changed their lives and instructed them to scatter and do the same. Eleven remaining disciples weren't enough, so seven courageous, young, outspoken radicals were chosen.

And Stephen's death launched the early church out into the world.

Wouldn't you like to be full of whatever he possessed?

In today's verse the New Testament Greek word used is *plērēs*, translated "full, abounding in, complete, and thoroughly permeated with." This very word is used to show that God had completely imbued this man with all he would need to live a powerful yet short life.

Stephen had the faith in Christ to speak out and speak up, not only giving testimony to what he believed, but to call others to also follow the way of Christ. And when this message fell on deaf ears, Stephen determined to continue his mission filled with another great gift from God—grace.

No anger, no vengeance, no retaliation. Grace. Even toward those who were killing him in a fury of rage.

"As the rocks rained down, Stephen prayed, 'Master Jesus, take my life.' Then he knelt down, praying loudly, 'Master, don't blame them for this sin'—his last words. Then he died" (Acts 7:59 MSG).

While this was happening, Stephen experienced the glory of God. "At that point they went wild, a rioting mob of catcalls and whistles and invective. But Stephen, full of the Holy Spirit, hardly noticed—he only had eyes for God, whom he saw in all his glory with Jesus standing at his side. He said, 'Oh! I see heaven wide open and the Son of Man standing at God's side!'" (Acts 7:56 MSG).

Divine approval. The people damned Stephen as a blasphemer, but God gave him the face of an angel.

I doubt many of us will be called to the same story as Stephen, but I know that even today we might be falsely accused, personally attacked, or chosen to serve others and speak up. When that happens, it will make a difference what we are filled with.

Are you full of Jesus?

My child, when life squeezes, what comes out? Depends on what you have been filled with. When you are filled with Me, what comes out are responses that honor and serve and heal. Grace extended even to your accusers. Calm in the midst of chaos. Love and forgiveness. Stephen was full of what I am waiting to fill you with today.

3. *Consecrate*

*"**Consecrate** yourselves, for tomorrow the LORD will do wonders among you."*

~ Joshua 3:5 NASB

As I write today, it is a brand-new year. A clean slate. A fresh start. Three hundred sixty-five blank pages on which to write the story of my life. The question becomes, what do I want that story to convey?

Miracles.

Wouldn't it be amazing if the way I lived this year were somehow transformed by God into lots of small, yet incredible, manifestations of His power, His grace, His glory?

Wonders. I want my story this year to be one where I participate as "the Lord will do wonders among you."

You too?

Then we must begin with today's word—*consecrate*.

> The word *consecrate* means to *set yourself apart*. By definition, consecration demands *full devotion*. It's dethroning yourself and enthroning Jesus Christ. It's the complete divestiture of all self-interest. It's giving God veto power. It's surrendering *all of you* to *all of Him*. It's a simple recognition that every second of time, every ounce of energy, and every penny of money is a gift *from* God and *for* God. Consecration is an ever-deepening love for Jesus, a childlike trust in the heavenly Father, and a blind obedience to the Holy Spirit.[6]

The first step in going all out is to surrender ALL. Total relinquishment to the One who knows you best and loves you most. The problem comes when we hold back pockets of our lives, those areas we cling to for control, unwilling to trust God in those tender areas.

Because we know that God not only can, but will, do exactly as He pleases with a surrendered soul.

My friend Jennifer gets this message from the Lord when she starts to wiggle on the Potter's wheel:

> I know that sometimes My sculpting hurts. Sometimes you feel as though you are looking less like Me rather than more like Me. Don't worry. There are intervals in the work of precisely shaping you during which you look like a shapeless, formless lump of clay. Your old shape has been destroyed, but your new shape has not yet emerged. Those are My hands you feel squeezing you and pushing you. I know exactly what I'm doing. Blessed one, part of the shaping is done by fire. It is going to burn away the earth stuff still clinging to you. It is going to set the work I have finished so the shape is stable.[7]

Will you offer yourself back to God today? To do wonders and miracles as He sees fit?

Then, join me in praying the words of this hymn from Frances Ridley Havergal:

> Take my life and let it be
> consecrated, Lord, to thee.
> Take my moments and my days;
> let them flow in endless praise,
> let them flow in endless praise.
>
> Take my love; my Lord, I pour
> at thy feet its treasure store.
> Take myself and I will be
> ever, only, all for thee,
> ever, only, all for thee.[8]

My child, I have called you to be set apart for My use—whatever that ends up being at any given time. As you surrender yourself to Me, I will so equip you for every task. This does not mean you are unapproachable or beyond others. In fact, your very act of consecration is one that dies to self. Be real and be ready.

4. Guide

"But I'll take the hand of those who don't know the way,
    who can't see where they're going.
*I'll be a personal **guide** to them,*
    directing them through unknown country.
I'll be right there to show them what roads to take,
    make sure they don't fall into the ditch.
These are the things I'll be doing for them—
    sticking with them, not leaving them for a minute."

~ Isaiah 42:16 MSG

I entered the British Museum and was both awestruck and overwhelmed. After all, this huge structure contains eight million objects, has two miles of exhibition space, and covers 990,000 square feet. How would I even begin to start exploring and find my way to the mummies and the Elgin marbles?

The British Museum Audio Guide.

This handy tool is available in ten different languages, plus British sign language. Not only does an invisible guide speak directly into your ear, but the guide also provides complete descriptions of what you are seeing, while you are seeing it! Expert commentaries teach you the background and provenance of the displays. And as a bonus, the audio guide even keeps track of what you see and creates a digital souvenir of your visit!

Could I just raise my hand here right now and say, "Enough with the museum already. I need one of these guides for life!"

The good news is that we do actually have access to a Life Audio Guide. His name is God.

And the prophet Isaiah promised that if we make an intentional choice for the "with God" life,

> Your own ears will hear him.
>> Right behind you a voice will say,
> *"This is the way you should go"*

whether to the right or to the left.
(Isaiah 30:21 NLT, emphasis added)

But how do I know His voice?

"When you open your Bible, God opens His mouth. The surest way to get a word from the Lord is by getting into God's Word. God will speak to you. Then God will speak through you."[9]

Each of us has a unique voiceprint. I know this because people come up to me frequently and say they recognized my voice from the next hall (not because I was too loud, mind you) due to the uniqueness of it. Each author has a certain "voice" to her writings, and one of the things I often mentor others on is seeking their personal writing voices, not trying to copy someone else.

But this also occurs spiritually. God will speak through your voice differently than those around you—use you in different ways with a different audience. If you want to find your own voice, you must first hear the voice of God.

> Sometimes walking with the Lord can feel like walking in a fog. We have to keep our eyes on Scripture with every step we take so we don't get lost or sidetracked down some dark road, ending up at the edge of a cliff with a pit below. God has promised that His Word will guide us and light our way; it will be "a lamp to guide our feet and a light for our path" (Psalm 119:105). It may not function like high-wattage beams that help us see yards ahead. In fact, His Word may be more like a candle, giving off a gentle light that illuminates only our next step. But we can trust that when His Word is guiding us, we won't take a wrong turn.[10]

Keep going.

My child, you have come to a juncture in your journey and are seeking guidance on the next step. And I am here as the Voice in your ear. But you need to plug in to My Word and listen to My Voice. There are many winding paths and dangerous detours. Never forget you have a Guide as close as a whisper. I know the way.

5. *Lose*

*"If you try to hang onto your life, you will **lose** it. But if you give up your life for my sake, you will save it."*

~ Luke 9:24 NLT

"All I can offer you is a chance to die."

These are the terms outlined by Amy Carmichael as she responded to letters from English women who were considering missionary life with her in India. In 1903, rescuing young girls from temple prostitution was groundbreaking early work in human trafficking.

Challenging. Dangerous. Humbling.

Yet Amy served there for fifty-five years without a furlough, establishing the Dohnavur Fellowship, which housed nine hundred children at the time of her death in 1951. These wounded and broken children called her "Amma," the Tamil word for "Mother."

Amy Carmichael understood the paradox in today's verse: "If you give up your life for my sake, you will save it." Early in her missionary career, when crossed by a coworker, she had clearly heard the voice of God before she reacted in defense: "See in this a chance to die." And thus began her journey of dying to self in order to give life to others.

In the middle of her vibrant ministry, Amy suffered a fall and was bedridden the last half of her life. She kept her windows and doors constantly open to the children, and she wrote volumes of poetry. (The epigraphs for sections in both *Ordinary Graces* and *Dwelling Places* are from Amy Carmichael's poems.)

In today's text Jesus is reminding us that as we release with open hands of surrender, we will be filled with grace gifts we never dared hope for. Give up your perceived right to control, and discover that God's sovereignty will orchestrate everything better than you possibly imagined.

Early missionaries did not pack trunks as they set off on long voyages across the world to take the gospel to hidden tribes. Instead, they each packed a coffin, one that would eventually be used to bury them in their new land. What does this say about commitment? They knew their venture would end in death, yet they still chose to do it—the loss was worth the hopeful kingdom gain.

Flannery O'Connor once said, "What people don't realize is how much religion costs. They think faith is a big electric blanket, when of course it is the cross."[11]

Do you realize that every gain comes through loss?

Today was the thirty-fifth anniversary of the death of a young wife and mother of three. What a loss this was to all who loved and needed her.

But it was my eventual gain. Only God.

Three years after her death, I received a priceless gift when I went to court in Seattle and adopted those three precious children. They have filled this mama's life with more joy, purpose, on-my-knees-prayer, and hopes than you can imagine.

"The only way anyone gets to adoption is through a door of loss and unless you fully feel the depth of that loss, the door you're walking through *leads to nowhere honest.*"[12]

Jesus made it clear that to live fully we must first lose our life. What are we willing to lose in order to know Him more fully? Our reputation? Our stuff? Our control? Our own dreams?

Only God.

My child, your hands are empty and your heart is too. That's what loss usually feels like. But the good news is that in My kingdom economy, all will yet again be filled. With someone or something new. So keep giving away your life because I assure you that more life in more people will be the by-product of your pouring out for Me.

6. Baggage

So then let's also run the race that is laid out in front of us, since
we have such a great cloud of witnesses surrounding us. Let's
*throw off any extra **baggage**, get rid of the sin that trips us up,*
and fix our eyes on Jesus, faith's pioneer and perfecter.

~ Hebrews 12:1-2

Can you imagine running a race while dragging a suitcase behind you? Everyone knows the less burdened we are, the easier the journey.

And yet, how many of us are still dragging around baggage from the past—and wondering why we can't reach our goals?

Today's verse offers three suggestions for running the race of life: (1) "throw off any extra baggage," (2) "get rid of the sin that trips us up," and (3) "fix our eyes on Jesus."

I once saw these principles vividly portrayed in a movie called *The Mission*. This 1986 film tells the true story of Jesuit priests ministering to the Guarani community of Argentina, Paraguay, and Brazil in 1750. Jeremy Irons plays the brave priest who risks everything to bring Christ to the jungle people above the waterfall. Robert DeNiro portrays the mercenary, Captain Mendoza, who has spent his life killing and enslaving those very same people. In a jealous fit of rage, he kills his own brother in a duel. Faced with his sin, he retreats into solitude for six months and then, as a redeemed man, decides to help the priests with the mission work above the falls.

Only Mendoza decides to punish himself by carrying on his back a large cargo net full of the vestiges of his old life—heavy swords, armor, and guns. This makes the climb torturous and dangerous. Halfway up, his companions ask each other how long the man will continue to carry his "baggage."

The priest replies, "Until *he* believes he has carried it enough."

Finally, covered in mud and exhausted from the strain, Mendoza staggers into the Guarani village and collapses. The natives, recognizing him for the killer he once was, hold a knife over the head of this almost-defeated, broken, repentant man.

A tense moment ensues. Will they get their revenge and kill him? As his former enemies cut off the burden and toss it over the waterfall, Mendoza breaks into tears of relief—finally free to embrace the forgiveness of God and the natives.

What baggage are you still carrying?

Mary had suffered years of abuse. "We all have baggage like mine. It may differ in proportion or type, but the truth is we struggle to understand God's wildly audacious love for us. I easily listened to lies that sounded like truth: *You aren't worth love. . . . You don't deserve attention or affection.*"[13]

How can we throw off such a huge cargo net of lies?

By doing what our verse says: "fix our eyes on Jesus." Look to God's Word for guidance. Pray for strength and purpose. Keep Christ's life and mandate always in your sight. And let the past fall away.

> My chains fell off. My heart was free.
> I rose, went forth and followed Thee.[14]

My child, you seem to have a knack for filling suitcases until they hardly close. Surely lugging all that around is getting tiresome. Why not unpack and leave it with Me? I will help you take out each piece and let it go. Then you will continue your journey with a much lighter step.

7. One Thing

*"**One thing** is necessary. Mary has chosen the better part. It won't be taken away from her."*

~ Luke 10:42

"Want to get closer to Jesus? What I can give you is *one thing* you absolutely must do," the young pastor said.

What? I thought.

Surely he means *twelve* things or *seven* keys. Some biblical number. Even reducing spiritual disciplines to *three* points would be a stretch. After all, I had spent a lifetime of sorting through the equivalent of *Quiet Time for Dummies,* looking for the magic bullet that would ensure my spiritual growth.

One thing? Had my prayers finally been answered?

I hung on his next words.

"If you are sick and tired of feeling so dreadfully busy and are looking for a one-point plan to help restore order to your life, this is the best advice I know: devote yourself to the Word of God and prayer."[15]

Time in prayer and Scripture—today's equivalent of "sitting at the feet of Jesus."

I can do that. I can do what Mary did.

"We have to believe that the most significant opportunity before us every day is the opportunity to sit at the feet of Jesus. We won't rearrange our priorities until we believe this is the best one."[16]

Sometimes I believe the most significant opportunity is the one in which I do more, like Martha. That's my default—*git 'er done*! But upon rereading today's story from the Gospels, I recognize that it's not so much what Mary *did*, but the manner in which she did it—receptivity, hunger for whatever Jesus was offering.

> Mary's posture tells the story. Her posture is that of a student, of someone who wants to listen to what Jesus has to say, of

someone who can wait for dinner. It is the posture; in fact, of someone who is so enthralled with Jesus that dinner might not even happen. . . . At the feet of Jesus, Mary is seemingly serene. Mary's serenity derives from attending to Jesus, an expression that sums up Mary's posture. Humans, Jesus says, are defined not by their labor for him, as Martha thinks, but by their relationship to him, as Mary learns.[17]

It's far easier to identify with Martha, who was busy getting stuff done.

But the simple fact was that Mary had discovered the way to get to know her friend Jesus was to sit with Him, and that was a higher priority for her than running around like a crazy woman. Sitting means choosing to spend time praying, meditating, being still, and communing with God through the power of the Holy Spirit.[18]

If you struggle with being more of a Martha than a Mary, remember today how much Jesus loves you. He created you with strengths and passions. He does not want you to become your sister, Mary.

He just wants you to be a Martha, who pays attention and sits close.

My child, there is room at My side for both—Martha and Mary. All I want is for you to sit still and heed My words. But in your own unique way. Tailor your prayer time to your personality and responsibilities. It doesn't matter when or what—I will be here to meet you. But don't forget the one thing necessary.

8. Plans

*"My **plans** aren't your **plans**, nor are your ways my ways, says the Lord. Just as the heavens are higher than the earth, so are my ways higher than your ways, and my **plans** than your **plans**."*

~ Isaiah 55:8-9

Cornelius had plans, but God had other plans.

As a Roman army officer in Caesarea, Cornelius gave generously to the poor and prayed regularly to God. One afternoon Cornelius was minding his business when an angel appeared with new instructions from God.

"My plans aren't your plans" is what God says when He calls us to a new task, assuring us, that "My ways are higher than your ways." God's plan is probably even better than we could imagine.

The angel told Cornelius to send his men to Joppa and bring back a man named Peter. This praying man didn't know Peter, but he knew God.

That next day at lunch, a vision came to Peter—God wanted him to know that what had previously been considered "unclean" was now clean. "Peter was very perplexed" (Acts 10:17 NLT).

What did it all mean?

After the surprise visit from Cornelius's men, Peter decided to accompany them back to Caesarea, not knowing the reason for the trip. When Cornelius tried to worship him, Peter explained that he was just a man, like him, but Jewish. However, being in the home of a Gentile was against the law for Peter.

Peter shared his vision of the day before, one that clearly set up this very meeting. "But God has shown me that I should no longer think of anyone as impure or unclean" (v. 28 NLT).

God's plan was to break down walls between two people groups that avoided each other.

Do you think His plans for us today might also include reconciliation—reaching out to people we have previously avoided?

As the men talked, Peter concluded, "I see very clearly that God shows no favoritism. In every nation he accepts those who fear him and do what is right . . . There is peace with God through Jesus Christ, who is Lord of all" (Acts 10:34-36 NLT).

Because of their reaching out to one another, Peter preached the gospel and the Holy Spirit fell on the Gentiles, just as it had on the day of Pentecost. As the book of Acts unfolds, we discover more people from other places were added to the numbers of the early church. And remember those who scattered after Stephen was martyred? It was their dispersion that helped spread the gospel.

God's ultimate plan prevailed because He used prayerful men to make it happen.

Do you pray about where God wants you and what He wants you to do? Do you consider open doors that appear in divine ways, even if you don't always understand?

"The plans of God are only revealed in the presence of God. We don't get our marching orders until we get on our knees! But if we hit our knees, God will take us places we never imagined going by paths we didn't even know existed."[19]

Be willing to go . . . beyond.

My child, sometimes I smile at your calendar. You have so many plans—good things, beneficial endeavors, loving outreach. But keep writing in pencil, because I may surprise you with better plans of My own. Always heed My voice and follow where I lead. Then you will be in just the right place at the right time.

9. Footsteps

You were called to this kind of endurance, because Christ suffered on your behalf. He left you an example so that you might follow in his footsteps.

~ 1 Peter 2:21

At the age of twenty-three, Norman Vaughan dropped out of Harvard because he had a different dream.

He wanted something more.

Boldly approaching Admiral Richard Byrd, this college student volunteered to become a dogsledder on his first expedition to the South Pole. Byrd was so pleased with his teamwork that he named a mountain in Antarctica after him—Mount Vaughan.

Norman never did return to Harvard.

But he did evacuate wounded fellow soldiers from the Battle of the Bulge in World War II as a US army colonel in charge of sled dog rescue units. And he finished thirteenth in the Iditarod Trail Sled Dog Races, as well as competing in the 1932 Olympics.

Norman spent sixty-five years longing to climb the mountain bearing his name. When he was eighty-eight, he finally began the arduous journey up the 10,302-foot peak.

As he began to zigzag up the mountain in normal mountaineering style, Norman's bad right leg was strained too much. So his mountaineering guide, Vernon, decided to take him straight up the mountain by cutting steps in the ice ahead of Norman.

Vernon cut 7,128 steps into the ice mountain for his friend.

It was slow; some days they climbed only three hours. But because he could put each foot on those steps, one at a time, Norman Vaughan made it to the peak of Mount Vaughan and celebrated a lifelong dream.[20]

In today's verse we are reminded that we too can endure—because of Christ's example.

The footsteps God left for us work in a similar way to those many, many steps cut into the ice mountain. They provide a means for us to climb the heights—to go farther, enduring beyond our own physical age and strength.

There is a path. And it is clearly laid out in the Bible.

You may not find the exact challenge you will have at the office today, but you will discover transferable principles for your own life and time.

You might even call them footsteps.

Not only do I seek to follow in Christ's footsteps, but I can also cut some steps in the ice for those behind me who are struggling on the path. I may be the one who shows the way.

One Monday morning, little Zoe began following her mother around the house.

As Mama moved from room to room, preparing lunch, working at her computer, even changing the bed linens, there was Zoe on her heels. Finally a bit frustrated, Mama suggested Zoe go play outside in the backyard.

But Zoe kept shadowing her.

Exasperated, Mama knelt down and cupped her little girl's face in her hands, "Honey, what's the matter—why are you following everywhere I go?"

"It's okay, Mama," Zoe replied. "Nothing's wrong. It's just that my Sunday school teacher told us to walk in Jesus' footsteps. And since I can't see Jesus, I'm walking in yours."

Oh, may all who come behind us find us faithful.

My child, little eyes and little ears and little feet are following your every word and every step. You are setting forth a path for others, whether or not you realize it, just as the older generation paved the way for you to come this far. So be alert and be diligent in following My path. Then help others climb to the peaks. For My glory.

10. Descendants

*"For I will pour out water to quench your thirst and to irrigate
your parched fields.
And I will pour out my Spirit on your **descendants**, and my
blessing on your children."*

~ Isaiah 44:3 NLT

I prayed a dedication over each of my children—that they would know God and that He would always guide and protect them throughout life.

From then on, my role as a mama was to hold on loosely, even when I wanted to squeeze tight. Long ago I promised all four of them (and eventually my two sons-in-law as well) that by the time they awakened each morning, I would have already prayed for them by name.

My mother-heart gift to them forever.

Sometimes friends comment on how spread out my children are now—doing amazing things all over the world. I reply, "Well, if you raise your children to become adventurers, don't be surprised if they live an adventure!"

I love that God promised "my blessing on your children." But what is a comfort to me might be a great puzzle for those whose children are far from God right now.

Are you thirsty for the salvation of your family members?

Monica's heart was broken as only a Christian mother's heart can be. When her son reached adolescence, he began to follow in the footsteps of his pagan, lustful, violent father. She wanted to see him settling down with a godly wife, but instead he moved in with a mistress and they had a son. Monica begged her son to join the church and take hold of the life-changing truths of Christ, but instead he fell in with a cult and dabbled in dark heresies.

The young man moved to Rome, and when his mother tried to follow him, he tricked her into missing the boat. He thought he could escape her, but he didn't realize the power of her prayers and perseverance. This

mother prayed for fifteen years, and every day she went to church to pour out her heart to God.

Monica never lost confidence that her prayers for her son would be answered.

Finally the young man repented and gave his life to Christ. Augustine's faithful mother, Monica, lived from AD 331 to AD 387, and her son is known today as Saint Augustine.

Because of a mother's prayers, this brilliant theologian's passion for God and profound spiritual wisdom shaped the entire course of Western civilization.[21]

The young man himself later wrote in his *Confessions* some of his own experience of God's pursuit during his youth: "Too late I loved Thee, O Thou Beauty of ancient days, yet ever new! Too late I loved Thee! And behold, Thou wert within, and I abroad, and there I searched for Thee. . . . Thou didst call, and shout, and burst my deafness. Thou didst flash, shine, and scatter my blindness. . . . I tasted, and *hunger and thirst*. Thou touchedst me, and I burned for Thy peace."[22]

God provided Living Water to quench the thirst of this wayward young man.

Will you keep praying and trusting and persevering for your descendants? The story is not over yet.

My child, perhaps your holiest moment of the day is when you come to Me and lay the names of all your children before My throne of grace, that I might bless, protect, and guide them. This is a sacred service, and I will honor your sacrifice of love and praise. Never forget that I love your loved ones even more than you do. I have a plan for them as well. It is good.

11. Ordinary

*So here's what I want you to do, God helping you: Take your everyday, **ordinary** life—your sleeping, eating, going-to-work, and walking-around life—and place it before God as an offering.*

~ Romans 12:1 MSG

Tish hated making her bed.

One Lent, she felt God saying that instead of giving up something, she should change her first-thing-in-the-morning habit from checking her cell phone to making her bed and sitting on it quietly, beginning the day with prayer and reflection.

Could you do that?

Trish found that not only was she able to do that for the forty days of Lent, but that the practice so transformed her days (and her heart) that she has continued it for years. "Instead of going to a device for my morning fix of instant infotainment, I'd invite God into the day and just sit. Silent. Sort of listening. Sort of just sitting. But I sat expectantly. It taught me to slow down, to embrace daily life, believing that in these small moments God meets us and brings meaning to our average day."[23]

One day a woman came up to me at a large conference in Boston. She said that when she was a young mom, I spoke to her MOPS group. "Something you said really changed my life, and I wanted to thank you for it."

I couldn't wait to hear what pearls of wisdom I had uttered back in the day. Which deep theological truth had I imparted? What clever story had I woven with great meaning?

"You told our group of young mamas that the way you were able to find order in your ordinary day with four kids was to first make your bed."

And to think I got a seminary degree to prepare me to say that!

All I could do was smile.

Because it was true. In those chaotic days of raising kids and working, writing, speaking, and running a home, I found very few projects that shouted, "Finished!" to me. But making the bed was one of them.

A glimpse that one day even my part in the raising of those kids would be substantially "finished." Each time I passed the bed, it became a touchstone to the ordinary graces God had for me, scattered in unexpected places.

And that the ordinary person I was really could be used to help change the world—my deepest prayer at age twenty and even today.

> Biblically there is no divide between "radical" and "ordinary" believers. We are all called to be willing to follow Christ in radical ways, to answer the call of the one who told us to deny ourselves and take up our cross. And yet we are also called to stability, to the daily grind of responsibility for those nearest us, to the challenge of a mundane, well-lived Christian life. We must also learn to follow Jesus in this workaday world of raising kids, caring for our neighbors, budgeting, doing laundry, and living our days responsibly with stability, generosity, and faithfulness.[24]

My life is actually quite ordinary. But my God is anything but.

Somehow we partner to bring light to a dark world. But first I must take my life "and place it before God as an offering."

He will do the rest.

ന്ദ്ര

My child, what often seems quite ordinary is actually extraordinary. Including your life. Will you view it as such—noticing every encounter and gift as from a heavenly Father's loving hand? You are just the kind of person I use to help change the world—made in My image and living in the midst of fellow travelers. Offer yourself to Me, and I will do the rest.

12. *Approved*

*For we speak as messengers **approved** by God to be entrusted
with the Good News.
Our purpose is to please God, not people. He alone examines the
motives of our hearts.*

~ 1 Thessalonians 2:4 NLT

My need for approval is deeply rooted in my lovely Georgia hometown, where "being nice" is a cultivated art form.

It seemed to me, growing up, that to be approved of was success; to experience disapproval meant to be ostracized.

Having experienced a bit of both, I left home a year early for a faraway college where no one knew me or had preconceived expectations.

Free to find my own way.

But as my personal faith in Christ grew deeper, I began trying to win approval as a "good Christian." I had simply exchanged one kind of approval (social acceptance) for another (acceptance in the Christian world).

Achievement in that milieu soon became the barometer for acceptance. Was I reading the *right* theology books, becoming active in the *right* causes, wearing clothes that made the *right* statement of my chosen lifestyle?

"For am I now seeking the approval of man, or of God? Or am I trying to please man? If I were still trying to please man, I would not be a servant of Christ" (Galatians 1:10 ESV). I knew Paul's words were in the Bible just for me. But a decade later my struggle became the catalyst that would save my life.

By then I had married an incredible man and gone to court to adopt three amazing children, ages nine, seven, and four. Since all four had been through grief and loss, I decided that I would make up for those years by being the Best Wife and Best Mother.

In the whole wide world.

Which included being room mother at three different schools, a Special Olympics volunteer with my eldest son, a Cub Scout den mother, and a Brownie Scout leader. I also enrolled in a university course to learn how to advocate for disabled children and took my kids to swim lessons, the library, and reading enrichment. Whew! All this in the early stages of marriage and motherhood.

Needless to say, I was trying too hard. But for all the right reasons—to be the best for my new little family. And to please God as a faithful wife and mother. I was desperate for approval from everyone.

And so I imploded.

It was not pretty. My failures at being perfect almost paralyzed me. But God stooped (the Hebrew word for *grace* means "to stoop"), picked me up, and reminded me I can never *do* enough.

This use of "approved" is translated from the New Testament Greek word *dokimos,* which literally means "tested and fit for service." It's the whole idea of putting metal through the fire so that it comes through the test purified, emerging strong and cleansed of alloy.

This same word *dokimos* is used to remind us of God's blessing: "Those who stand firm during testing are blessed. They are tried and true" (James 1:12).

Grace was the gift that changed my life.

I no longer live for approval. I'm already approved.

My child, of course you want approval. It is the human means whereby you feel affirmed for a job well done. There's nothing wrong with that—until it becomes more important than pleasing Me. I have tested you already and found you worthy to be My child and witness. So stop dancing for everyone else. Serve Me alone, and others will benefit as well.

211

13. Overflow

*May the God of hope fill you with all joy and peace in faith so that you **overflow** with hope by the power of the Holy Spirit.*
~ Romans 15:13

What does it mean to live from the overflow?

Imagine your life as a Mason jar filled to the brim with water. Now, add some stones, one by one. Each has a name—one might be your latest medical challenge, another your prodigal child, three more stones are those projects due at work, and perhaps the biggest one of all is that ongoing conflict with your spouse.

As each stone drops into your life (the jar of water) what happens? It displaces what's inside, and the water begins to overflow the jar.

What's inside is what comes out when life bombards us with one thing after another.

Do you think that is what Paul was thinking when he asked God to fill us with "all joy and peace and faith" so that what comes out in our overflow is "hope by the power of the Holy Spirit"?

Absolutely!

Do you want to live from the inside out?

Here are two words that keep me focused on developing an overflow life:

Rooted: That water in the jar represents living vibrancy of daily deposits of communion with God through prayer and Bible study—all those spiritual disciplines that go toward forming our own character *rooted* in the character of Christ. We are told to "be rooted and built up in him, be established in faith, and *overflow* with thanksgiving" (Colossians 2:7, emphasis added).

> I am more and more convinced that what gives a ministry its motivation, perseverance, humility, joy, tenderness, passion, and grace is the devotional life of the one doing ministry.

> When I daily admit how needy I am, daily meditate on the grace of the Lord Jesus Christ, and daily feed on the restorative wisdom of his Word, I am propelled to share with others the grace that I am daily receiving at the hands of my Savior.[25]

Released: But we were not created to be transformed from the inside out for no purpose beyond ourselves. The endgame is giving it all away—being *released* to a broken world. "And may the Lord make your love for one another and for all people grow and *overflow*, just as our love for you overflows" (1 Thessalonians 3:12 NLT, emphasis added).

> Spiritual growth is the process of becoming more like Jesus, becoming more conformed to his image inside and out. . . . He never looked at human need without being moved. It was this deep compassion and love, along with his desire to glorify the Father, that caused him to minister grace, healing, and life to others. That means there's no living the Christian life unless we feel deeply for others and, being moved by love, care for them and their needs.[26]

As a variety of pebbles drop into your life today, may what overflows be pleasing to God and others.

My child, how you react or respond to the unexpecteds of life may depend on what fills your heart and mind. If you take time to fill up with My love and wisdom daily, then when life squeezes, all kinds of goodness will overflow to others. And your caring and compassion will be evident to all.

14. Way

*"Don't look for shortcuts to God. . . . The **way** to life—to God!—is vigorous and requires total attention."*

~ Matthew 7:14 MSG

The Smythes have a code word they share whenever complaining begins. One says, "Long walk." Immediately there is a change in attitude.

When asked why these two words are so transformational, they share of a time many years earlier when they had been ministering in Africa and received from one of the villagers a beautiful polished shell—unique to a faraway beach.

As Mrs. Smythe exclaimed her joy and gratitude for such a lovely gift, the African merely replied, "Long walk."

Puzzled, she said, "Pardon?"

He then explained, "Long walk *part* of gift."

As today's verse reiterates, the "way to life—to God" includes the actual journey itself. *How* we reach our destination is just as important as where we are going.

God uses the process, often slow and treacherous, to equip us for the next destination. This may include slowing down or even waiting in the interim.

For the African giver, the walk was hard and long, and that gave the shell gift even more value.

"We cannot shortcut the journey. We cannot avoid the wait. No, it is God who is working, in his timing, in his way. First God heals, first he is enough, first we flounder and fail and allow him to remake us through our failings. First he works in the waiting. Then the promise comes, the gift, the outpouring from his love that he always intended."[27]

Where are you on the journey? Are you ever impatient to just get there?

Life is not a sprint; it is a marathon. A long obedience in the same direction.

> In going to God Christians travel the same ground that every-one else walks on, breathe the same air, drink the same water, shop in the same stores, read the same newspapers, fear the same dangers, are subject to the same pressures, are buried in the same ground. The difference is that each step we walk, each breath we breathe, we know we are preserved by God, we know we are accompanied by God, we know we are ruled by God.[28]

So "don't look for shortcuts to God." The Greek word used in this verse is *hodos*, which literally means "a path or road," or the way a person travels "on his way." It's a metaphor for our thinking, behavior, or way of life.

What way are you following?

I recently talked with a young woman who is trying to follow two different paths; one a strong outer pull from secular culture and the other an inner tug from Christ inside. While these two are not always in conflict, sometimes they go in two different directions. And then she must choose.

Before they were known as Christians, those in the early church were called "followers of the Way" (see Acts 9:2; 22:4-5 NLT).

If you don't know where you're going, you'll get there every time.

The path is clear. The way is long. But we are never alone on the journey.

My child, it does matter how you journey through this life, which way you take. There are no shortcuts to My kingdom. Only step-by-step obedience. But it helps to remember that some of the best lessons are learned in the process of walking. All you have to do today is take that next step forward. I am here beside you.

15. Anger

*Don't sin by letting **anger** control you. Don't let the sun go down while you are still angry.*

~ Ephesians 4:26 NLT

Twenty-five years ago, a marriage counselor looked into my eyes and said, "Cindy, you are a very angry person."

"Me, angry? How preposterous." I exclaimed, thinking, *This man just met me. What does he know?*

Frankly, it made me furious!

But since I've always tried to examine whatever truth might lie in an admonition from a fellow Christian, I calmed down and looked for a small kernel of truth here.

"Uh, I guess I have stuffed a lot of feelings—disappointment over unmet expectations, grief at losses, guilt from failure, and resentment when things seem unfair . . ." I trailed off.

"But that's just it," he pointed out. "Situations left unresolved and struggles not yet surrendered to the Lord build up inside, only to be eventually released in unhealthy ways. Anger is merely an emotion, but God's Word says 'Don't sin by letting anger control you.'"

My own anger was merely a symptom of yet-unnamed sins—pride, lack of trust in God, self-centeredness. Why trust when I could worry? Why surrender when I could control? Why show compassion when I could stand in judgment? Why accept responsibility when I could blame others?

Without realizing it, I had joined a statistic. A recent *Time* magazine states clearly that "Americans are angry." More than half of the three thousand adults surveyed said they are angrier today than last year.

Does all this anger alarm you? It should.

> Angry people are poor communicators and even worse listeners. Their empathy is foreshortened, and they have trou-

ble imagining the other's point of view. It makes people less healthy, and when both parties are angry, fewer are likely to find middle ground. If the only way people feel they will be heard is when they are angry, then our public discourse will be an arena for shouting past one another. Now . . . perhaps we can have a reasoned public discussion about how to calm the rage and begin the work. You can be principled even when you speak in a soft voice.[29]

Perhaps it's time for all of us to begin to speak in a softer, kinder voice.

And maybe the first person we should speak to about it is God, who may respond, as in this poem: "In telling Me the anger you genuinely feel / It loses power over you, permitting you to heal."[30]

God knows anger can be part of our emotional makeup, but warns us as well. "Fools vent their anger, but the wise quietly hold it back" (Proverbs 29:11 NLT).

Do you really want someone (say, a counselor) to call you an angry person?

Calm down.

My child, everyone seems to be angry about something these days. And the fall-out of that emotion is crippling our world. Will you bring your anger to Me and allow healing to occur? I so long for you to be free from negative emotions that only tear you down. Face the source and find full release only through Me.

16. Fragrance

*As far as God is concerned there is a sweet, wholesome **fragrance** in our lives. It is the **fragrance** of Christ in us, an aroma to both the saved and the unsaved all around us.*

~ 2 Corinthians 2:15 TLB

To a fourteen-year-old girl, a French perfume factory is unforgettable.

I still remember visiting the Parfumerie Fragonard in Grasse, France, so long ago. This town near the French Riviera, known as the perfume capital of the world, is surrounded by fields of roses, jasmine, violet, mimosa, and lavender.

As a teenager I loved wearing fragrance—Wind Song was my favorite. To this day, when I smell that scent, I am immediately taken back to the days of braces and cheerleading, insecurity and dreams.

Smell plays an important role in memory, mood, and emotion.

First our noses send a signal to the olfactory nerve, which then passes along smell information to the limbic system. These are structures inside the brain controlling long-term memory, behavior, and emotion. In fact, a diminishing sense of smell can sometimes be an early sign of Alzheimer's and Parkinson's disease. Losing one's sense of smell often results in losing sentimental pathway to memories.

Paul uses this imagery in today's verse, knowing that people respond to fragrance in a visceral way. What would the "fragrance of Christ" look like (smell like) in your life?

If you were to make an appointment at the Parfumerie to design your own personal scent, the expert there—called The Nose—would describe fragrance notes. He might present more than a hundred to choose from, explaining the various families of scents, such as floral, fruity, or musk. Your signature scent would then be narrowed down to the *peak note* (top scent), the *heart note* (middle scent), and the *base note* (lowest scent). After the three were combined in varying amounts, they would be allowed to settle for a time in order to mix together. Voilà!

Perfume is a combination of oils, herbs, spices, and flowers that have been crushed—that process is what releases the strongest fragrance.

> God is creating you to be a one-of-a-kind Designer fragrance. He has brought all the ingredients together, orchestrated all the details of your life—causing some and allowing others— to bring out the best in you, to help you live strong and to fulfill His purposes for you. As you surrender to the process, you become more and more like Jesus. You bring glory to Him— and you bring others to Him.[31]

Do you smell like Jesus?

"Live your life with love, following the example of Christ, who loved us and gave himself for us. He was a sacrificial offering that smelled sweet to God" (Ephesians 5:2).

Our Lord was crushed as well. "He became a pleasing aroma when He suffered and died on the cross. He gave off the fragrance of obedience, submission, and devotion to the will of God."[32]

Can you identify your own peak note, heart note, and base note—the combination of characteristics that put forth your unique spiritual fragrance? If the first two are God-honoring, such as faith and grace, but the base note is something like impatience or judgment, then the whole scent is less than sweet.

What are the three primary ingredients to your signature life fragrance? Because people will remember your aroma for a long time.

My child, whether or not you realize it, you spread a scent everywhere you go. For better, or worse. People always remember how they felt when they were in your presence. Don't you want them to remember the sweetness, not the sour? Then cling to Me and soak in My grace. You will be long remembered for it.

17. Restore

Though you have made me see troubles, many and bitter, you
*will **restore** my life again; from the depths of the earth you will*
again bring me up.

~ Psalm 71:20 NIV

My husband swears by glue. All kinds. With it he restores a variety of household items beginning to crumble after a thirty-three-year marriage. Lamp bases. Cabinet knobs. Chair-back rungs. One dab of glue and they are good as new.

Restored.

"Man is born broken," playwright Eugene O'Neill famously said. "He lives by mending. The *grace of God* is glue."[33]

Our verse today illustrates the restorative power of God's grace. In fact, the Hebrew word we often translate as grace literally means "to stoop"—as in, "you will again bring me up."

Did you see how the psalmist blames God for his plight—"you have made me see troubles, many and bitter"? Sometimes God indeed allows hardship and suffering into our lives, but often we are the ones who have dug the pit we fall into. Either way, we can count on the fact that our lives can be restored.

Made good as new.

Of course, there will be a few scars, a limp here and there. Just to remind us of how far God brought us up from the bottom.

God knows we might fail. But He doesn't leave us there.

One man who knew great failure and great grace shared what he felt Jesus was saying to him:

> I witnessed a Peter who claimed that he did not know Me,
> a James who wanted power in return for service to the king-
> dom, a Philip who failed to see the Father in Me, and scores

of disciples who were convinced I was finished on Calvary. Yet on Easter night I appeared to Peter. James is remembered for the sacrifice of his life for Me. Philip did see the Father in Me when I pointed the way, and the disciples who despaired had enough courage to recognize Me when we broke bread at the end of the road to Emmaus.[34]

Do you believe God can restore you as He did these men?

In today's verse the psalmist concludes with deciding to trust God's sovereign wisdom and love, even after sending bitter trouble into his life—"you will restore my life again."

Tim Keller points out that David "knows that in the end everything that happens is for the ultimate purpose of restoring our life—by deepening the love, wisdom, and joy of our spiritual life."[35]

My child, everyone is broken. And grace can be the glue that helps restore people and lives. You know this because I did it for you. Not once, but several times already. Sometimes my choicest servants are those who go through life with a limp. Bringing others to the Mender. Who will you help restore today?

18. Attend

If people can't see what God is doing,
*   they stumble all over themselves;*
*But when they **attend** to what he reveals,*
*   they are most blessed.*

~ Proverbs 29:18 MSG

"Cindy, pay attention!"

This was all too often the soundtrack of my childhood because I was all over the place—curious to explore and try new things. Distracted. Prone to multitasking. Off on adventures in my head even while holding on to Mama's hand.

I needed focus. To "attend" to the matter at hand. But my brain would rather wander than pay attention because it takes more energy to focus.

Where do you need to pay attention today? To God?

Our Christian friends in the Orthodox Church begin each reading of Scripture with a call of "Wisdom. Let us attend!"

And no wonder. "The average attention span has dropped from 12 seconds in 2000 to just 8.25 seconds in 2015. An American on social media receives 54,000 words and 443 minutes of video every day."[36]

"We live in a hyper-connected world. Linda Stone, a leadership consultant, describes our current distracted culture with the phrase 'continual partial attention,' a semi-attentive state in which people continuously 'scan for opportunities, activities, and contacts.'"[37]

Let us attend.

If we want to focus our hearts on God, we will learn how to focus.

> When we say "stay" to a new puppy, we want her to wait, to abide in the same place. Waiting implies attentiveness, listening and expectation. We sit in the waiting room as we're in line for the doctor's care. Are we in the physician's office? Yes.

Are we talking with him? Not yet, but we are attuned to his expected presence. We do something similar when we wait on God. We're focused on him, expecting him to act or to give us guidance or instruction. Sitting in the doctor's waiting room indicates we know we're needy, we know the doctor is able to help us, and we know he cares about us and will take care of our needs.[38]

Randy wanted to know what would happen if he gave God his full attention for forty days. So he went to a house of prayer in the South Texas desert. His sojourn began as a struggle.

At first the "nothing to do" was maddening. But a deeper communion with God came when he gave in to the silence. . . . A big question came to him in the desert: "How can I, a person who can talk about salvation by grace from Romans in a way that will make people weep, understand it so little?" What Randy discovered is if you are willing to invest time with God, what he will do is teach you the gospel. Not with the head, but with the heart.[39]

Are you listening and focusing—with both your heart and mind?

Jesus said, "Pay close attention to what you hear. The closer you listen, the more understanding you will be given—and you will receive even more" (Mark 4:24 NLT).

Let us attend.

My child, listen up. Yes, you! The one juggling all those balls in the air. Could you just settle down and focus on Me? I know the world bombards you with data every single moment. But I have more than data; I have divine insight and eternal encouragement for your heart. All you have to do is look up. And listen.

19. Work

Let the favor of the Lord our God be upon us;
*and confirm for us the **work** of our hands;*
*yes, confirm the **work** of our hands.*

~ Psalm 90:17 NASB

Katherine was a human computer.

An African American woman in the mid-century America NASA space program. Among her responsibilities was calculating the trajectories for both the Mercury and Apollo missions.

But no one knew about her work.

Until the recent book and movie *Hidden Figures* revealed the true story of the "West Computers"—women who were at the heart of NASA's advancements. Including Katherine G. Johnson.

"They worked through equations that described every function of the plane, running the numbers often with no sense of the greater mission of the project. They contributed to the ever-changing design of a menagerie of wartime flying machines, making them faster, safer, and more aerodynamic. Unlike the male engineers, few of these women were acknowledged in academic publications or for their work on various projects."[40]

We all want our work to matter.

The psalmist in today's verse is Moses who prayed that God would "confirm for us the *work* of our hands" (emphasis added). I pray a similar prayer: "Make the small and large things You have called me to do help bring light and hope to the world."

In the Old Testament Hebrew, the word for *confirm* or *establish* means "firmly fixed, stable, secure." We all want to believe that all we have invested in during this life will be appreciated and, hopefully, will make a difference.

But there are no guarantees.

How do we ever know the results of "the work of our hands"? For author Philip Yancey, writing is a very isolated occupation. "We write in desperate hope that the sometimes-tedious tasks of researching, composing, and polishing words will eventually become a virtual chain that links us to others."

Still, he has been amazed at some responses.

> A woman in Lebanon told me how much my book, *Disappointment with God*, meant to her. She read it a few pages a night in the midst of the civil war there, in a bomb shelter by the light of a kerosene lamp. Another woman in Beirut wrote that my book *What's So Amazing About Grace?* helped her have a better attitude toward the P.L.O. guerrillas who had commandeered her apartment. . . . Again and again God has surprised me by using words written with mixed motives by my impure self to bear fruit in ways I never could have imagined.[41]

When I am tempted to wonder if my writing, speaking, and teaching will ever make a difference, invariably I will get a note from someone sharing the impact of my words. This spurs me on tremendously.

Writer Robert Benson points out, "The real reason we cannot quit is because of the friends, known and unknown to us, who have somehow come to expect that the bits and pieces of our personal lives . . . do indeed reveal the places where the One Who made us has made an appearance [and] will shed light on the ways such appearances are taking place in their own."[42]

Do your work—as unto the Lord.

My child, some people work in a computer lab, a hospital, a sound booth, a classroom, or a mine deep beneath the earth. And it all matters to Me because you are called and gifted to offer up your talents and time for the betterment of the world. Do every task with integrity and honor. Even if no one else ever knows. Do not quit. Your work matters.

20. Worthless Things

*Turn my eyes from looking at **worthless things**, and give me*
life in your ways.

~ Psalm 119:37 ESV

"I can't believe I just spent fifteen dollars and two hours of my life on such a terrible movie!"

My friend was regretting her use of money and time that can never be retrieved—wasted on "worthless things."

How much do you spend on the empty and unsatisfying? On things that tend to bring death, rather than life?

"Too much," is my own answer.

> The Bible tells us that we have chosen to build our lives on things that do not have the power to fulfill us or give us identity and purpose. That is why we are often left feeling empty, dissatisfied, and insecure. It is why our attempts at fulfillment never ultimately satisfy. Instead of loving and serving God, we have attempted to run our own lives. Since God is our Creator, that behavior is considered treason from God's point of view.[43]

The psalmist says, "Give me life in your ways." He calls us to live with holy priorities, not the latest flavor-of-the-week. But this will not happen without a deliberate, proactive plan.

This includes determining the kind of programming I want to put in my mind. Frankly, much of what is offered in the way of entertainment has literally no redeeming value at all. Likewise, if I'm committed to reaching out to others, I can't leave it all up to chance, but need to calendar in special times of participating in outreach or mission events, serving in tangible ways.

What are the nonnegotiables on your weekly calendar? What are the extras or the once-in-a-blue-moon activities? How will you set your priorities—for that which brings life?

One woman decided to define her own purpose with two simple words: *choose life*. For her, that succinct affirmation from Deuteronomy 30:19 was the barometer that helped her decide on her investments:

> "We can eat a candy bar or an apple," she said, "but which leads to a greater quality of health? We can watch TV or read a book, but which leads to a greater quality of growth? We can say a loving word or the critical word, but which conveys the quality of personal nourishment?" And so she chose to drive her purpose—a vital, healthy, growth-oriented life—through every action in the day. Ultimately her purpose is to help others choose life as well, life as Christ offers it.[44]

Who wants to reach the end of life, regretting all the time they wasted on idols—anything we substitute for the life and love that only Christ can bring?

"Our culture is hawking approval and it's a multibillion-dollar business. We get our fill, and then—*poof*—it is gone. For what end? Love idols rust. In a blink, this life will be over. And our popularity ratings will mean nothing on the other side of eternity."[45]

Poof! In an instant the worth-more-than-we-could-afford is revealed as yet one more worthless thing God warned us against.

Just turn your eyes away. And your heart.

My child, what are some of the things you have invested in that rust? I long for you to turn from the lures of worldly life and focus on people instead. Lives that need change or challenge. Or maybe just a bit of courage. Everything else is worthless. You can't take it with you when you die. So invest in people. I will show you how.

21. Wise

*So be careful how you live. Don't live like fools, but like those
who are wise.*

~ Ephesians 5:15 NLT

In reading today's verse I immediately began singing the old Sunday
school tune, "The wise man built his house upon the rock." It was a lesson I
learned early on. Don't be like the fool and build your house upon the sand,
because it's dangerous—"the rains came down and the floods came up . . .
and the house on the sand went 'splat!'"

Wisdom comes down to choices.

Fools make bad choices. Perhaps they even stumble into the bad rather
than intentionally pursuing it. Nonetheless, the consequences reveal them
as foolish, or at least ignorant.

Are you living wise?

How often I told my children, "It's not enough just to *know* the difference between right and wrong. You must then *choose* the right path."

Those who live wise make choices that bring life, not death. Light, not
darkness.

How can we know the wise path? Especially in a world where the lines
between "right" and "wrong" are blurry at best, opaque at worst.

There are at least eight significant characteristics listed in James 3:17
that comprise godly wisdom: "But the wisdom from above is first of all
pure. It is also *peace loving*, *gentle at all times*, and *willing to yield to others*. It
is *full of mercy* and the fruit of *good deeds*. It *shows no favoritism* and is *always
sincere*" (NLT, emphasis added).

Which of these characteristics are you strong in? Which ones could use
some work?

The original Greek word here is *sophia*, translated "wisdom, insight, skill
(human or divine), and intelligence." It is the root word of the English terms
sophistication (the art of using wisdom) and *philosophy* (affection for wisdom.)

But wisdom is not the same thing as intelligence.

One sociologist observed, "Typically people who can see beyond the information they've learned and apply it through analogies to other situations in their life or see other insights from it, those are the people we typically refer to as being exceptionally wise."[46]

King Solomon, the wisest man who ever lived, had some prime words for believers. Look to God's Word for ultimate wisdom. Here are some examples—which ones speak to you?

> "Tune your ears to wisdom, and concentrate on understanding." (Proverbs 2:2 NLT)
>
> "Cry out for insight, and ask for understanding. . . . For the Lord grants wisdom! From his mouth come knowledge and understanding." (Proverbs 2:3, 6 NLT)
>
> "Search for [wisdom] as you would for silver; seek [it] like hidden treasures." (Proverbs 2:4 NLT)
>
> "Get wisdom; develop good judgment." (Proverbs 4:5 NLT)
>
> "Fear of the Lord is the foundation of true knowledge, but fools despise wisdom and discipline." (Proverbs 1:7 NLT)

God promises to grow you in wisdom. Begin today.

My child, did you think you would be wise by the time you reached this age? The good news is, you probably are much wiser than before. But that can only increase as you seek these qualities of peace, gentleness, mercy, good deeds, and integrity. Turn to My Word as your guide to all wisdom. Prayer will reveal the way.

22. Obey

*"Choose to love the Lord your God and to **obey** him and to cling to him, for he is your life and the length of your days."*

~ Deuteronomy 30:20 TLB

Jonah didn't like what the Lord asked him to do. "Get up and go to Nineveh, that great city, and cry out against it, for their evil has come to my attention" (Jonah 1:2).

Thus he chose to disobey God—to run away. "So Jonah got up—to flee to Tarshish from the LORD!" (Jonah 1:3).

And he ended up in deep trouble. Bottom-of-the-sea-in-a-whale deep.

Have you ever run from God because you didn't want to obey Him?

> While you and I might not have gone to such extremes to run from God externally, we've all run at one time or another in ways less noticeable. It's far more simple and discreet to run away internally, isn't it? We head to Tarshish in our hearts so we can still pretend we are obeying God. We can pack our internal bags just as quickly as Jonah packed his and be on a boat headed in the opposite direction of God's will even while we are in the throes of everyday life.[47]

Jonah's disobedience set into play a series of very unexpected events—thrown overboard, swallowed by a whale, called urgently to God in prayer, released onto dry ground, and called a second time to visit Nineveh. You better believe he obeyed this time!

In order to obey, we first must hear.

We cannot hear without listening. The Latin word for *listen* is *audire*. Listening with our full and focused attention is *ob-audire*, from which comes the word *obedience*.

Are you open to hearing what God is asking of you—and obeying?

Or have you shut down and become *surdus*, the Latin word for *deaf*?

Henri Nouwen said, "Being formed in God's likeness involves the struggle to move from *absurd living* to *obedient listening*."[48] Harold Myra explains, "Nouwen defines absurd living as deafness in which we don't hear the voice of the Creator who calls us to new life. Such living is painful because it cuts us off from the essential source of our being."[49]

Frankly it's easier for me to talk than to listen. But to grow spiritually, I must hear and obey what God communicates through His Word.

"Trust and obey, for there's no other way . . ." says the old hymn. And it's still true today. When Jonah finally did go to Nineveh, God used Jonah's obedience to bring many people to Him.

"When Jonah chose to walk in obedience to the word of the Lord, the result was a harvest of amazing fruit he'd probably never seen coming. The story of Jonah testifies to the power of our willingness to yield to divine interruptions and leads us to consider two things: the effect the Word has on unbelievers and the effect our simple obedience has in our personal circumstances."[50]

May you strive to obey, "for he is your life and the length of your days."

My child, in order to obey, you must first hear My will, then follow it. Oh yes, you can run, but you cannot hide. Just like Jonah. Yet once you understand that I call you to the best, perhaps you will answer the first time, instead of having to experience the consequences. I will always use a willing servant.

23. Success

*We dare to say these good things about ourselves only because of
our great trust in God through Christ, that he will help us to be
true to what we say, and not because we think we can do anything of lasting value by ourselves. Our only power and **success**
comes from God.*

~ 2 Corinthians 3:4-5 TLB

I cried a little each day for the first four months of 1981.

I didn't cry due to homesickness—although I had just moved to Cal-
ifornia, three thousand miles from family and friends. I didn't cry due
to increased work demands—although becoming missions director at a
four-thousand-member church did have a tendency to overwhelm. And I
didn't cry due to challenging relationships—although I had discovered a
small group who had lobbied for their friend to get my position.

I cried for fear of failure.

Our congregation was located in the heart of Silicon Valley near Stan-
ford University. Success was all around, and I was dizzy.

"Here at Menlo Park, the staff is free to succeed!" a fellow pastor re-
marked with a twinkle in his eye.

It was a joke. But I wasn't laughing.

Our senior minister was one of the first Christians I'd encountered who
was willing to lead in a vulnerable way, offering a church full of grace and
acceptance. All around us, lives were being touched and healed. But I was
still young and full of a need to prove myself professionally.

There were times I failed at pioneering a new ministry. But I learned.
And by the grace of God, my work became a national church prototype for
local church missions by the time I left four years later.

"Not because we think we can do anything of lasting value by ourselves."
Success happened because of "our great trust in God through Christ."

Do you realize that true success comes only from God?

I'm usually eager to give my best, but in recent years I have also been able to give God my worst. And you know what? He can handle both!

Secure in that knowledge, I now leave the results to God. Yes, I still care about quality and the satisfaction of a job well done. But others' expectations no longer drive me.

Success is not as important as faithfulness. God has been right beside me in every triumph of my life. But I have also experienced dismal defeat only to find Him there as well.

"God's love doesn't depend on our performance. It depends on Jesus Christ. The reason Jesus stretched out His arms on the Cross was so He could reach them around people like you and me. . . . If you experience God at your lowest moment, you'll know it has nothing to do with your condition—and everything to do with God's amazing grace."[51]

One prominent musician says that God develops us in those unseen places where we hear His voice and keep going. "It's where the word *success* transitions to *call*, where you long to hear the voice of God over worrying about your reward. It's where you are free to dream big—but you consider all the parts along the way just as important as the final destination."[52]

No one really likes crying while on the way to rejoicing. But if that's an integral part of the journey, then please pass the tissues.

My child, what does success mean to you, and how will you know when you have achieved it? Success is fidelity and faithfulness. Honor and hope. Doing exactly what I've called you to do and being the person I created. It's usually swimming upstream in the process, but with a lot of divine power helping you surge. You are pleasing in My eyes today.

24. Memorial

*"These stones are to be a **memorial** to the people of Israel forever."*

~ Joshua 4:7 NIV

Today, for the third time in my life, I visited the grave of a woman I never met.

I helped my son and husband plant flowers, and we sang together the hymn inscribed on her tombstone "Thine Is the Glory." Except for our voices, it was strangely quiet in this small Dutch village churchyard as we dug and stood vigil for the birth mother of my first three children.

A grace gift of both joy and solemnity.

Before my youngest daughter married her husband, we stood in a Texas memorial garden honoring his father, and prayed with thanksgiving for Tom's life and our children who had come together to carry on his name and legacy.

And when I visit my Georgia family, I occasionally kneel at the grave of my childhood friend and chat about growing older without her. Sometimes I leave little gifts, like the Barbie Christmas ornament that reminds me of so many little-girl dreams—ones that she decided on her own would never come true.

Graves and tombstones are tangible memorials to someone's life. As believers we know our loved ones aren't actually there, in the ground or the vault. But these places provide a touchstone of remembering who they were and how they changed our lives.

"How often do we go to the cemetery and stand, kneel or sit in front of the place where our spouse, parents, brothers, sisters, aunts, uncles, or friends have been buried? Are we still in touch with those who have died, or are we living our lives as if those who lived before us never really existed?"[53]

When Joshua led the forty thousand Israelites out of the desert and into the Promised Land, God parted the waters of the churning Jordan River so they could cross safely. And God commanded that each of the twelve priests take a stone from the riverbed. Joshua told them exactly what to say when children in the future would ask about the memorial stones they left. "Then you will let your children know: 'Israel crossed over the Jordan here on dry ground.'" (Joshua 4:22).

The two lasting truths? God does the impossible and God's power is great.

How do you remember the life of a loved one who has died?

Perhaps you keep a possession, a recording, or a letter. Maybe you donate to a cause or ministry your loved one was passionate about, or establish a scholarship to encourage students in his or her field.

> What a gift it is to know deeply that we are all brothers and sisters in one human family and that, different as our cultures, languages, religions, life-styles, or work may be, we are all mortal beings called to surrender our lives into the hands of a loving God. What a gift it is to feel connected with the many who have died and to discover the joy and peace that flow from that connectedness.[54]

Because they lived, we are different.

All Saints' Day (November 1) and the anniversary of a death can be significant times for memorials. When I sang at that Dutch grave, I was witness to two lasting truths—Inka gave life to people I love the most, and she remained faithful to Christ until death.

My child, what will others remember most about you? That you were kind, encouraging, helpful, funny? Or that you were always too busy? I urge you to live each day as though everything you do, everything you say, and everyone you encounter builds the kingdom. Because it does. You don't have to worry about memorials. Just live.

25. Aim

*Make love your **aim**.*

~ 1 Corinthians 14:1 RSV

Daddy taught me how to shoot and hunt in south Georgia.

How to look through the scope of a rifle, aim, and fire. If I blinked or moved my attention from the target, then the shot went wild. It only hit the target if I kept my focus and didn't flinch.

When I read Paul's words in our verse today, I was reminded that too often I get sidetracked in my efforts to live out my faith—serving, listening, teaching, lifting up an urgent need, or counting the numbers of those who appear to be responding.

My eyes and heart, instead, need to stay targeted on the one thing that I am called to do—love.

"Love is our aim. It deserves our full attention, effort, and strength. Love is our whole agenda. We can get everything else right, but if we miss love, we miss it all."[55] What is one step you could take to extend love today?

How about prayerwalking?

> When I first began praying as I walked, my prayers were self-focused. But prayerwalking has opened my eyes to the needs of people I don't even know. Early each morning I pray for the business owners and employees up and down Main Street, for the people in the homes I pass, and for anyone who comes across my path. I am impassioned to bring the needs of others to God.[56]

Are you willing to love, even if your efforts are misunderstood, or rejected?

> You may not love me back. You may humble me, humiliate me, reject me, shatter my heart, and drive the shards into my

soul—but this is not the part that matters. . . . What matters most is not if our love makes other people change, but that in loving, we change . . . we become more like Someone.[57]

How can you and I begin to love like that?

We can be the hands and feet, mouth and ears, of Jesus to someone who has almost given up hope that anyone cares. And not worry if our efforts fail or seem insignificant.

Lori says she will never regret her feeble attempts to love others as God loved her:

It's a clumsy thing, my loving others. . . . But even the raw scribbles of the child da Vinci, were they discovered today, would be treasured because we would see them as the early works of a master. When I see God face to face, I'll notice that my first attempts to love as He loved are taped to His refrigerator.[58]

We all start somewhere. Keep aiming. You will hit the target, with God's help.

My child, since I have so freely loved you, it's time to return the favor. Love the ones who are prickly, those hardest to touch but who need it the most. Start small and nonthreateningly. A conversation. An offer of companionship or help. Eventually you can share where ultimate love is found—only through Me. And tell them I created them with love already.

26. *Everything*

Everything *that goes into a life of pleasing God has been miraculously given to us by getting to know, personally and intimately, the One who invited us to God.*

~ 2 Peter 1:3 MSG

Today is Crazy Christmas Sweater Day, and I am wearing one depicting my favorite scene from the movie *Elf*.

Pictured on the front is Buddy the Elf screaming with ecstasy, "Santa's coming! I *know* him!" Raised (by Santa) at the North Pole, Buddy works in the Christmas department of a New York City store. Though an upcoming visit from "Santa" is a humdrum for the other staff, Buddy spends all night excitedly decorating to welcome a person he both knows and loves.

I'm the same way around Christmas—but not for Santa. For Jesus.

You see, Christmas celebrates Jesus' coming. And since I *know* Him, that changes my whole motivation for celebration.

Do you truly know Jesus or do you just know *about* Him?

In our verse today we are promised that one of the greatest gifts we are given is the opportunity to get to know our Savior "personally and intimately." How? By taking hold of the "everything" that is needed to live a life of godliness.

It has already been given to us.

God's actions are the ultimate example of perfect giving.

"For it is by grace you have been saved, through faith—and this is not from yourselves, it is the gift of God." (Ephesians 2:8 NIV)

God's gift for you and me came to earth wrapped in a bundle—a baby named Jesus—and labeled grace. . . .

We have done nothing to deserve this gift of life. . . .

Yet, we only need to believe to accept what God offers.

. . . Remember God's gift of grace, through Jesus, is enough for you.[59]

The New Testament Greek word used in today's verse is *pas,* which is translated "everything, all things, complete." No exceptions. Here, the context refers to anything we need to grow spiritually—"a life of pleasing God." And the condition for this to be provided? We are to get to know the One "personally and intimately."

It's not enough just to *have* the gift; we must actually *use* it.

When Crowfoot, chief of the Blackfoot nation in Alberta, Canada, gave the Canadian Pacific Railway permission to lay train track from Medicine Hat to Calgary, he was given in exchange a lifetime railroad pass. A ticket he could use to go anywhere, anytime. Everything he needed for a journey.

For the rest of his life.

Chief Crowfoot was so pleased with the gift that he put it in a fine-tooled leather pouch and wore it around his neck. But he never used it. He never took a trip on the train. He had everything, but he didn't avail himself of the gift.

Don't waste the grace gifts God has given you. "In him lie hidden all the treasures of wisdom and knowledge" (Colossians 2:3 NLT). Simply draw near; read His Word; talk to Him in prayer.

That's everything.

My child, what do you most need from Me today? I want to gift you with it. Perhaps I already have. You see, I offer you everything to live your seemingly impossible life. Grace gifts abound, but you must actually make them a part of your daily life, not just carry them as a lovely present. The best gift of all? You have Me. Always.

27. Pieces

*As they were eating, Jesus took some bread and blessed it. Then
he broke it into **pieces** and gave it to the disciples, saying, "Take
this and eat it, for this is my body."*

~ Matthew 26:26 NLT

What can you do when your life is in pieces?

How well I remember laying out a myriad of small fabric squares in a
beautiful pattern on the floor of my mountain cottage. One day this would
be an artistic quilt, but for now, I was designing with hundreds of little
pieces.

I had just gathered them up, row by row, when I stumbled, and the
whole lot flew up into the air and scattered freely. What a mess!

I sat among the pieces and cried.

Not really for the quilt—I had the design on graph paper and would
eventually put it all back together again. What I was really crying about
was my twenty-three-year-old life—none of the pieces, neither personally
nor professionally, appeared to be forming any kind of hopeful pattern.
How could I fulfill my destiny when I didn't even know what that would
look like?

"GOD made my life complete when I placed all the pieces before him"
(Psalm 18:20 MSG).

So I made a list of three proactive ways I could move forward:

1. **Gather my pieces.** (Identify concerns, people,
   and situations.)
2. **Give them over to God.** (Offer them up in
   prayer to the Master Quilter for a pattern of His
   choosing.)
3. **Get ready to grow.** (Focus on going deeper in my
   faith, pursuing excellence in God's unique gifts.)

Don't despair if you also feel broken—into bits.

Pieces, when offered back to the Creator, can reveal an amazing pattern for new life. He takes all our experiences, losses, failures, and regrets. They may look like scraps to us, but each fits perfectly into the life pattern He is creating.[60]

Pieces of the broken can feed a multitude.

Jesus knew this. Look what He did with the little boy's simple lunch of fish and bread.

In a final act with friends, Jesus broke the bread into pieces, showing that He was offering Himself to feed others. "Take this and eat it, for this is my body."

Do you think that the pieces of your life can be used to bring others to wholeness?

Oswald Chambers said, "A Christian is not one who proclaims the gospel merely, but who *becomes* broken bread and poured out wine in the hands of Jesus Christ for others."[61]

Perhaps the first place to begin is to offer ourselves: "Here is my brokenness. Given. Here is my battered life, here is my bruised control, here are my fractured dreams, here is my open hand, here is all that I have, here is my fragile surrendered heart, here I am, a living sacrifice. Broken. Given."[62]

God will collect what we have given and bring about wholeness.

My child, sometimes all you have are leftover pieces. From a lost dream, a former life, or a broken relationship. And what good are pieces anyway? Good. Combined with a loving hand that crafts and molds them, a new image of whole emerges. To help others. Do not despair over your brokenness. Just give Me the pieces and I will make them beautiful.

28. Difficult Times

*In the last days there will be very **difficult times**. For people will love only themselves and their money. They will be boastful and proud, scoffing at God, disobedient to their parents, and ungrateful. They will consider nothing sacred. They will be unloving and unforgiving; they will slander others and have no self-control. They will be cruel and hate what is good. They will betray their friends, be reckless, be puffed up with pride, and love pleasure rather than God.*

~ 2 Timothy 3:1-4 NLT

Why are we so surprised to be living in such difficult times?

When I read today's text, Paul's final words to Timothy, I am amazed that in many ways, very little has changed in our world.

But if "difficult times" have been present off and on for two millennia and beyond, then why do we wring our hands, whining that surely *this* is the end of the world?

God is still on the throne.

Whatever is happening in your world today . . . it did not take Him by surprise. If God allows such difficulty to intersect with your life, be confident that He will put Himself right in the middle of it to provide for you.

I don't know what you are experiencing as you read these words. But as I write them, there is great change and upheaval in my own country. People are afraid. People are angry. And even some believers are forgetful.

That our Christian faith was not only born in the midst of political turmoil (murderous King Herod and Christian persecutor Nero) but has prevailed throughout time with both weak and strong leaders, believers and scoffers.

How should we conduct ourselves during difficult times, when all of the things listed in today's verse are truly personified in our daily news and our daily encounters?

We should do exactly what Paul exhorted Timothy to do: "But you must remain faithful to the things you have been taught" (2 Timothy 3:14 NLT).

One pastor offered these suggestions for living in difficult times:

> Pray repentance and saving faith "for kings and all
> who are in high positions" everywhere. (1 Timo-
> thy 2:2 RSV)
> Lift up Christ and gather with people, in beautiful
> diversity and harmony, to worship God together
> in healthy, holy, humble churches.
> Love each other "earnestly from a pure heart"
> (1 Peter 1:22 ESV), remaining "unstained from
> the world" (James 1:27 ESV).
> Spread the great good news of the saving grace of
> Jesus Christ to all people.[63]

These are characteristics of reconciliation. Isn't this who we are called to be?

> [Reconcilers] bring people together. They hate war, violence,
> contentiousness, division caused by race, economics, gender
> and ideology. They believe that being peaceable and making
> peace trumps all other efforts in one's lifetime. A Christian is
> mightily stirred into action when he sees those dividing walls
> that separate people, each of whom was made uniquely and
> loved by God. What an incredible example he is to . . . arrogant
> people who walk through every day dividing and diminish-
> ing people all around them. The transforming Christ-follower
> knows his natural human tendency and seeks God's power to
> replace it with another tendency: redeeming, healing love.[64]

Difficult times are inevitable. May our response bring reconciliation and peace.

My child, the world is at war—over politics, ideology, culture, religion, and economics. It has always been this way. And sometimes evil wins a few skirmishes. But I have empowered you to live in this very volatile world, armed with truth and hope that comes from knowing your God is the ultimate Victor. Do not give in to despair. Do not give up.

29. Season

*There's a **season** for everything and a time for every matter under the heavens.*

~ Ecclesiastes 3:1

A few years ago, when my friend Pam turned forty, she started a group called "Seasoned Sisters" to celebrate the wisdom, strength, and opportunities of women in the season of midlife.

Needless to say, I gladly joined the Seasoned Sisterhood, for I have indeed witnessed every season—several times over. And lived to tell about it.

Mostly what I bear witness to is this: timing is everything.

Embrace your current season, rather than wish you were in another one. Remember there is a season for everything that God has purposed for your life story.

Our words today were recorded by wise King Solomon. He knew something about timing. His illustrious life included both elaborate success and dismal failure. But one of the benefits of persevering over the long haul is that one eventually cues into the wisdom of God's creation of season, thus declaring, "God makes all things beautiful in His time" (see Ecclesiastes 3:11).

What season are you in today? If it's not where you wish you were, pray for God to change your heart and show you His will and way for today.

Gordon found wonderful liberation at midlife: "Liberation from feeling that I always had to be right, from always having to be more successful this year than last year, from fearing some people wouldn't like me. . . . In part, that liberation came from the grace and kindness of Jesus and also from having to clean up after failure."[65]

Susan, grandmother of twenty-one, discovered that every season includes both challenges and blessings.

> We have biological seasons: childhood, single years, marriage
> for some, parenting years, empty nest, bungee cord season

(when you only thought you were an empty nester), the golden years, and perhaps singleness again. We also have seasons of loss: a death, the loss of a dream, the loss of health. We have mixed up seasons, like caring for an elderly parent while raising a toddler. And we have seasons of transition, of change. It is important to articulate the challenges but then choose to focus on the blessings.[66]

Whether you are busy getting your degree, running around after a houseful of littles, building a business, or reinventing yourself in retirement, there are always blessings to experience in every season. Why not list them?

I'll go first with some blessings of my current season:

- I know who I am (and who I'm not). Very freeing.
- My children still want to visit me!
- I'm enjoying sweet companionship with my husband of thirty-three years.
- I have no major health challenges.
- I'm eager to learn new things, meet new people, read new books.
- God still allows me the privilege of writing and speaking for Him.
- I don't need a bucket list; I'd rather empty my bucket for others.

Now, your turn.

My child, while it is a worthy thing to reflect on the blessings of each season, I also know that each one holds challenges as well. Growing older can be rife with frustration and diminishing ability. But perhaps it can also be a time of clinging to that which is most important. Don't wish you were elsewhere. Live here. Live now. It is good.

30. Remained Faithful

I have fought the good fight, I have finished the race, and I have **remained faithful**.

~ 2 Timothy 4:7 NLT

Tears were streaming down my face as I watched the short video clip Pete made—his final message prepared to be shown at his funeral. My friend, who spent much of his life in a wheelchair, knew that he would soon join his brother in heaven.

We had connected on several occasions, but I was especially impressed with his excellent emceeing at a Joni and Friends Family Retreat where Mike and I had been the speakers. Confident, compassionate, funny, and articulate was Pete Lafferty.

In the video, he urged us to continue our lives with faith in Christ, counting on divine power to do impossible things. Then looking straight at the camera, he quoted the apostle Paul: "I have fought the good fight, I have finished the race, and I have remained faithful."

Will you and I be able to say at the end of our lives that we have indeed "remained faithful"?

> What makes authentic disciples is not visions, ecstasies, biblical mastery of chapter and verse, or spectacular success in the ministry, but a capacity for faithfulness. Buffeted by the fickle winds of failure, battered by their own unruly emotions, and bruised by rejection and ridicule, authentic disciples may have stumbled and frequently fallen, endured lapses and relapses, and wandered into a far country. Yet they kept coming back to Jesus.[67]

Perhaps one of the best grace gifts of all.

Paul's words "remained faithful" were originally written in Greek. *Meno,* for "remain" can also mean "to continue, endure or dwell." To remain is to be steadfast, and Jesus promised that if we remain in Him, He will remain in us. Every day we make that choice—to remain on God's path, or to go our own way. *Pistos* is the word for "faithful," which can be either a noun or an adjective meaning one of firm persuasion. In the New Testament this word always connotes "conviction, commitment and confidence."

So how then should we live today?

Put one foot in front of the other. By faith.

And when we do join that great host of those who have gone before us, perhaps it will be as one man imagined:

> I think we will feel humbled by what we see. And honored to be given a glimpse of the grand sweep of God's story. Humbled to know that we have played a part in the story, however small a part, and for however brief a time. . . . We will look on the rewards that have been stored up for us, rewards for our faithfulness as stewards of the heavy talents of suffering that were entrusted to us. And we will be startled to see that the exchange rate of heaven is not measured out to us pound for pound because the thumb of a generous God is on those scales, weighting them in our favor.[68]

Embrace each day as a gift of faith.

My child, I urge you to keep moving forward in faith. Holding tight to the many grace gifts you encounter in your ordinary life. As a result, you will emerge as a person of deep faith and compassion. I will inhabit your words, your actions, your desires, and your friendships. You will know Me as close as your very breath. Remain in Me. I am with you. Always.

Gratitudes

This entire book is full of the words of gratitude that I offer back to God and to you. When we actually take time to notice the innumerable grace gifts appearing in our ordinary days, how can we do anything else but say *thank you*?

For an author, the opportunity to write a book is a huge cause for thanksgiving, and I am forever grateful to my Abingdon Press publishing family for yet again entrusting such a privilege to me. Thank you, Susan Salley, Dawn Woods, Susan Cornell, Brenda Smotherman, Russ Sellars, and the entire cast of marketing, sales, and support. It takes a team to launch a book into the world, and you are one of the best!

I also want to personally thank everyone who has taught me through the years about grace, mercy, and God's gifts. Too numerous to mention, I will also just say that I am humbled to be able to pass along so many of your words to others. Writers must be readers, and I read a variety of amazing books each year. I hope you do too.

Here in New England I am so very grateful for Tessa and Lauren in my writers' group; Rachel and the entire reNEW—retreat for New England Writing community; Karen, Jessica, and Judy, my Daybreak prayer/birthday team; the Andersons, Charettes, Coopers, and Phillipses, our couples growth group; my First Church congregation; and my Tuesday night women's Bible study. You have been the community of Christ support and encouragement I have needed and relied upon.

A special shout-out of thanks to everyone I have met, studied under, spoken next to, and had the privilege of teaching as I travel to conferences, writer events, book conventions, retreats, and family camps. And to my sisters who know what my life is like in the Advanced Writers and Speakers Association.

Prayer is powerful, and I would not even be able to attempt writing or speaking without my precious SpaSisters (you know who you are) behind me all the way. This amazing group of women know me, believe in me, and storm the gates of heaven so that I might be used for the kingdom. I do the same for them, and am utterly humbled and grateful for the privilege.

I am also grateful to my colleagues and students at Wethersfield High School. Daily, they provide an atmosphere in which I seek to live out the principles in this book. Because I don't always "pass the test," I'm glad that even public high schools can be a grace place.

My ninety-year-old praying mama, Sarah Secrest, is the wind beneath my wings and always has been. I would not be who I am today if not for both my parents—Daddy, I still hear your voice in my ear every day saying, "You can do this!" And so I did.

But honey, I got kinfolk. And each of them leaves a mark on me, so "Appreciate it" goes to all the Secrests, Hastys, McDowells, Van Seventers, Stallingses, and Karpoffs for still claiming me as one of your own.

Special thanks to sisters Cathy and Susan, and sisters-of-my-heart Maggie and Claire. What would we do without each other?

My six children and three grandchildren may not always know what Mama/Granny is working on and writing on and speaking on any given day. But all of them offer me love, support, understanding, and whenever possible, their presence and prayers. Hugs and kisses of gratitude to Justin, Tim, Fiona, Tim K., Saoirse, Hugh, Maggie, Stephen, and New Baby. You are the greatest gifts I ever received and have had to hold loosely. Please know that every word in here I learned the hard way. And now I pass them on to you.

No one is more grateful at the completion of this project (nor has prayed as much for it) than my dear husband of thirty-three years—Michael. Honey, thanks for covering home base these past months. You take good care of me and love me well. I am the luckiest girl to be able to journey through life with you at my side.

Jesus, Lover of my soul, You hold me close, fill me up, then launch me back into a broken world—to share the grace gifts I have received. I don't deserve them. But You give anyway. So I hope to spend the remaining days of my life loving You, loving others, and flinging ordinary graces far and wide.

Lucinda Secrest McDowell
"Sunnyside," February 2017

Notes

GRACE

1. Tod Bolsinger, "The Words We Most Want to Hear," March 7, 2005, Tod Bolsinger online, accessed December 1, 2016, http://bolsinger.blogs.com /weblog/2005/03/the_words_we_mo.html.

2. Barry Corey, *Love Kindness: Discover the Power of a Forgotten Christian Virtue* (Carol Stream, IL: Tyndale, 2016), 170.

3. Shane Claiborne, Jonathan Wilson-Hartgrove, and Enuma Okoro, *Common Prayer* (Grand Rapids: Zondervan, 2010), 202.

4. Tracie Miles, *Unsinkable Faith: God-Filled Strategies to Transform the Way You Think, Feel, and Live* (Colorado Springs: David C. Cook, 2017), 171–72.

5. Jennifer Dukes Lee, *The Happiness Dare: Pursuing Your Heart's Deepest, Holiest, and Most Vulnerable Desire* (Carol Stream, IL: Tyndale, 2016), 221.

6. Lori Stanley Roeleveld, *Jesus and the Beanstalk* (Nashville: Abingdon Press, 2016), 244.

7. Gail MacDonald, *A Step Farther and Higher* (Sisters, OR: Questar, 1993), 177.

8. Oswald Chambers, *My Utmost for His Highest* (Ulrichsville, OH: Barbour, 1987), 17.

9. Tish Harrison Warren, "Courage in the Ordinary," The Well (blog), April 3, 2013, http://thewell.intervarsity.org/blog/courage-ordinary.

10. Miles, *Unsinkable Faith*, 65–66.

11. Lysa Terkeurst, *Uninvited: Living Loved When You Feel Less Than, Left Out, and Lonely* (Nashville: Thomas Nelson, 2016), 46.

12. G. B. Hallock, "The Cultivation of Humility," *Herald and Presbyter* 90 (December 24, 1919).

13. Andrew Wilson, "Jesus Is the Best Gift," *Christianity Today* (September 2016): 34.

14. Ken Gire, *Seeing What Is Sacred* (Nashville: Thomas Nelson, 2006), 15.

15. Terkeurst, *Uninvited*, 40.

16. Fil Anderson, *Running on Empty* (Colorado Springs: WaterBrook, 2004), 49.

17. Henri J. M. Nouwen, *Finding My Way Home* (New York: Crossroad, 2001), 131–32.

18. Frederick Buechner, *The Clown in the Belfry* (San Francisco: Harper, 1992), 171.

19. Rob Renfroe, *The Trouble with the Truth: Balancing Truth and Grace* (Nashville: Abingdon Press, 2014), 32.

20. Ibid.

21. Jonathan Merritt, "Becca Stevens Believes Her 'Farmer's Theology' Can Change the World," RNS, July 17, 2015, http://religionnews.com/2015/07/17/becca-stevens-promotes-a-farmers-theology/.

22. Ann Voskamp, "How to Always Make Your Life Bearable: The 1 Question You Have to Ask," AnnVoskamp.com, January 16, 2017, http://annvoskamp.com/2017/01/how-to-always-make-your-life-bearable-the-1-question-you-have-to-ask/.

23. Kathryn Westcott, "What Is Stockholm Syndrome?" *BBC News Magazine* (August 2013): 4.

24. Brennan Manning, *The Ragamuffin Gospel* (Sisters, OR: Multnomah, 1990), 180.

25. Harold Myra, *One Year Book of Encouragement: 365 Days of Inspiration and Wisdom for Your Spiritual Journey* (Carol Stream, IL: Tyndale, 2010), 141.

26. Ruth Haley Barton, "Advent 1: The Importance of Waking Up," Transforming Center (blog), November 21, 2016, www.transformingcenter.org/2016/11/importance-waking/.

27. Charles H. Spurgeon, "Pray Without Ceasing," Spurgeon Archive, accessed March 31, 2017, http://www.spurgeon.org/sermons/1039.php.

28. Terkeurst, *Uninvited*, 8.

29. Corey, *Love Kindness*, 113, 115.

30. Shauna Niequist, *Present Over Perfect: Leaving Behind Frantic for a Simpler, More Soulful Way of Living* (Grand Rapids: Zondervan, 2016), 221.

31. Placide Cappeau, "O Holy Night" (1847) www.hymnary.org/text/o_holy_night_the_stars_are_brightly_shin.

32. Niequist, *Present Over Perfect*, 54.

33. Ibid., 55.

34. Henri J. M. Nouwen, *The Return of the Prodigal Son* (New York: Doubleday, 1994), 17; Henri J. M. Nouwen, *Spiritual Direction: Wisdom for the Long Walk of Faith*, repr. ed. (New York: HarperOne, 2015), 111.

35. Manning, *Ragamuffin Gospel*, 183.

36. Pete Briscoe, "Ministry Strong," *Leadership Journal* (Winter 2014): 22.

37. Charles Stone, "What's Wrong with People Pleasing?" *Leadership Journal* (Winter 2014): 84.

38. Kevin DeYoung, *Crazy Busy: A (Mercifully) Short Book about a (Really) Big Problem* (Grand Rapids: Zondervan, 2013), 35.

39. *Orthodox Study Bible* (Nashville: Thomas Nelson, 2008), 799.

40. Keri Wyatt Kent, *Deeper into the Word: Reflections on 100 Words from the New Testament* (Minneapolis: Bethany, 2011), 193.

41. Rebecca Manley Pippert, *Live* (Surrey, UK: Good Book, 2014), 47.

42. Renfroe, *Trouble with the Truth*, 52.

43. John Galt, *The Life and Studies of Benjamin West*, 2d ed. (London: T. Cadell, 1817), 10.

44. Gordon MacDonald and Mark MacDonald, *BeScrooged: Imagining a Full Life of Generosity* (Melbourne: Canterbury Partners, 2015), 92.

45. Miles, *Unsinkable Faith*, 43.

46. Tish Harrison Warren, "We're So Unashamed We Wrote a Book on It. Three of Them Actually" *Christianity Today*, September 12, 2016, www.christianitytoday.com/ct/2016/september-web-only/were-so-unashamed-we-wrote-book-on-it-three-of-them-actuall.html.

47. Ellen Vaughan, *Come, Sit, Stay: Finding Rest for Your Soul* (Brentwood, TN: Worthy, 2012), 57.

48. Joseph Hart, "Come, Ye Sinners, Poor and Needy" (public domain).

49. Andy Crouch, "The Return of Shame," *Christianity Today*, March 10, 2015, www.christianitytoday.com/ct/2015/march/andy-crouch-gospel-in-age-of-public-shame.html.

50. Bob Hostetler, *The Red Letter Life: 17 Words from Jesus to Inspire Simple, Practical, Purposeful Living* (Ulrichsville, OH: Barbour, 2014), 1999.

51. Eugene H. Peterson, "Learning to Love the Church," CT Pastors, accessed March 31, 2017, www.christianitytoday.com/pastors/2016/state-of-church-ministry-2017/learning-to-love-church.html.

52. Kent, *Deeper into the Word (NT)*, 226.

53. Harry Kraus, *Breathing Grace* (Wheaton, IL: Crossway, 2007), 14.

54. Steve Reynolds, "Confessions of a Recovering Legalist," PTM (Plain Truth Ministries), accessed April 5, 2017, www.ptm.org/quad/legalism Confessions.htm.

55. Manning, *Ragamuffin Gospel*, 214.

56. Kraus, *Breathing Grace*, 29.

57. Mark Batterson, *Going All In: One Decision Can Change Everything* (Grand Rapids: Zondervan, 2013), 35–36.

58. Kathy Howard, *Lavish Grace: Poured Out, Poured Through, and Overflowing* (Birmingham: New Hope, 2016), 73.

59. Susan Alexander Yates, *Risky Faith: Becoming Brave Enough to Trust the God Who Is Bigger Than Your World* (Bend, OR: Loyal Arts Media, 2016), 162.

60. Howard, *Lavish Grace*, 73.

61. Karen Ehman, *Listen, Love, Repeat: Other-Centered Living in a Self-Centered World* (Grand Rapids: Zondervan, 2016), 197.

62. *Oxford Living Dictionaries*, *s.v.* "FOMO," accessed March 31, 2017.

63. Melody Wilding, "How to Stop 'Fear of Missing Out' from Ruining Your Happiness," *Forbes*, July 6, 2016, www.forbes.com/sites/melodywilding /2016/07/06/career-fomo-how-to-stop-fear-of-missing-out-from-ruining -your-happiness/#5d2604262924.

64. Jen Hatmaker, "Belong," Jen Hatmaker (blog), November 23, 2015, http://jenhatmaker.com/blog/2015/11/23/belong.

65. Francine Rivers, *Earth Psalms: Reflections on How God Speaks through Nature* (Wheaton, IL: Tyndale, 2016), 75.

66. Vaughan, *Come, Sit, Stay*, 118.

67. Andrew Murray, *The Prayer Life* (Chicago: Moody, 2013), 17–18.

68. Henri J. M. Nouwen, *Gracias* (New York: Harper & Row, 1983), 20.

69. Ann Voskamp, *The Broken Way* (Grand Rapids: Zondervan, 2016), 201.

70. Madeleine L'Engle, *Walking on Water* (Wheaton, IL: Harold Shaw, 1980), 61–62.

STRENGTH

1. J. R. Briggs, "Redeeming Failure," *Leadership Journal* (Spring 2014): 23.

2. Ann Voskamp, *The Broken Way* (Grand Rapids: Zondervan, 2016), 263.

3. Keri Wyatt Kent, *Deeper into the Word: Reflections on 100 Words from the Old Testament* (Minneapolis: Bethany, 2011), 184.

4. Mary DeMuth, *Worth Living: How God's Wild Love for You Makes You Worthy* (Grand Rapids: Baker, 2016), 108.

5. Ibid., 81.

6. Frederick Buechner, *The Hungering Dark* (New York: HarperCollins, 1969), 13–14.

7. Suzanne Eller, *Come with Me* (Minneapolis: Bethany, 2016), 179.

8. Bert Crabbe, "A Seaworthy Soul," *Leadership Journal* (Winter 2014): 81.

9. Ibid.

10. Liz Curtis Higgs, *31 Verses to Write on Your Heart* (Colorado Springs: WaterBrook, 2016), 56.

11. Cheri Fuller and Jennifer Kennedy Dean, *The One Year Praying the Promises of God* (Carol Stream, IL: Tyndale, 2012), August 23.

12. Philip Yancey, *Prayer: Does It Make Any Difference?* (Grand Rapids: Zondervan, 2010), 112.

13. "Pals Carry Friend with Muscular Dystrophy Across Europe and to Skellig Michael in a Backpack," *IrishCentral*, September 26, 2016, www.irishcentral.com/travel/pals-carry-friend-with-muscular-dystrophy-across-europe-and-to-skellig-michael-in-a-backpack-video.

14. Johanna Li, "Man with Muscular Dystrophy Plans to Travel Through Europe on Friends' Backs," *Inside Edition*, March 21, 2016, www.insideedition.com/headlines/15381-man-with-muscular-dystrophy-plans-backpacking-trip-through-europe. See also We Carry Kevan, at http://wecarrykevan.com/.

15. Steve Brown, *Overcoming Setbacks* (Colorado Springs: NavPress, 1994), 60.

16. Voskamp, *Broken Way*, 190.

17. Ibid., 191

18. C. S. Lewis, *Surprised by Joy: The Shape of My Early Life*, reissue ed. (New York: HarperOne, 2017), 19.

19. Fil Anderson, *Running on Empty* (Colorado Springs: WaterBrook, 2004), 185.

20. Jennifer Dukes Lee, *The Happiness Dare: Pursuing Your Heart's Deepest, Holiest, and Most Vulnerable Desire* (Carol Stream, IL: Tyndale, 2016), 232.

21. Mark Batterson, *Draw the Circle: The 40 Day Prayer Challenge* (Grand Rapids: Zondervan, 2012), 79–81.

22. Jennie Allen, "Kicking in the Barbie Dream House," Jennie Allen (blog), December 1, 2016, www.jennieallen.com/kicking-barbie-dream-house/.

23. Fuller and Dean, *One Year Praying the Promises*, October 22.

24. Timothy Keller, *The Songs of Jesus: A Year of Daily Devotions in the Psalms* (New York: Viking, 2015), 331.

25. Statista, "Statistics and Facts on Health & Fitness Clubs," Statista.com, accessed April 3, 2017, www.statista.com/topics/1141/health-and-fitness-clubs/.

26. Eugene H. Peterson, "Learning to Love the Church," CTPastors, accessed April 3, 2017, www.christianitytoday.com/pastors/2016/state-of-church-ministry-2017/learning-to-love-church.html.

27. Higgs, *31 Verses*, 42.

28. Susan Alexander Yates, *Risky Faith: Becoming Brave Enough to Trust the God Who Is Bigger Than Your World* (Bend, OR: Loyal Arts Media, 2016), 209.

29. Shauna Niequist, *Present Over Perfect: Leaving Behind Frantic for a Simpler, More Soulful Way of Living* (Grand Rapids: Zondervan, 2016), 229.

30. Buechner, *Hungering Dark*, 104.

31. Ann Voskamp, "The Secret Truth That Cures Feelings of Abandonment & What Has to Be Said About Advent," Ann Voskamp (blog), December 6, 2016, http://annvoskamp.com/2016/12/the-secret-truth-that-cures-feelings-of-abandonment-what-has-to-be-said-about-advent/.

32. Henri J. M. Nouwen, *Our Greatest Gift: A Meditation on Dying and Caring* (New York: HarperOne: 2009), 58–59.

33. Max Lucado, "Coming Clean," *Leadership Journal* (Summer 2012): 48.

34. Anthony M. Coniaris, ed. *My Daily Orthodox Prayer Book* (Minneapolis: Light and Life, 2001).

35. Ellen Vaughan, *Come, Sit, Stay: Finding Rest for Your Soul* (Brentwood, TN: Worthy, 2012), 198.

36. Ray Stedman, "Jesus Is Our Sabbath Rest," ldolphin,org, accessed April 3, 2017, www.ldolphin.org/sabbathrest.html.

37. Vaughan, *Come, Sit, Stay*, 204.

38. Gail MacDonald, *In His Everlasting Arms: Learning to Trust God in All Circumstances* (Ann Arbor: Servant, 2000), 15.

39. Oswald Chambers, *My Utmost for His Highest Journal* (Ulrichsville OH: Barbour, 1963), February 22.

40. Mark Batterson, *Going All In: One Decision Can Change Everything* (Grand Rapids: Zondervan, 2013), 32.

41. *Christianity Today*, "Who Is Holding Up Your Arms?" womenleaders.com, July 13, 2007, www.christianitytoday.com/gifted-for-leadership/2007/july/whos-holding-up-your-arms.html?paging=off.

42. Sandra Levy, "Texting While Walking More Common, More Dangerous," Healthline, July 29, 2016, www.healthline.com/health-news/tech-texting-while-walking-causes-accidents-031014.

43. "I Sought the Lord," *The United Methodist Hymnal* (Nashville: The United Methodist Publishing House, 1989), 341.

44. Keri Wyatt Kent, *Deeper into the Word: Reflections on 100 Words from the New Testament* (Minneapolis: Bethany, 2011), 184.

45. Macrina Wiederkehr, *Behold Your Life* (Notre Dame, IN: Ave Maria, 1999), 11.

46. Vaughan, *Come, Sit, Stay*, 37.

47. Charles Spurgeon, *Spurgeon's Sermons* (Grand Rapids: Baker, 1996), sermon delivered March 5, 1893.

48. Marlo Schalesky, *Waiting for Wonder* (Nashville: Abingdon Press, 2016), 190–91.

49. Rob Renfroe, *The Trouble with the Truth: Balancing Truth and Grace* (Nashville: Abingdon Press, 2014), 15.

50. Ibid., 16.

51. WITW Staff, "Michelle Obama Says America Is Entering a Time of Hopelessness," *New York Times*, December 16, 2016, nytlive.nytimes.com /womenintheworld/2016/12/16/michelle-obama-says-america-is-entering-a -time-of-hopelessness/.

52. Kent, *Deeper into the Word (NT)*, 98.

53. For more information, see "reNEW—retreat for New England Writing," https://renewwriting.com/.

54. Frederick Buechner, *Wishful Thinking: A Theological ABC* (New York: Harper & Row, 1973), 95.

55. Oliver Wendell Holmes, "Lord of All Being" (1848) www.cyberhymnal .org/htm/l/a/lalbeing.htm).

56. Bob Hostetler, *The Red Letter Life: 17 Words from Jesus to Inspire Simple, Practical, Purposeful Living* (Ulrichsville OH: Barbour, 2014), 151.

57. Robert Benson, *Punching Holes in the Dark* (Nashville: Abingdon Press, 2016), 144.58. Jack Voelkel, "Helen Roseveare: Courageous Doctor in the Congo," Urbana (blog), February 18, 2007, https://urbana.org/blog/helen-roseveare.

59. Paula Spencer Scott, "Let's Make 2017 the Year of Being Kind," *Parade* (January 1, 2017): 8.

60. Barry Corey, *Love Kindness* (Carol Stream, IL: Tyndale, 2016, 30–31.

61. DeMuth, *Worth Living*, 145.

Gratitude

1. Jonathan Edwards, *A Treatise Concerning Religion Affections*, pt. 3.2, www .covenantofgrace.com/religious_affections_part3_2.htm.

2. Ed Dobson, *Seeing Through the Fog: Hope When Your World Falls Apart* (Colorado Springs: David C. Cook, 2012), 69–70.

3. Jennifer Dukes Lee, *The Happiness Dare: Pursuing Your Heart's Deepest, Holiest, and Most Vulnerable Desire* (Carol Stream, IL: Tyndale, 2016), 221.

4. Barnabas Powell, "A Commentary on the Inauguration," Facebook post, January 20, 2017, www.facebook.com/notes/barnabas-powell/a-commentary -on-the-inauguration/10154149751336606.

5. Johnson Oatman, "Count Your Blessings," 1897.

6. Adapted from John Trent and Gary Smalley, *The Blessing* (Nashville: Thomas Nelson, 1993; 2011).

7. John Ortberg, *Soul Keeping: Caring for the Most Important Part of You* (Grand Rapids: Zondervan, 2014), 20.

8. Shauna Niequist, *Present Over Perfect: Leaving Behind Frantic for a Simpler, More Soulful Way of Living* (Grand Rapids: Zondervan, 2016), 224.

9. Ortberg, *Soul Keeping*, 174.

10. Ibid., 136.

11. Marlo Schalesky, *Waiting for Wonder* (Nashville: Abingdon Press, 2016), 130.

12. Keri Wyatt Kent, *Deeper into the Word: Reflections on 100 Words from the New Testament* (Minneapolis: Bethany, 2011), 153.

13. Cheri Fuller and Jennifer Kennedy Dean, *The One Year Praying the Promises of God* (Carol Stream. IL: Tyndale, 2012), August 26.

14. Timothy Keller, *The Songs of Jesus: A Year of Daily Devotions in the Psalms* (New York: Viking, 2015), 149.

15. Mary DeMuth, *Worth Living: How God's Wild Love for You Makes You Worthy* (Grand Rapids: Baker, 2016), 142.

16. Henri J. M. Nouwen, *Life of the Beloved: Spiritual Living in a Secular World* (New York: Crossroad, 2002).

17. Tish Harrison Warren, *Liturgy of the Ordinary: Sacred Practices in Everyday Life* (Downers Grove, IL: InterVarsity, 2016), 76.

18. Schalesky, *Waiting for Wonder*, 133.

19. Warren, *Liturgy of the Ordinary*, 79.

20. Lee, *Happiness Dare*, 253.

21. Elisabeth Elliot, *Keep a Quiet Heart* (Grand Rapids: Baker, 2004).

22. J. Ron Blue, "Habakkuk," in John F. Walvoord and.Roy B. Zuck, eds., *The Bible Knowledge Commentary: An Exposition of the Scriptures by Dallas Seminary Faculty: Old Testament* (Colorado Springs: David C. Cook, 1983), 1507.

23. "Prayer of Teilhard de Chardin," IgnatianSpirituality.com, accessed April 4, 2017, www.ignatianspirituality.com/8078/prayer-of-theilhard-de-chardin.

24. "Unquenchable Faith—Interview with Author Carol Kent," *Kids Life* magazine, January 8, 2014, www.kidslifemagazine.com/2014/01/08/20136/unquenchable-faith-interview-with-author-carol-kent.

25. Christine Caine, *Undaunted* (Grand Rapids: Zondervan, 2012).

26. Emily Belz, "Ann Voskamp—Upside-Down Kingdom," *World Magazine*, December 31, 2016, https://world.wng.org/2016/11/upside_down_kingdom.

27. Carol Kent, *Waiting Together: Hope and Healing for Families of Prisoners* (Grand Rapids: Discovery, 2016), 230.

28. Denise Marie Salino, *In Her Steps* (Nashville: B & H, 2005), 13.

29. Fuller and Dean, *One Year Praying the Promises*, April 12.

30. Lee, *Happiness Dare*, 203.

31. Fuller and Dean, *One Year Praying the Promises*, March 7.

32. Dallas Willard, *The Divine Conspiracy* (New York: HarperCollins, 1998), 347–48.

33. Nancie Carmichael, *Selah* (Grand Rapids: Revell, 2004), 11.

34. Ibid.

35. Dallas Willard, *The Spirit of the Disciplines* (New York: HarperOne, 1999), viii, 8.

36. Jennifer Weaver, "When God Says No," Jen Weaver (blog), January 27, 2017, http://thejenweaver.com/when-god-says-no/.

37. Kimberly M. Drew and Jocelyn Green, *Refresh: Spiritual Nourishment for Parents of Children with Special Needs* (Grand Rapids: Kregel, 2016), 64–65.

38. Belz, "Ann Voskamp," https://world.wng.org/2016/11/upside_down _kingdom.

39. Abby Phillip, "Why Some People Just Can't Dance or Clap to the Beat," *Washington Post*, November 12, 2014, www.washingtonpost.com/news/to -your-health/wp/2014/11/12/why-some-people-just-cant-dance-or-clap-to -the-beat/?utm_term=.d4f52e12d43e.

40. Geri Scazzero, with Peter Scazzero, *I Quit: Stop Pretending Everything Is Fine and Change Your Life* (Grand Rapids: Zondervan, 2010), 201.

41. Elisabeth Elliot, *A Lamp unto My Feet* (Grand Rapids: Baker, 2013).

42. Susan Alexander Yates, *Risky Faith: Becoming Brave Enough to Trust the God Who Is Bigger Than Your World* (Bend, OR: Loyal Arts Media, 2016), 172–73.

43. Andrew Murray, *Abide in Christ* (New Kensington, PA: Whitaker, 2002), 200–201.

44. Mark Buchanan, "It's All in Your Head," *Leadership Journal* (Summer 2014): 94.

45. Tracie Miles, *Unsinkable Faith: God-Filled Strategies to Transform the Way You Think, Feel, and Live* (Colorado Springs: David C. Cook, 2017), 68.

46. Priscilla Shirer, *The Armor of God* (Nashville: Lifeway, 2015), 167.

47. Ibid.

48. Gordon MacDonald and Mark MacDonald, *BeScrooged: Imagining a Full Life of Generosity* (Melbourne: Canterbury Partners, 2015), 78.

49. Henri J. M. Nouwen, *Our Greatest Gift: A Meditation on Dying and Caring* (New York: HarperCollins, 1994), 3.

50. Gail MacDonald, *Keep Climbing: Turning the Challenges of Life into Adventures of the Spirit* (Carol Stream, IL: Tyndale, 1989), 42.

51. Gail MacDonald, *In His Everlasting Arms: Learning to Trust God in All Circumstances* (Los Angeles: Regal, 2003), 152–53.

52. Isaac of Nineveh, "Lover of Silence," Friends of Silence 2, no. 1 (January 1989), http://friendsofsilence.net/quote/author/isaac-niniveh.

53. Henry Francis Lyte, "Praise My Soul the King of Heaven," 1834.

54. Yates, *Risky Faith*, 175.

55. Helen Lemmel, "Turn Your Eyes upon Jesus," 1922.

56. "A Testament to Mercy," interview with Kay Arthur by Leslie Basham, Revive Our Hearts Radio, December 16, 2008, www.reviveourhearts.com /radio/revive-our-hearts/a-testament-to-mercy/.

57. Peter Scazzero, *Emotionally Healthy Spirituality: It's Impossible to Be Spiritually Mature, While Remaining Emotionally Immature* (Grand Rapids: Zondervan, 2014), 93.

58. Sharon Hodde Miller, "Real, Authentic Authenticity" *Christianity Today*, September 22, 2011.

59. Scazzero and Scazzero, *I Quit*, 208.

60. Maya Angelou, *Letters to My Daughter* (New York: Random House, 2009), 66.

61. Lisa Powell, "Grateful for the Gift of Maya Angelou," 8 Women Dream, May 29, 2014, 8womendream.com/6527/how-to-be-grateful-no-matter-what.

62. Harold Myra, *One Year Book of Encouragement: 365 Days of Inspiration and Wisdom for Your Spiritual Journey* (Carol Stream, IL: Tyndale, 2010), 92.

63. Janet Holm McHenry, *Prayerstreaming: Staying in Touch with God All Day Long* (Colorado Springs: WaterBrook, 2005), 120.

64. Cleland Boyd McAfee, "Near to the Heart of God," 1903, www.hymnary .org/text/there_is_a_place_of_quiet_rest.

65. McHenry, *Prayerstreaming*, 125.

66. Anne Lamott, Facebook status update, April 8, 2015, www.facebook .com/AnneLamott/posts/662177577245222.

67. Warren, *Liturgy of the Ordinary*, 86.

68. Kent, *Deeper into the Word (NT)*, 77.

69. Bob Hostetler, *The Red Letter Life: 17 Words from Jesus to Inspire Simple, Practical, Purposeful Living* (Ulrichsville OH: Barbour, 2014), 119.

70. Ibid.

71. "Princess Diana: 10 Most Inspiring Quotes from the 'People's Princess,'" *Hello!* magazine, August 31, 2015, http://us.hellomagazine.com/royalty/1201 411051084/princess-diana-s-10-most-inspiring-quotes/.

72. Raj Raghunathan, PhD, "The Need to Love," *Psychology Today*, January 8, 2014, www.psychologytoday.com/blog/sapient-nature/201401/the-need-love.

73. Ibid.

74. DeMuth, *Worth Living*, 37.

75. Czarina Ong, "Evangelist Beth Moore Says True Peace Comes in Situations That Are Completely Surrendered to Christ," *Christian Today*, June 4, 2016, www.christiantoday.com/article/evangelist.beth.moore.says.true.peace .comes.in.situations.that.are.completely.surrendered.to.christ/87492.htm.

76. Ken Gire, *Winter's Promise: Hope-Filled Reflections for the Difficult Seasons* (Eugene, OR: Harvest House, 2014), 26.

77. Joni Eareckson Tada, "From the Heart," Joni and Friends (blog), January 2, 2017, www.joniandfriends.org/blog/heart-jan-2017/.

78. Margaret Feinberg, *Wonderstruck* (Brentwood, TN: Worthy, 2012), 151.

79. Ibid., 148.

80. Ellen Vaughan, *Radical Gratitude: Discovering Joy Through Everyday Thankfulness* (Grand Rapids: Zondervan, 2005).

LIFE

1. G. K. Chesterton, *Collected Works of G. K. Chesterton Volume X* (San Francisco: Ignatius, 2008), 38.

2. John Ortberg, *The Life You've Always Wanted: Spiritual Disciplines for Ordinary People* (Grand Rapids: Zondervan, 1997), 60.

3. Kenneth Boa, "John—Chapter 10," Bible.org, accessed April 5, 2017, https://bible.org/seriespage/john-chapter-10.

4. Ken Gire, *Winter's Promise: Hope-Filled Reflections for the Difficult Seasons* (Eugene, OR: Harvest House, 2014), 105.

5. Mary Oliver, "The Summer Day," www.loc.gov/poetry/180/133.html.

6. Mark Batterson, *Going All In: One Decision Can Change Everything* (Grand Rapids: Zondervan, 2013), 24.

7. Jennifer Kennedy Dean, *Set Apart* (Birmingham: New Hope, 2009), 156–57.

8. Frances Ridley Havergal, "Take My Life and Let It Be," 1864, www.hymnary .org/text/take_my_life_and_let_it_be.

9. Mark Batterson, *Draw the Circle* (Grand Rapids: Zondervan, 2012), 137.

10. Francine Rivers, *Earth Psalms: Reflections on How God Speaks Through Nature* (Carol Stream, IL: Tyndale, 2016), 35.

11. Shane Claiborne, Jonathan Wilson-Hartgrove, and Enuma Okoro, *Common Prayer* (Grand Rapids: Zondervan, 2010), 122.

12. Ann Voskamp, "How to Catch a Falling Star: An Adoption Story," Ann Voskamp (blog), June 29, 2016, http://annvoskamp.com/2016/06/how-to-catch-a-falling-star-an-adoption-story-or-why-you-thought-should-not-adopt-or-care-for-an-orphan-and-were-wrong/.

13. Mary DeMuth, *Worth Living: How God's Wild Love for You Makes You Worthy* (Grand Rapids: Baker, 2016), 35.

14. Charles Wesley, "And Can It Be that I Should Gain," *The United Methodist Hymnal* (Nashville: The United Methodist Publishing House, 1989), 363.

15. Kevin DeYoung, *Crazy Busy: A (Mercifully) Short Book About a (Really) Big Problem* (Grand Rapids: Zondervan, 2013), 113.

16. Ibid., 115.

17. Scot McKnight, *The Jesus Creed* (Brewster, MA: Paraclete, 2004).

18. Ellen Vaughan, *Come, Sit, Stay: Finding Rest for Your Soul* (Brentwood, TN: Worthy, 2012), 8.

19. Batterson, *Draw the Circle*, 15.

20. Ken Ringle, "In Hot Pursuit of a Frozen Dream," *Washington Post*, January 7, 1995.

21. Paul Thigpen, "Monica," *Discipleship Journal* (November/December 1994): 51.

22. William G. T. Shedd, ed., *The Confessions of Augustine* (Andover, MA: Warren F. Draper, 1860), 273.

23. Tish Harrison Warren, *Liturgy of the Ordinary: Sacred Practices in Everyday Life* (Downers Grove, IL: InterVarsity, 2016), 28.

24. Ibid., 84.

25. Paul Tripp, *Dangerous Calling* (Wheaton, IL: Crossway, 2012), 35.

26. Rob Renfroe, *The Trouble with the Truth: Balancing Truth and Grace* (Nashville: Abingdon Press, 2014), 37, 39.

27. Marlo Schalesky, *Waiting for Wonder* (Nashville: Abingdon Press, 2016), 160.

28. Eugene Peterson, *A Long Obedience in the Same Direction* (Downers Grove, IL: InterVarsity, 1980), 40-41.

29. Rabbi David Wolpe, "Why Americans Are So Angry About Everything," *Time*, January 5, 2016, http://time.com/4166326/why-americans-are-so-angry-about-everything/.

30. Jessica Shaver, "A Prayer for Freedom," *Virtue* (January/February 1996).

31. Christin Ditchfield, *Praying Ephesians* (Brentwood, TN: Worthy, 2012). 145.

32. Ibid.,146.

33. Eugene O'Neill, *Thirst: "Man Is Born Broken. He Lives by Mending. The Grace of God Is Glue,"* Kindle ed. (n.p.: Stage Door, 2014).

34. Brennan Manning, *The Ragamuffin Gospel* (Sisters, OR: Multnomah, 1990), 187.

35. Timothy Keller, *The Songs of Jesus: A Year of Daily Devotions in the Psalms* (New York: Viking, 2015), 162.

36. Matthew Woodley, "Deep Preaching in a Distracted Age," CT Pastors, accessed April 6, 2017, www.christianitytoday.com/pastors/2016/state-of -church-ministry-2017/deep-preaching-in-distracted-age.html.

37. Charles Stone, "Communicating with the Brain in Mind" *Leadership Journal* (Summer 2014): 48.

38. Janet Holm McHenry, *Prayerstreaming: Staying in Touch with God All Day Long* (Colorado Springs: WaterBrook, 2005), 79.

39. Greg Taylor, "The New Monk Warriors," *Leadership Journal* (Summer 2012): 89.

40. Maya Wei-Haas, "The True Story of 'Hidden Figures,' the Forgotten Women Who Helped Win the Space Race," Smithsonian.com, September 8, 2016, www.smithsonianmag.com/history/forgotten-black-women-mathemati cians-who-helped-win-wars-and-send-astronauts-space-180960393/.

41. Philip Yancey, "Why I Write," Philip Yancey (blog), June 19, 2016, http://philipyancey.com/why-i-write.

42. Robert Benson, in a newsletter for the Florida Christian Writers Conference, December 2016.

43. Rebecca Manley Pippert, *Live* (Surrey, UK: Good Book, 2014), 27.

44. Gail MacDonald, *In His Everlasting Arms: Learning to Trust God in All Circumstances* (Los Angeles: Regal, 2003), 151.

45. Jennifer Dukes Lee, *Love Idol* (Carol Stream, IL: Tyndale, 2014), 55.

46. Huffpost Video, "The Difference Between Wisdom and Intelligence Explained," *Huffington Post*, March 26, 2014, www.huffingtonpost .com/2014/03/26/difference-between-wisdom-intelligence_n_5037134.html.

47. Priscilla Shirer, *Jonah* (Nashville: Lifeway, 2010), 36.

48. Henri J. M. Nouwen, *Spiritual Direction: Wisdom for the Long Walk of Faith* (New York: HarperOne, 2006), 17.

49. Harold Myra, *The One Year Book of Encouragement: 365 Days of Inspiration and Wisdom for Your Spiritual Journey* (Carol Stream, IL: Tyndale, 2010), 38.

50. Shirer, *Jonah*, 119.

51. Kevin Miller, "Do You REALLY Believe God Loves You?" *Today's Christian Woman* (November/December 1993): 62–63.

52. Suzanne Eller, speaking of Christine Caine, *Come with Me* (Minneapolis: Bethany, 2016), 141.

53. Henri J. M. Nouwen, *Our Greatest Gift: A Meditation on Dying and Caring* (New York: HarperCollins, 1994), 71.

54. Ibid., 74.

55. Lori Stanley Roeleveld, *Jesus and the Beanstalk* (Nashville: Abingdon Press, 2016), 246.

56. McHenry, *Prayerstreaming*, 106.

57. Ann Voskamp, *The Broken Way* (Grand Rapids: Zondervan, 2016), 119.

58. Roeleveld, *Jesus and the Beanstalk*, 212.

59. Rachel Britton, "How to Accept a Gift of Grace," Rachel Britton (blog), December 22, 2016, https://rachelbritton.com/how-to-accept-a-gift-of-grace/.

60. Adapted from Lucinda Secrest McDowell, *Quilts from Heaven* (Nashville: B & H, 2007).

61. Oswald Chambers, *My Utmost for His Highest* (New York: Dodd, Mead, 1935), 46.

62. Voskamp, *Broken Way*, 258.

63. Adapted from John Piper, "How to Live Under an Unqualified President," Desiring God, January 20, 2017, www.desiringgod.org/articles/how-to-live-under-an-unqualified-president.

64. Gordon MacDonald, "How to Spot a Transformed Christian." *Leadership Journal* (Summer 2012): 34.

65. Gordon MacDonald, *Building Below the Waterline* (Peabody, MA: Hendrickson, 2011).

66. Susan Alexander Yates, *Risky Faith: Becoming Brave Enough to Trust the God Who Is Bigger Than Your World* (Bend, OR: Loyal Arts Media, 2016), 157.

67. Manning, *Ragamuffin Gospel*, 176.

68. Gire, *Winter's Promise*, 133.

About the Author

Lucinda Secrest McDowell is passionate about embracing life—both through deep soul care from drawing closer to God, as well as living courageously in order to touch a needy world. A storyteller who engages both heart and mind, she offers *Encouraging Words* to all on the journey. A graduate of Gordon-Conwell Theological Seminary and Furman University, Lucinda is the author of thirteen books, including *Ordinary Graces*, *Dwelling Places*, *Live These Words, Role of a Lifetime, Refresh,* and *Quilts from Heaven*.

Whether codirecting reNEW—retreat for New England Writing, pouring into young leaders, or guiding a restorative day of prayer, she is energized by investing in people of all ages.

Lucinda's favorites include tea parties, good books, laughing friends, ancient prayers, country music, cozy quilts, musical theatre, and especially her family scattered around the world, doing amazing things. She writes from "Sunnyside" cottage in New England and blogs weekly at EncouragingWords.net.

Mission: "To glorify God and live in His grace and freedom, and through the power of the Holy Spirit to use my gifts to communicate God's faithfulness, extend His grace, and encourage others to trust Him fully."

Every word you give me is a miracle word—
  how could I help but obey?
Break open your words, let the light shine out,
  let ordinary people see the meaning.

—Psalm 119:129-130 MSG

Website/Blog www.EncouragingWords.net
E-mail cindy@encouragingwords.net
Phone (860) 402-9551
Twitter @LucindaSMcDowell
Instagram LucindaSecrestMcDowell
Facebook Encouraging Words—Lucinda Secrest McDowell
Mail Encouraging Words, P.O. Box 290707, Wethersfield CT 06129

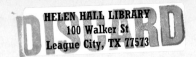
What if a Thriving, Active Faith Were as Simple as Reading One Word a Day?

In *Dwelling Places: Words to Live in Every Season*, author Lucinda Secrest McDowell uses short and inspiring readings to unpack a single word - such as mercy, beauty, gratitude, or grace - to reveal a biblical blessing or challenge relevant to where you are. Full of stories and illustrations to empower you to live the word you have just read, each devotional ends with a benediction, written as if God were speaking directly to you. These "dwelling places," that offer the joy of God's promise and presence, cover four seasons: fall, Advent, Lent, and summer. Whether in the midst of busy holiday schedules, holy days, ordinary moments, or changing seasons, a deeper faith can be as simple as a single word.

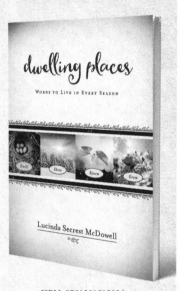

ISBN: 9781501815324

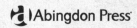